T0328441

Law and the Borders of Belonging in the Long Nineteenth Century United States

For more than a generation, historians and legal scholars have documented inequalities at the heart of American law and daily life and exposed inconsistencies in the generic category of "American citizenship." Barbara Young Welke draws on that wealth of historical, legal, and theoretical scholarship to offer a new paradigm of liberal selfhood and citizenship from the founding of the United States through the 1920s. *Law and the Borders of Belonging in the Long Nineteenth Century United States* questions understanding this period as a progressive narrative of expanding rights, revealing that it was characterized instead by a sustained commitment to borders of belonging of liberal selfhood, citizenship, and nation in which able white men's privilege depended on the subject status of disabled persons, racialized others, and women. Welke's conclusions pose challenging questions about the modern liberal democratic state that extend well beyond the temporal and geographic boundaries of the long nineteenth century United States.

Barbara Young Welke is Associate Professor of History and Professor of Law at the University of Minnesota. She is the author of *Recasting American Liberty: Gender, Race, Law and the Railroad Revolution, 1865–1920* (Cambridge University Press).

New Histories of American Law

Series Editors

Michael Grossberg, Indiana University
Christopher L. Tomlins, University of California-Irvine

New Histories of American Law is a series of bold, synthetic, and path-breaking interpretive books that will address the key topics in the field of American legal history, written by the leaders of the field and designed for scholars and students throughout universities, colleges, and law schools.

Law and the Borders of Belonging in the Long Nineteenth Century United States

BARBARA YOUNG WELKE

University of Minnesota

CAMBRIDGE UNIVERSITY PRESS

CAMBRIDGE
UNIVERSITY PRESS

University Printing House, Cambridge CB2 8BS, United Kingdom

One Liberty Plaza, 20th Floor, New York, NY 10006, USA

477 Williamstown Road, Port Melbourne, VIC 3207, Australia

314-321, 3rd Floor, Plot 3, Splendor Forum, Jasola District Centre, New Delhi - 110025, India

79 Anson Road, #06-04/06, Singapore 079906

Cambridge University Press is part of the University of Cambridge.

It furthers the University's mission by disseminating knowledge in the pursuit of education, learning and research at the highest international levels of excellence.

www.cambridge.org
Information on this title: www.cambridge.org/9780521152259

First published 2010

A catalogue record for this publication is available from the British Library

Library of Congress Cataloging in Publication data
Welke, Barbara Young, 1958–
Law and the borders of belonging in the long nineteenth century
United States / Barbara Young Welke.
p. cm. – (New histories of American law)
Includes bibliographical references and index.
ISBN 978-0-521-76188-8 (hardback)
1. Equality – United States – History – 19th century. 2. Citizenship –
United States – History – 19th century. 3. Liberalism – United States –
History – 19th century. 4. Discrimination – Law and legislation –
United States – History – 19th century.
I. Title. II. Series.
HM821.W45 2010
323.608´0907309034–dc22   2009048862

ISBN 978-0-521-76188-8 Hardback
ISBN 978-0-521-15225-9 Paperback

CONTENTS

ACKNOWLEDGMENTS

This book began almost a decade ago not as a book but with an invitation from Michael Grossberg and Christopher Tomlins to write an essay for *The Cambridge History of Law in America*. Editorship is its own craft. It requires being able to read less than fully articulated and often conflicting ideas expressed in muddy, disorganized, incomplete prose and see the potential, and then, through equal parts questioning, probing, seeing, encouraging, and where necessary redirecting, to help an author to fully realize and express her ideas. Mike and Chris bring all these skills to editing. They responded to more long, reflective emails, read more versions of the essay and then the book, and welcomed more follow-up phone calls than any author would have a right to ask. At every stage, they offered support, pushed me to be clear about what I was saying, and challenged me where they were unconvinced. It is with the deepest respect and gratitude that I acknowledge their knowledge, skill, support, and friendship.

Mike and Chris got me into this thing and helped me see it through, but I could write *Law and the Borders of Belonging* only because of the original archival work and scholarly articles and monographs of the many scholars who came before me. "All works of history are in a sense collaborative endeavors, for no matter how original, they necessarily build on previous scholarship. This is even more true for books, like [this], based largely on secondary literature. My greatest debt is to the legions of American historians on whose work I have relied." Eric Foner opens the acknowledgments of *The Story of American Freedom* with these words and sentiments. Agreeing with them entirely and unable to improve upon them, I repeat them here. I have tried to convey something of my intellectual debt, as well as providing a resource for further reading, in the bibliographic essay.

Completing this book required reading far beyond the boundaries of my own areas of expertise. I benefited immensely from the generosity of many individuals who read the manuscript at various stages and supported me throughout. Their suggestions of other works I should read and comments on parts of the work that most closely touched on their own fields of study broadened my field of vision. It is with deep pleasure that I acknowledge all those who gave so generously of their time and knowledge. Margot Canaday, Kirsten Fischer, Linda Kerber, Erika Lee, Jeff Ostler, and Peggy Pascoe all read the first long version of what ultimately became (in a dramatically shortened version) the CHLA essay. Their generosity in volunteering to read kept me going; their comments made both the essay and the book far better. It was Kirsten, Erika, and Linda who independently each suggested that they thought this was a book, not just an essay. I thank them for their specific comments on the manuscript, but also for first seeing that this might be a book and then supporting me in the additional years of work that endeavor required. Peggy's thoughtful comments, as always, filled many single-spaced pages. Jeff's reading was absolutely crucial for his expertise in Native American history. Next to Chris and Mike, Margot Canaday read more drafts of the book than anyone. Her generosity in offering to read again and again and the fresh eye and important critiques she brought to every reading both meant a great deal to me and have made this a better book. The students in my U.S. Women's Legal History course at the University of Minnesota enthusiastically read an early draft of the book;

their reading was key in helping me see the book through undergraduates' eyes. Conversations about the project with Susan Rugh while paddling in the BWCAW improved both the book and my quality of life.

Additional readers came later, including Josh Barkan whose careful reading among other things pushed me to clarify the relationship between legal personhood and citizenship; the members of the Women, Law, and Public Policy Reading Group at the University of Minnesota (including Liz Boyle, Carolyn Chalmers, Carol Chomsky, Sally Kenney, and Mary Lay Schuster); and, Kathleen Neils Conzen, Hendrik Hartog, Laura Weinrib, Rebecca Rix, Jonathan Levy, and Nate Holdren. Kathy Conzen's thoughtful reading of the penultimate draft pushed me to tackle the manuscript as a whole one more time, gave me the confidence that I had it in me to address her hard questions, and encouraged me to consider the relevance of the borders of belonging beyond the long nineteenth century United States. Dirk not only offered thoughtful comments of his own, but also generously made space for *Law and the Borders of Belonging* in his graduate readings seminar at Princeton, as did Linda Kerber in her graduate class at the University of Iowa. I appreciated the seriousness with which both groups of students engaged the manuscript. Their questions helped me bring fresh eyes to the final set of revisions. Rebecca Rix and Jon Levy both took part in the discussion at Princeton and engaged in extended email conversations afterwards that were very productive. Laura Weinrib, whose juggling of graduate school and motherhood I understand only too well, nonetheless carved out time to carefully read and share a long, helpful set of comments. Nate Holdren's close reading of and thoughtful comments on the manuscript just as it was about to go to press captures the wonderful mutuality that I have found in graduate teaching at the University of Minnesota. I look forward to returning the favor as he completes work on his dissertation.

Books depend not only on generous colleagues, but also on presses, editors, and reviewers. I am delighted to have this be the first book in a new series in legal history by Cambridge University Press, edited by Michael Grossberg and Christopher Tomlins. Three anonymous reviewers read the book for Cambridge University Press. I am grateful to all of them. Publishing has changed dramatically in the decade since Cambridge published my first book in 2001. It is now, like so much else, a largely global electronic enterprise. I appreciate having had as my guides in this new world Eric Crahan, Editor, History & Politics; Emily Spangler, Senior Editorial Assistant, History & Politics; Marielle Poss, Senior Production Controller; the team at Newgen Imaging Systems, Chennai, India; Robert Swanson and Gerald McLenahan in navigating Cambridge's distinctive indexing system; and in copyediting the manuscript, Sue Spiegel.

I am also grateful to Suzanne Thorpe and the library staff more generally at the University of Minnesota Law School for their assistance in gathering various legal materials and to the work that Jeff Manuel spent on important details in the final version of the manuscript.

I have saved to the end my family, but of course, they've been with me throughout this project. My children, Wilder and Frances, were born, developed into people of their own, and began school over the course of my work on my dissertation and first book. With this one, they have passed from boy- and girlhood, through their teenage years, high school, one successful launch into college and another just a year away. This makes me sound awfully slow, and I suppose I am. Children take time and what a joy that time has been. My scholarship and teaching are better for their presence in my life, and my life beyond scholarship and teaching are better as well because of them. My husband Bill listened to me talk about this book for years. His greatest gifts to me have been not just his love and companionship over 26 years, but his unwavering support of my teaching, service, research, and writing. His reading of and comments on the manuscript near the end forced me to explain myself in matters large and small that have made this a better book. I think my family will be glad to say goodbye to *Law and the Borders of*

Belonging or, as we've called it for short, "BoB." That they all support yet more book projects tells you that I am as lucky in my home life as I am in my professional life.

Barbara Young Welke

St. Paul, Minnesota
September 2009

INTRODUCTION

Questions of belonging rest at the heart of the modern liberal democratic state. What does belonging mean? Who belongs? Does belonging depend on there being others who do not belong? What is their relationship to the polity? Does it matter what the basis for belonging is, what the defining characteristics of belonging are? Who decides? What does law have to do with it? The answers to these questions are critical in establishing who can make claims on the polity and who cannot; on relationships among those who live in a polity; and in making a population a people. They highlight, what I call, "borders of belonging." Though borders of belonging have been fundamental to the human condition throughout history, they are of particular significance in the modern world and especially to the modern liberal democratic state with its assumptions of the sovereign individual, universal equality, and the authority of the rule of law.

This book traces the borders of belonging at a particular, formative moment in the long history of the development of the modern liberal democratic state: the nineteenth-century establishment and consolidation of the United States. The language of the Declaration of Independence and the preamble to the U.S. Constitution expressed a powerful vision of the fundamental right to freedom, liberty, and equality. Looked at one way, that vision was incrementally transformed into a lived reality for a broader and broader number of Americans over the course of the long nineteenth century.[1] The American Revolution transformed subjects into citizens; between the 1820s and the 1840s, states removed property qualifications for voting, extending the franchise to most white men; the 1860s brought freedom to the roughly four million Americans held in chattel slavery and a constitutional revolution in individual rights; married women's property reform and ultimately suffrage in 1920 gave women a fuller individuality; and millions emigrated to America's shores and became citizens. One can look at this history and believe in some fundamental way in America's liberalism.

And yet, taking the story as a whole, one cannot escape a different narrative. From the outset, personhood, citizenship, and nation were imagined in abled, racialized, and gendered terms: able white men alone were fully embodied legal persons, they were America's "first citizens," they were the nation. Able white male legal authority was fundamental to the very nature and meaning of nineteenth-century American law in both conceptual and constitutive terms. It created law's borders; it defined belonging. As this suggests, the universal human legal person imagined by liberalism and equally imbedded in capitalism was in fact highly particularized. More important, however much change there was on the surface over the course of the long nineteenth century, the borders of belonging never escaped their initial imagining. Abled, racialized, and gendered identities – simply assumed at the beginning as the foundation or justification for the granting or denial of personhood and citizenship – came to be self-consciously embraced, marked in law, and manipulated, protecting able white male privilege not simply up to the Civil War, but after it as well. In turn, the founding assumptions that imagined legal personhood and from it citizenship in abled, racialized, and gendered terms fundamentally shaped

---

[1] The term long nineteenth century here refers to the period from 1789 through the 1920s. I explain why I use the long nineteenth century as the frame of reference later in the introduction.

the development of the American legal and constitutional order for the twentieth century.

Law, Personhood, Citizenship, and the Borders of Belonging

Concepts are useful because they offer a mental symbol, an evocative explanation that captures an underlying symmetry in what might otherwise appear to be without pattern or form. With this in mind, it seems advisable to provide greater explanation of what I mean by and the relationship among "personhood," "citizenship," "borders of belonging," and law's centrality to all three.

The free, self-owning, rights-bearing, sovereign individual stands at the foundation of the modern liberal state. Scholars have used a range of terms to describe the self-owning individual – "possessive individualism," "the liberal individual," or, as I do here, simply "personhood" or "legal personhood." *Personhood*, as I use the term, rests most fundamentally on legal recognition and protection of *self*-ownership, that is, of a right to one's person, one's body, and one's labor. Other elements of personhood stem from this starting point: a right to freedom of movement, to marry, to procreate (or not), to be free from physical abuse or coercion without due process of law, to contract, to inherit and devise property, and so on. Protection of these basic rights of personhood requires, in turn, basic civil rights, including the right to sue and be sued, the right to suffrage, and the right to serve on juries and be eligible for elective office. These characteristics bring us to citizenship.

Citizenship is often defined in terms of a set of formal rights and obligations, for example, the right to sue in national courts, the right to the protection of the state when traveling abroad, and so on. But what such a definition fails to capture is the reflexive relationship in the liberal state between personhood and citizenship. Citizenship and personhood are interdependent. Thinking about citizenship in this way enables us to see how one might formally be a citizen and even enjoy particular rights and share obligations associated with citizenship and yet not enjoy effective citizenship because one is not invested by law with full personhood. Moreover, the extension of citizenship could itself be or become an instrument of authority and subordination.

Several decades of scholarship have accustomed us to thinking of race and gender as constructed in part through law. What I am suggesting is that we think more generally of how law *constructs*, that is, lends consequence to elements of individual identity – race, sex, age, ability, religion, birth status and place of birth, marital status, and so on. Thinking in these terms helps us to keep in mind that elements of individual identity do not have any set meaning. They are given meaning socially, culturally, and, most importantly here, legally. They are thus set apart; they are given borders. The meaning attached to these characteristics in turn is articulated to personhood, citizenship, and nation, and through them to the ability to both substantively participate in society and to have a corresponding legal status as someone who can participate in society. Law in this way has been fundamental in the construction of personhood, citizenship, and hence borders of belonging. As this suggests, the term *borders of belonging* offers a conceptual tool for describing the commonality in the meaning or consequences attached to ability, race, and gender that otherwise appear distinct, different, or particular.

There are other terms I might have used in place of "belonging"; dignity, capacity, and standing all capture part of what I am after here, but each only incompletely and with troubling elisions. "Belonging," and especially "borders of belonging," allows me to get at the intersections and interdependence of the individual, relationships between/among individuals, and the space of the individual within and as representative of the nation. As I have conceived the term, *borders of belonging*, both borders *and* belonging have a spatial (bodily and territorially) and figurative meaning. In a territorial sense, "borders" refers to the borders of the nation. But it likewise refers to the borders between individuals and the state, and between different levels of governing authority. In the case of the United

States, for example, "borders," in this sense, refers to a complex set of relationships among individuals, states, the federal government, incorporated and unincorporated territories, and Indian tribes. "Borders" also though refers to physical and psychic personhood (self-ownership). The term "belonging," likewise, refers to self-ownership or belonging to oneself, as well as meaning "to be a member of" or "to be part of" as in citizenship. Tracing borders of belonging reveals the ways in which recognition of personhood establishes the preconditions of effective citizenship.

Part of the value of borders of belonging as a conceptual tool is its power to expose instances in which belonging for some is achieved through the subordination or exclusion of others. No figure in the liberal state was self-defining; privilege and subordination, as the term suggests, were interlocked and interdependent. Seen in this light, both "belonging" and "borders" can be charged negatively, as well as positively. So, for example, in addition to its positive valence, belonging also connotes, less positively, the realities of "belonging to" as in legal relationships of ownership, authority, and/or protection and subordination (e.g., master/slave, master/servant, husband/wife, guardian/ward). Even in its positive sense – that of being a part of – belonging can be a negative tool. In the nineteenth century United States, state recognition of freedmen's and freedwomen's right to marry and the sanctity of their familial bonds in the aftermath of emancipation and ratification of the Thirteenth Amendment following the American Civil War, granted African Americans two of the most fundamental elements of personhood, yet simultaneously proved a tool for forcing African Americans to conform to a particular definition of family and a basis for expropriating the labor of those who did not. So too with "borders." The Dawes Act, for example, which gave the U.S. president authority to divide tribal lands and allot 160 acres to each family and smaller plots to individuals, brought American Indians closer to full-fledged U.S. citizenship. It also was intended to and effectively did dispossess them of their tribal sovereignty and cultural identity. "Belonging" and "borders" came together in this negative sense in the nonconsensual reproductive sterilization of those institutionalized for mental and congenital disability in the early twentieth century United States. These examples challenge a reading of "borders of belonging" in terms simply of a positively charged interior and a negatively charged exterior, a reading that holds out the promise of a progressive, liberal narrative: as the borders of belonging expand, those outside are brought inside. Finally, the concept is productive for helping us visualize ways in which exclusion from borders of belonging, voluntary and involuntary, may offer benefits.

In highlighting the legal construction of personhood and citizenship, I do not mean to suggest that individuals' only source of selfhood, personhood, or belonging is through law; in fact, other cultural sources of selfhood and belonging become especially important for those marginalized or subordinated by borders of belonging established through law. It is to say that with the creation and expansion of the modern liberal state, law has operated as an authoritative discourse, that it fundamentally shapes individual identity and rights, relationships among individuals, and the relationship of the individual to the state. And while the particulars have differed over time and space, borders of belonging have been integral to the modern liberal order.

Categories of Belonging

Even if thinking about race or gender as elements of legal personhood is new to readers, recognizing that privilege and subordination rested along axes of race and gender in American history most certainly is not new. Several decades of scholarship, moreover, have accustomed us to seeing race and gender (and, more recently, sexuality) as analytical categories. We are less accustomed to thinking of ability and disability as equally critical historically in shaping privilege and subordination. I argue here that ability, no less than race and gender, was fundamental to personhood and citizenship, that it was a constituent element of the borders of belonging

from the nation's founding and that it remained so throughout the long nineteenth century. Fundamental rights of personhood, including freedom of movement, immigration, the
right to contract, to devise one's property, to marry, to procreate, even the right to be in public depended on individual
capacity, on being defined in law as "able." Elements of civic
personhood – the right to testify, jury and military service,
suffrage – likewise were limited to the "able."

Understanding the fundamental nature of ability in shaping the borders of belonging requires letting go of our long-
established conditioning to think of disability in medical
terms. There were most certainly individuals who were deaf,
blind, and crippled, who suffered from epilepsy or who suffered from varying degrees of mental incapacity. Just as in
thinking about sex, skin color, and heredity, it is not the
characteristic, but the *legal* significance, the legal disability
(or in the case of ability, the legal capacity) attached to the
characteristic that must be denaturalized and historicized.
What counted as evidence of mental capacity and incapacity too must be historicized. Nineteenth century Americans
correlated epilepsy with feeblemindedness. Elizabeth Ware
Packard's refusal to submit to her husband's authority provided the foundation for her commitment in 1860 to a state
insane asylum where she would spend the next three years
of her life against her will. Poverty coupled with behavior
that challenged gender or other social norms could and regularly did translate into labels of feeblemindedness and idiocy that would justify placement in a state facility for the
feebleminded.

The work we have to do to shake the sense that physi-
cal/cognitive abilities and disabilities are different from sex
and race helps us to more fully enter into and understand the
mindset of the nineteenth century. In the nineteenth century,
there was a deep correlation between gender, race, and ability.
White men were assumed to have capacity, to be able, unless
proven otherwise; for women and racialized others the beginning assumption was the reverse. Medical and legal scholars (by definition white and male) understood the incapacity

or disability of women ("the sex") and racialized others as
marked on their minds and bodies as certainly as was that
of the "feebleminded," the epileptic, the "cripple," and the
"idiot." Think, for example, of justifications for women's
exclusion from civic society on the grounds, in John Adams's
words, that "their delicacy renders them unfit for practice
and experience in the great business of life, and the hardy
enterprises of war, as well as the arduous cares of the state....
[T]hat nature has made them fittest for domestic cares."[2]
Think also of justifications for slavery based on Africans'
asserted mental inferiority and physical adaptedness for
field labor. As historian Douglas Baynton notes, "Disability
has functioned historically to justify inequality for disabled
people themselves, but it has also done so for women and
minority groups."[3] The difference of each of these groups –
whether of ability, race, or sex – from able white men was
the foundation for denying them through law equal rights of
personhood and citizenship.

Each category here – male, female, white, nonwhite, abled,
disabled – combines individuals marked as certainly by their
differences as by their shared identity. What I wish for the
reader to see is that law played a fundamental part in creating shared identity, that it did so by investing elements of
identity with legal consequences of inclusion and privilege
or exclusion and subordination, and that the inclusion and
privilege of some, in part, was defined by and depended upon
the exclusion and subordination of others. Deep differences
of class and religion divided able white men at every point
in the nineteenth century United States, but law created a
shared identity rooted in ability, race, and gender that cut
across, bridged these differences. Able white men's shared
identity as heads of household provided the foundation for

[2] John Adams to James Sullivan, Philadelphia, May 26, 1776, reprinted
in *The Feminist Papers: From Adams to de Beauvoir*, ed. Alice S. Rossi
(Boston, 1988), 13–14.
[3] Douglas C. Baynton, "Disability and the Justification of Inequality
in American History," in *The New Disability History: American
Perspectives*, eds. Paul K. Longmore and Lauri Umansky (New York,
2001), 33.

their shared civic identity as voters, jurors, and citizens. Each sphere of capacity was the product of law and each reinforced the other. Able white men's capacity, their sense of self, their independence was expanded materially and psychically by the authority law gave them over others – wives, children, servants, slaves, wards.

Just as seeing the way in which law accorded personhood and citizenship on the basis of ability, race, and gender requires looking past the differences that divided able white men, seeing how law denied personhood and citizenship requires looking across differences among women, among people of different racial backgrounds, among people with a range of disabilities. Not all women were equally subjects of law. There were women who were free and women who were enslaved, women of every race, women who were formally citizens and those who were not, single, married, and widowed women, women who were mothers and those who were not, women who were able and those with mental and physical disabilities. These differences mattered in daily life and law. Yet, to acknowledge that enslavement, race, marital status, citizenship, and ableness shaped women's legal status should not let us overlook that women by virtue of sex shared a set of legal disabilities and that men's independence rested on women's legally structured dependence. Moreover, within the qualities that divided women, sex shaped the law in form and practice so that women were treated differently from men who shared the same qualities. As a matter of law through most or all of the long nineteenth century, women could not vote; a married woman had no right to her labor or to her body; the category of exclusion "likely to become a public charge" targeted single women; "feebleminded" women were the special targets of sterilization laws, and so on.

The same point applies for race. I use the term "racialized others" to refer collectively to the many diverse tribal nations that peopled the continent; slaves, free blacks, freedmen and freedwomen; Chinese, Japanese, and other Asian immigrants, as well as Chinese-, Japanese-, and other Asian-Americans; Mexicans who became U.S. citizens by virtue of the Treaty of Guadalupe-Hidalgo; Mexican-Americans who became citizens by virtue of birth in the United States; and Mexican immigrants. And so on. These groups did not share an identity any more than all women shared an identity. Nor were they identified in law as a single group. Recognizing these differences must not, though, obscure the fundamental fact that law *made* skin color and heredity the foundation for personhood and citizenship. My use of the term "racialized others" rather than "race" recognizes just this: race is constructed. Moreover, individual racial groups – African Americans, the Chinese, and so on – in part developed a group identity in the United States by being marked in law as a group.

The same was true with the category of disability. While there were terms used to speak of disabled persons as a group ("defectives," the "unfit," etc.), there was not a shared or group identity that crossed disability categories. I use "disabled persons" as a legal category referring collectively to those who in the nineteenth century were variously labeled "cripples," "idiots," "the insane," "the feebleminded," "the blind," "the deaf," "epileptics," "defective," and "unfit." While some individual groups (the blind, the deaf) developed a group identity over the course of the nineteenth century, they most certainly did not consider themselves like others who were labeled defective. The same could be said, as I have suggested, of race and sex. Laws relating to skin color and heredity targeted groups by particular racial categories. And individuals of different racial groups did not, in the nineteenth century, share cross-racial identity. So, for example, black men in San Francisco in the 1860s sought to have the testimony ban barring blacks from testifying against whites eliminated from the state constitution; they did not make common cause with Chinese persons who were also banned from testifying against whites. It was only beginning in the mid-twentieth century, largely embedded in Fourteenth Amendment Equal Protection analysis, that "race," then "sex," and most recently "disability" became unitary *legal* categories.

I highlight three characteristics – ability (mental and physical ableness), race (white), and gender (male) – as defining the borders of belonging in America's long nineteenth century. Each of the three is deeply rooted not just in U.S. history, but in the political theory of liberalism and republicanism and the historical contexts in which they were articulated. Capitalism also assumed the free, self-owning, rights-bearing sovereign individual, the "liberal" self while also depending on the unwaged household labor of wives. Other characteristics deeply divided, at the same time that they provided a sense of fellow-belonging to, nineteenth century Americans. Most important here are religion and class. Religion shaped the borders of belonging at important moments in the long nineteenth century. A pervading issue in debates over the extent of the land the United States would acquire following the Mexican-American war was the fear not simply of racial others who would become citizens, but that they were Catholic. Mormons were violently chased out of Illinois and Utah statehood blocked until Mormons disavowed polygamy; restrictive covenants almost uniformly targeted racialized others, but many excluded Jews as well; prohibition was directed at Catholic, working-class Americans.

And yet, the U.S. Census, which from the beginning marked the population by sex and race, and, beginning in the 1830s by disability, never inquired as to religious identity. The Constitution specifically proscribed religious tests for office holding; the First Amendment barred the establishment of religion and protected the free exercise of religion, and states moved early in the nineteenth century in the same direction. While many Americans assumed that the United States was not simply a white nation, but a Protestant one, and Catholics, Jews, Mormons, and other religious minorities faced hostility, exclusion, and violence at many points in the century, Protestantism, it seems to me, was not fundamental to *individual legal capacity*, to *legal personhood*, in the way that ability, race, and gender were. Catholics, Jews, Mormons, and other religious minorities to the extent they were able, white, and male were acknowledged in law as persons and citizens.

Like religion, class also deeply divided Americans, underlay violent clashes, and was the basis for subordinating many Americans. It has long been central in narratives of American history. It most certainly divided able white men in ways that makes it jarring to hear able white men referred to as a group. That I do not include it here, like religion, is not intended as a statement diminishing its significance in American history. Yet, like religion, class, seems to me different from ability, race, and gender. One can identify certain groups defined in some particulars as something less than free men in the law (e.g., seamen, miners, beggars, and paupers), but it is important to recognize that that status was connected to occupation or the complete failure of or refusal to pursue labor; it was not a matter of personal identity. Whatever their differences, and I acknowledge that they were many, able white men shared a legal identity as persons and as citizens. That shared legal identity and the privileges it offers have been, I would argue, a critical element in the failure, not simply in the nineteenth century but since, of laboring white men to see in their situation commonalities with that of disabled persons, racialized others, and women. Privilege, based on however thin a reed, is nonetheless a powerful force.

A third characteristic I might have included as an element of the borders of belonging, but have not, is age. Unlike religion or class, legal personhood did depend on age. Though the age of majority varied by state and changed over time, children did not own themselves, they could not enter into contracts, sue in their own name, and so on. They were subject to the authority and discipline of a father. Children could not vote, serve on juries, or hold elective office. But children did not remain children. They aged out. Disabled persons, racialized others, and women never escaped the legal disabilities defined by ableness, race, and gender. Age at the other end of the life spectrum is, in this respect, different: one only ages out of old age by death. My exclusion of age here rests on the fact that even in old age, the law assumed the capacity of white men. In the most classic of examples, that of wills, judges expressed tremendous reluctance to find that a man's last testament did not express "his will."

Law and the Long Nineteenth Century

American legal historians – from Roscoe Pound to Willard Hurst, Morton Horwitz, and William Nelson – have long recognized the nineteenth century as the formative era of American law. My argument here is that the stories of transformation they have charted overlook a more fundamental continuity, one that in fact provided stability in the American republic in the face of "the transformations of law" that they and others chart. Tracing that fundamental continuity requires looking across the long nineteenth century: a view that traces the long arc from the nation's birth through its full flowering as a capitalist, industrial world power, that takes in, in other words, the political *and* economic coming of age of the United States, the world's first self-professed liberal, democratic republic.

Historians divide time into distinct periods as a way of making sense of the past, as a way of highlighting larger continuities or defining qualities that otherwise might be missed. Traditional divisions – periods we know by shorthand phrases such as "the Revolutionary Era," "the Early Republic" and "the Age of Jackson," "the Civil War Era," "the Gilded Age," and "the Progressive Era" – mask the fundamental continuities of abled, racialized, and gendered privilege and subordination. The American Revolution was not simply incomplete or failed; abled, racialized, and gendered privilege was deliberately constructed and embraced as the embodiment of independence, self-ownership, citizenship, and nationhood. Progressive narratives creep all too comfortably into chronologically driven accounts, broader continuities lost in the chronicle of a single era. Thus, we are told, the achievement of the Revolutionary Era is throwing off the status of colonial subjects and the founding of a republic of citizens. The achievement of Western Expansion and the

Age of Jackson is the addition of new states and expansion
of democracy in the extension of suffrage to white men without regard to property ownership. The achievement of the
Civil War Era is ending the contradiction of slavery in the
American Republic. And so on.

Historians have not been insensible to the contradictions
of each era. So, for example, historians have highlighted
that the Revolution was most certainly not a revolution
for women or slaves. They have stressed that the corollary
of Western expansion in the Age of Jackson was the brutal
removal of Native Americans. More recently, they have highlighted the repressive legal regimes targeting disabled persons
in the Progressive Era. But it is only by including *both* ends of
this longer continuum that we are able to see the underlying
continuity in the borders of belonging. Focusing here on the
years from the Revolutionary era through the 1920s takes
in the nation's founding, in which able white men's privileged legal identity became the template for the nation, as
well as the early decades of the twentieth century in which
land expropriation within the continental boundaries of the
United States, empire, and immigration restriction reached
full flowering and in which legal denial of basic human rights
of those categorized as "defective" or "unfit" (the disabled)
took their most egregious forms. What is too easily elided in
a more traditional framing of the nineteenth century is the
fundamental continuity of able, white, male legal authority,
the way in which each challenge to abled, racialized and gendered privilege, each challenge to the borders of belonging
was successfully parried.

It is equally critical to acknowledge what the argument
here assumes and what it does not. Privilege and subordination were never complete; the boundaries did not always
hold; belonging was not all or nothing; resistance mattered
psychically and in fact. There was most certainly fuzziness
and porosity in administration and even more in actual social
life. Yet acknowledging each of these points, one can never-
theless trace a fundamental continuity of legal personhood
and citizenship imagined in abled, racialized, and gendered

terms, thus privileging ableness, whiteness, and manhood, privilege that depended on subordinating disabled persons, racialized others, and women. Seen in this light, the years from the ratification of the Constitution in 1789 to the resolution of quotas under the Immigration Act of 1924 in 1929 are not the *long* nineteenth century: they are *the* nineteenth century.

Organization and Sources

The argument is developed over three chapters that are organized interpretively and analytically rather than chronologically for the basic reason, as noted earlier, that chronology has served to obscure the fundamental continuity in the borders of belonging. Each chapter opens with a set of epigraphs that establish the scope and frame of reference of the chapter, orienting the reader to the work of each chapter. Chapters 1 and 2 focus primarily on documenting privilege and inclusion on the one hand and the impact of subordination and exclusion on the other.

Chapter 1, "Constructing a Universal Legal Person: Able White Manhood," traces what often remains least examined: the capacities that law gave able white men on the basis of their ability, race, and gender as persons and as citizens. Law accorded able white men ownership of self, citizenship, and likewise gave them a superior claim to the land. In part, men's independence rested on the legally forced dependence, subjection, ownership, and exclusion of others. In this chapter, I trace both: privilege granted to able white men by law as persons and as citizens and the privilege they gained through the legally enforced dependence, subjection, ownership, and exclusion of others. The chapter begins with self-ownership and citizenship and then turns to able white men's superior claim to the land and to the space of the nation. Chapter 2, "Subjects of Law: Disabled Persons, Racialized Others, and Women," shifts perspective to focus on those excluded by the borders of belonging. The chapter focuses on two key elements of the consequences of laws' imagining of "people" as able, white, and male: the submergence of individual identity for everyone else and the daily indignities of being "subjects of" or "other" in law.

The picture Chapters 1 and 2 present is one of continuity in the borders of belonging across the long nineteenth century. But this picture raises fundamental questions: Why? How? Despite what? Chapter 3, "Borders: Resistance, Defense, Structure and Ideology," focuses on explanation. It begins by considering how those othered in law challenged their exclusion and subordination, the paths of reappropriation of self, dissemblance, confrontation, and other "weapons of the weak,"[4] and the pursuit of right through law. But privilege, as we know, generally has deep roots and is not easily surrendered. With this in mind, the chapter turns to tracing the legal and theoretical underpinnings of law's imagining of personhood and citizenship in abled, racialized, and gendered terms and considers how each challenge to the borders of belonging was parried, so that while particulars changed, the abled, racialized, and gendered foundations of the borders of belonging remained intact. The final two sections of the chapter focus on the significance of the structure of the American legal system and those who made, interpreted, and enforced the law in supporting the borders of belonging. The borders of belonging were constructed, masked, and reinforced through the structure of the American legal system: the multiplicity of sites of law, ideology, and the fundamental fact that white men made, interpreted, and enforced the law.

In reading, you will encounter the same topics and time periods at multiple points within a chapter and across chapters. Repetition is an intentional strategy. In each case where I revisit a subject or story, the focus is different the point for which an example or reference stands distinct. So, for example, I discuss slavery in multiple places within each chapter. In Chapter 1, I highlight how slavery augmented white men's shared independence and how it facilitated white men's claims

---

[4] See James C. Scott, *Weapons of the Weak: Everyday Forms of Peasant Resistance* (New Haven, 1985); Scott, *Domination and the Arts of Resistance: Hidden Transcripts* (New Haven, 1990).

to the land. The focus is not on the slave, but on how slavery augmented white men's independence. In Chapter 2, the perspective is different: that of the experience of the slave, what it meant as a daily matter to be legally subject to, and the property of, another and the hierarchies of privilege within subordination. And, in Chapter 3, I return to slavery, tracing the path of resistance, reappropriation of self, strategic dissemblance, and pursuit of right through law; the tools used to preserve white privilege and black subordination in the wake of emancipation; and the way slavery extended its ugly hand into every facet of the legal system. The organization gives primacy to the interpretive and the analytical over the comprehensive or chronological. It puts topics together that are not normally thought of together to highlight their shared qualities within the larger analytical frame.

The argument draws on many subfields of law including the law of domestic relations and law regulating reproduction; property, inheritance, zoning, tax, contract, and tort law; labor law and the regulation of industries and professions; law relating to public order and safety; the law of race and law relating to Native Americans; law regulating involuntary commitment and sterilization; law relating to military service; law regulating immigration, naturalization, and citizenship; constitutional law; law relating to civil and political rights; criminal law; the law of empire; and so on. The goal is not to trace in full any of these areas of law. Rather, it is to seek patterns to capture the multiplicity of sites and levels (local, state, federal; common law, statutory, administrative, treaty) within law that gave shape to legal personhood, citizenship, and the borders of belonging in the long nineteenth century. It requires recognition that law operates affirmatively and negatively, by inclusion and exclusion, by expression and omission, and that extralegal assumptions, norms, and practices take shape in the shadow of the law.[5] Law, of course, does not simply exist or emerge from nowhere, nor is

[5] The phrase "shadow of the law" is from Tocqueville. *Democracy in America, In Two Volumes with a Critical Appraisal of Each Volume by John Stuart Mill* (New York, 1970), trans. Henry Reeve, 1:151–2.

it simply an instrument or tool. So that, one must consider as well the structures and institutions of law and the lawmakers; the dynamics of social, political, cultural, and economic change over time that shape law and that law also shapes; the exercise of power and the agency of the disempowered; and law's unintended, as well as its intended, consequences.

The argument here, while not synthetic, incorporates and draws on the work of many, many scholars. In the body of the work itself, the reader will find few footnotes. In keeping with the format of the series, I have limited footnotes to direct citations of cases, statutes, quotations, and to instances where an idea is fundamentally associated with a particular author. At the volume's end, there is an extensive bibliographic essay and alphabetical listing of secondary sources that highlight my intellectual debts and provide a guide for further reading.

There is an understandable appeal or desire to relegate the story told here to history. It is less comfortable, but I believe worth considering the impact of borders of belonging for modern American history and for modern liberal democratic states more generally, not simply historically, but in the present. The Conclusion sketches the ways in which abled, racialized, and gendered power shaped the twentieth century American state. The brief Coda with which the volume closes reflects my hope that the history traced here of America's long nineteenth century can provide a foundation for broader engagement with the borders of belonging at the heart of the liberal ideal, for thinking about the relationship between privilege and subordination, for considering the role of law in their construction and perpetuation, and for the possibility of crafting more equitable polities.

"As to your extraordinary Code of Laws, I cannot but laugh... Depend upon it, We know better than to repeal our Masculine systems." (John Adams to Abigail Adams, Letter, 14 April 1776)

****

"Rightly considered, the policy of the General Government toward the red man is not only liberal, but generous. He is unwilling to submit to the laws of the States and mingle with their population. To save him from this alternative, or perhaps utter annihilation, the General Government kindly offers him a new home, and proposes to pay the whole expense of his removal and settlement." (President Andrew Jackson, Second Annual Message to Congress, 8 December 1830)

****

"We do not regard [slavery] as an evil, on the contrary, we think that our prosperity, our happiness, our very political existence, is inseparably connected with it ....We will not yield it." (John A. Quitman, Governor of Mississippi, Inaugural Address, 10 January 1850)

****

"I am willing to admit that all men are created equal, but how are they equal?.... I do not believe that a superior race is bound to receive among it those of an inferior race if the mingling of them can only tend to the detriment of the mass." (Peter Van Winkle, Republican Senator, West Virginia, Congressional Debate re Amending Naturalization Law, 30 January 1866)

****

"Well, sir; it is to protect a man in his business... [and] for the accom'odation of the passengers generally, the white people... the traveling public." (John G. Benson, Master, *The Governor Allen*, explanation of the object of racial segregation, 11 February 1878)

****

"It is said that our holding the Philippines is a violation of the Declaration of Independence.... The instrument is to be restrained to the fitness and the reason of things. All people are not capable of self-government." (William H. Taft, 26 August 1904)

****

"We have seen more than once that the public welfare may call upon the best citizens for their lives. It would be strange if it could not call upon those who already sap the strength of the State for these lesser sacrifices ... in order to prevent our being swamped with incompetence.... Three generations of imbeciles are enough." (Justice Oliver Wendell Holmes, *Buck v. Bell*, 2 May 1927)

I

CONSTRUCTING A UNIVERSAL
LEGAL PERSON

Able White Manhood

The space of legal privilege all too often remains unmarked altogether or is incompletely sketched, the shadows cast by particular examples of subordination. Yet as the epigraphs to this chapter suggest, able white men understood, embraced, and defended their privilege and others' subordination. Their words provide an entry into tracing the creation, the stakes, and the borders of the legal privilege held by able white men across the full sweep of the long nineteenth century. Their privilege was both positively marked in law and constructed through the subordination, ownership, marginalization, and exclusion of disabled persons, racialized others, and women. Law made full personhood and citizenship dependent on ability, race, and gender. It gave able white men claim to the land both in positive terms and by denying others' rights to it. Collectively, personhood, citizenship, and their claim to the land allowed able white men to see themselves as the embodiment of the nation not simply at the founding, but across the long nineteenth century.

Self-Ownership and Citizenship

The American Revolution effected a dramatic political transformation – the establishment of the first modern republic – but it was fought, like the Glorious Revolution that preceded

it by a century, for the rights of propertied Englishmen as
men. The political theory of liberalism and republicanism
on which the revolution rested assumed inequality: in fact,
depended on it. Deeply rooted in the expansive rhetoric of
the Declaration of Independence – "all men are created equal;
that they are endowed by their Creator with certain unalienable rights; that among these are Life, Liberty, and the pursuit of Happiness" – was the seventeenth century project of
the American revolutionaries' English forebears asserting the
rights of parliament, of landed, that is, propertied, English
men, as against the authority of the king. John Locke wrote
and published his *Two Treatises of Government* (1689), from
which the American patriots found so much to justify the
cause of independence, in the context of and in support of
events that led to the Glorious Revolution. "[E]very man,"
Locke explained in his *Second Treatise*, "has a *Property* in his
own *Person*. This no Body has any Right to but himself. The
Labour of his Body, and the Work of his Hands, we may say,
are properly his." His property extended, moreover, to property produced through labor that was his by ownership ("my
horse") and by contract ("my servant").[1] Locke's vision of
property, the state of nature, and civil society focused on men,
able white men; women, slaves, idiots, and the insane were
not part of the civil society he envisioned. Like Locke and his
contemporaries, the leaders of the American Revolution were
able, white, and male; they were propertied in both senses that
Locke understood the term: they were self-owning individuals
and they held landed wealth. And they fought the Revolution,
and, a decade later in 1789, crafted the Constitution in defense
of their rights as propertied men.

Fundamentally underlying those rights was the English
common law. Between 1776 and 1784, every one of the former colonies, except Rhode Island and Connecticut (and they
followed in 1798 and 1818, respectively), adopted the English
common law as their law. Why? There was, as the Vermont
legislature explained in 1782, the immediate need for law and

---

[1] John Locke, *Second Treatise*, sec. 27–28, John Locke, *Two Treatises of
Government*, ed. Peter Laslett (New York, 1960), 287–9.

the challenge of crafting a new code of laws while fighting a war of independence. There were, after all, no published American law reports to which courts might easily turn. And there was also the matter of familiarity – again, as the Vermont legislature put it: "whereas the inhabitants of this State have been habituated to conform their manners to the English laws, and hold their real estate by English tenures."[2] But as fundamental was the basic fact that the American Revolution was not fought to change the law. Early in his now classic text *The Americanization of the Common Law*, William E. Nelson notes, "There is no evidence that any of the men who led Massachusetts into the War of Independence or any of those who followed acted for the purpose of bringing about fundamental changes in the rules and institutions of which the legal system was comprised."[3] In this respect, the men of Massachusetts were no different from the landed gentry of Virginia, or the men who led the independence movement in any of the thirteen states. This is enough perhaps to show the conservatism of the Revolution, but the import of the new states embrace of the common law goes deeper. The common law in its origins was the law articulated by the royal central courts; it applied to a fraction of the English population, the landed gentry, and took as its central preoccupation the protection of property.

From the outset of the new republic then, law privileged able white men's ownership of self, according full personhood and belonging only to those who were able, white, and male. Here law protected his real and personal property through the law of property, his reputation through the law of slander and libel, his "property" in his wife through the law of coverture and the unwritten law of husbands' rights, his property in his children through the law of patriarchy, and in his human chattel through the law of slavery. Only able

---

[2] Vermont reception statute of 1782, quoted from Elizabeth Gaspar Brown, in consultation with William Wirt Blume, *British Statutes in American Law, 1776–1836* (Ann Arbor, 1964), 23–4.

[3] William E. Nelson, *The Americanization of the Common Law: The Impact of Legal Change on Massachusetts Society, 1760–1830* (Athens, GA, 1994, 1974), 67.

white men enjoyed the full panoply of civil rights – the right to inherit, own, and devise (dispose of) property; to contract; to sue and be sued; and to enjoy the fruits of their own labor.

The common law did not, of course, remain static over the nineteenth century. And yet, vast areas of common law newly forged in the nineteenth century in response to industrialization including contract law, the law of accidental injury, and the law of corporations' presumed self-ownership. "In order to surrender rights and accept duties," Amy Stanley notes, "parties to contracts had to be sovereigns of themselves, possessive individuals *entitled to* their own persons, labor, and faculties."[4] As a matter of law, though, only able white men were self-owning individuals. Contract doctrines like caveat emptor, "buyer beware," rested on an assumption of capacity that, in fact, only able white men had. So too, the founding assumption of the law of negligence was that the actor was, in fact, "his own master and judge, of what was, and was not prudent."[5] Courts and legal commentators explained the standard of conduct against which the conduct of the actors was judged as that of the "reasonable man."

In long-established areas of the law as well, nineteenth century American courts backed men's capacity to conduct their legal affairs and dispose of their property as they saw fit. "The rights of property depend upon the law," the judge explained to the jury in a typical mid-century case involving a challenge to a man's will. "The law has not committed to us the power of disposing of men's property as we please.... A rich old man may marry a young wife or a handsome and obliging housekeeper, or maid servant – he may disinherit his own children and leave them beggars. You and I may think his conduct oppressive and unjust in the highest sense; yet if it be his will, we have no power to set it aside."[6] Where legal doctrine and courts' application of it in will contests

---

[4] Amy Stanley, *From Bondage to Contract: Wage Labor, Marriage, and the Market in the Age of Slave Emancipation* (New York, 1998), 3 (emphasis added).

[5] *Chicago, Burlington and Quincy R.R. v. Hazzard*, 26 Ill. 373 (1861).

[6] *Turner v. Hand*, 24 F. Cas. 355, 360–61 (C.C.D.N.J. 1855) (No. 14,257).

and contract cases assumed the capacity of white men, the incapacity of the disabled, women, and racialized others was written into the law.

In other particulars as well, law accorded able white men an expanded right of self, while denying it to others. Over the course of the nineteenth century, state courts created an American doctrine of self-defense that sharply repudiated the English common law doctrine that one must retreat "to the wall" at one's back before legitimately killing in self-defense, adopting in its place a rule of no duty to retreat. The Ohio Supreme Court held in *Erwin v. State* in 1876 that a "true man" was "not obliged to fly" from his assailant. The U.S. Supreme Court followed the path that the state supreme courts had forged.[7] Justice Holmes, the author of the Supreme Court's opinion, later privately wrote "a man is not born to run away;" the law "must consider human nature and make some allowances for the fighting instinct at critical moments."[8] Holmes phrased his comment in terms of "human nature," but what he in fact meant was white men. The American doctrine of self-defense was shaped in cases involving white men; it presumed and further fostered an independence that only they had under the law. The black slave and the married woman had no right to resist with deadly force a master's or husband's physical assault. The slave's only protection was not the hollow proscriptions written into law, but a master's economic self-interest. What a man did to his wife within the marriage relation was, in large measure, defined by law as private.

So complete was a husband's dominion over his wife and home that an unwritten corollary of the law of self-defense extended to a man who killed his wife's lover. As Hendrik Hartog notes, "if a man found his wife in the arms of another man and he killed the other man on the spot, he would never be convicted of

---

[7] *Erwin v. State*, 29 Ohio St. 186 (1876); *Brown v. U.S.*, 256 U.S. 335 (1921).

[8] Mark DeWolfe Howe, ed., *Holmes-Laski Letters: The Correspondence of Mr. Justice Holmes and Harold J. Laski, 1916–1935*, 2 vols. (Cambridge, MA, 1953), 1:339–40.

murder."[9] He was not a murderer, but a man acting in defense of his home; his "momentary madness" proved only that he was a real man doing what any man would be compelled to do were he to face the same situation. In practice, jurors did not even require a man to have acted in the heat of the moment. In celebrated cases at mid-century known by the names of both assailant and victim – Sickles-Key, Cole-Hiscock, McFarland-Richardson – jurors acquitted each assailant despite the fact that none of the men's acts met the requirement of having come upon his wife in the arms of her lover.

As the examples of husbands and masters suggest, men's independence rested from the outset on the legally structured dependence and subjection of others. No regime was more fundamental to preserving the established social and political order than the law of coverture. One of the most famous private exchanges of the Revolutionary Era was that between John Adams and his wife, Abigail, relating to the power the common law gave husbands over wives. "I long to hear that you have declared an independency," Abigail wrote in spring 1776, "and by the way in the new Code of Laws which I suppose it will be necessary for you to make I desire you would Remember the Ladies." His response: "As to your extraordinary Code of Law, I cannot but laugh.... Depend upon it, We know better than to repeal our Masculine systems." Describing her husband's response in a letter to her friend Mercy Otis Warren, Abigail again noted that surely independence would require a new code of laws: "I thought it was very probable our wise Statesmen would erect a New Government and form a new code of Laws." And she pointed specifically to the harshness of the common law toward women: "I ventured to speak a word in behalf of our Sex, who are rather hardly dealt with by the Laws of England which gives such unlimited power to the Husband to use his wife Ill."[10] But

---

9 Hendrik Hartog, "Lawyering, Husbands' Rights, and the 'the Unwritten Law' in Nineteenth-Century America," *Journal of American History* 84 (June 1997): 67.

10 L. H. Butterfield, ed., *The Adams Papers, Series II, Adams Family Correspondence* (Cambridge, MA, 1963), 370, 382, 397.

the states of the fledgling nation did not draft a new code of laws, embracing the common law instead. Moreover, lacking published reports of their own, they looked for interpretation of the common law to English reports of cases decided after, as well as before, the Declaration of Independence, and to the common law's most famous expositor, William Blackstone's *Commentaries on the Laws of England* completed in the 1760s on the eve of the American Revolution. Blackstone, Holly Brewer notes, was cited more in American newspapers of the 1790s "than any other thinker, including Locke and Montesquieu."[11]

Nowhere was Blackstone's work in rendering the common law seamless and timeless more important than in his explication of the law of domestic relations. There were three parallel "Great Relations in Private Life," Blackstone explained, that of master and servant, husband and wife, parent and child, and then a fourth in the event of the loss of the latter, that of guardian and ward. Blackstone took a certain liberty in describing the three relations as "parallel"; in so doing, Brewer notes, he extended to husbands and fathers the near absolute authority that had been the sphere of masters only, so that husbands acquired stronger authority over wives, fathers greater rights to their children. Blackstone's *Commentaries*, in turn, became the foundation from which American treatise writers would then expand.

Blackstone defined men's and women's relative rights and obligations in the following terms: "By marriage, the husband and wife are one person in law; that is, the very being or legal existence of the woman is suspended during the marriage, or at least is incorporated and consolidated into that of the husband."[12] As applied by American courts, under the law of coverture, a woman, by virtue of marriage, lost her right to contract, to sue or be sued in her own right, or to write a will. Her earnings were his, because her labor was his. An injury

---

[11] Holly Brewer, "The Transformation of Domestic Law," in *The Cambridge History of Law in America, 3 vols.*, eds. Michael Grossberg and Christopher Tomlins (New York, 2008), 1:289–90.

[12] William Blackstone, *Commentaries on the Laws of England*, 1:430.

to her body was an injury to him, because he was responsible for the medical costs of her care, but also because her labor and right to sexual relations were his. Children born to their union were his, not hers. The obligation to obey was hers, the right to discipline his. His place of residence became hers, because a married woman could have no settlement separate from her husband. Married women's loss of legal personhood under the law of coverture augmented men's personhood; her dependence defined his independence. As Nancy Cott notes of marriage in the nineteenth century, "Men's civil and political status grew, then, from being independent heads of units that included dependents."[13]

The narrow conditions for divorce (or, in the case of South Carolina the refusal to grant divorce on any grounds) sealed men's domestic authority. As one South Carolina court explained, the law would not require a husband to support his wife if she left him no matter how grave the abuse, if "the husband offer to take her back ... she is bound to return." "The only 'necessity,'" Stephanie McCurry notes of ante-bellum South Carolina, "justifying separation was the husband's refusal to have her in his – and it was his – house." If a woman chose to "starve rather than submit," a prominent South Carolina lawyer noted, the state would not intervene to protect her.[14] The law in South Carolina was not so much an aberration as one end of a more general continuum. Whether in South Carolina or Massachusetts, judges understood the "peace and happiness of families" and the "best interests of society" as dependent upon placing "the husband and father at the head of the household."[15]

Even in death, the law constructed men as providers and women as dependents. Under the common law, a right of

---

[13] Nancy F. Cott, "Giving Character to Our Whole Civil Polity: Marriage and the Public Order in the Late Nineteenth Century," in *U.S. History as Women's History*, eds. Linda K. Kerber, Alice Kessler-Harris, Kathryn Kish Sklar (Chapel Hill, 1995), 111.

[14] Stephanie McCurry, *Masters of Small Worlds: Yeoman Households, Gender Relations, and the Political Culture of the Antebellum South Carolina Law Country* (New York, 1995), 87–8.

[15] Ibid., 88.

action for accidental injury belonged to the individual and, hence, if the individual was killed in an accident or died from the injuries sustained, the right of action died with him. The growing death toll from industrial accidents in the nineteenth century led to the passage of wrongful death statutes modifying the common law. But, whereas England's pioneering wrongful death laws provided a right of action for the benefit of "wife, husband, parent, and child" of the deceased, a majority of American states limited wrongful death actions to cases involving the death of a man. As in New York's statute (1847), damages were limited to the "pecuniary injury resulting from such death to the wife and next of kin."[16]

Men's shared legal status as heads of families bridged deep economic differences. Stephanie McCurry captures, in the lives of yeoman in the antebellum South Carolina low country, a world in which slaves were the majority of the population and the lives of planters and yeoman were divided by glaring economic inequality. Yet yeomen and planters shared a legal status as masters of their households.

In the daily exercise of power and authority within the household, in the authority conferred [by law] on household heads and the subordination demanded of dependents, yeoman farmers not only produced the material basis of independence; they laid claim as well, even in the absence of slaves, to the identity of freemen and masters....[17]

In a nation fundamentally premised on independence, it is a telling contradiction that women's legally enforced dependence under coverture was not part of the constitutional debates. It is equally telling that slavery was preserved, even given constitutional protection, despite having been so debated. What greater evidence could there be of law's power

---

[16] Quoted in John Fabian Witt, *The Accidental Republic: Crippled Workingmen, Destitute Widows, and the Remaking of American Law* (Cambridge, MA, 2004), 53–54; Witt, "From Loss of Services to Loss of Support: The Wrongful Death Statutes, the Origins of Modern Tort Law, and the Making of the Nineteenth Century Family," *Law and Social Inquiry* 25 (2000): 733–7.

[17] McCurry, *Masters of Small Worlds*, 91.

than slavery? Through it human beings were transformed into property, chattel owned by other men. But the economic interest in slavery extended far beyond the master class to those who leased slaves, who insured human chattel, who ran slave markets, who bought cotton, who ran the inns and taverns that serviced the slave trade on market days and court week, and so on. In the sense that a court of equity would use the term, all had unclean hands. Moreover, slaves represented more than a pool of unfree labor, they became, quite literally, the coin of the realm. Easily convertible to cold cash, they were the best collateral a man could offer or ask for; they were, as Ariela Gross notes, "the cornerstone of the Southern credit economy."[18] And, in this regard, commercial law complemented the law of slavery; indeed, as Gross shows, in some counties in the antebellum South the commercial law of slavery made up as much as half of the business of circuit courts.[19] The market in slaves held another benefit, as well: it held out the promise that even the most marginal of white men might acquire a slave and thus secure his own independence, his full citizenship, his inclusion in the master class.[20] Moreover, the racial privileges of the borders of belonging stretched across the slavery divide geographically and chronologically.

Whiteness, in the American republic, was itself a form of property.[21] It had been made so, in the first instance, by the legal regime of slavery. Because only blacks could be slaves, the law of slavery created a property interest in being white. As Thomas R. R. Cobb noted in *An Inquiry Into the Law of Negro Slavery in the United States* (1858), to be white created a presumption of freedom matched by the presumption of slavery that came with being black.[22] The property interest in

[18] Ariela J. Gross, *Double Character: Slavery and Mastery in the Antebellum Southern Courtroom* (Princeton, 2000), 32.
[19] Ibid., 23.
[20] Walter Johnson, *Soul by Soul: Life inside the Antebellum Slave Market* (Cambridge, MA), 80.
[21] Cheryl I. Harris, "Whiteness as Property," *Harvard Law Review* 106 (1993): 1709–91.
[22] Thomas R. R. Cobb, *An Inquiry into the Law of Negro Slavery in the United States* (Philadelphia, 1858), 66–7 (sec. 68–9).

whiteness forged through slavery survived abolition. "How much would it be worth," Homer Plessy's lawyer in *Plessy v. Ferguson* (1896), Albion Tourgee argued,

> To a young man entering upon the practice of law, to be regarded as a white man rather than a colored one? Six-sevenths of the population are white. Nineteen-twentieths of the property of the country is owned by white people. Ninety-nine hundredths of the business opportunities are in the control of white people.... Indeed, is [reputation for being white] not the most valuable sort of property, being the master-key that unlocks the golden door of opportunity?[23]

As Tourgee so clearly understood, the end of slavery did not end the property interest in whiteness; legalized discriminations rendered whiteness the "master key." But what Tourgee assumed or overlooked must also be made explicit: whiteness was a form of property when coupled with manhood and mental and physical ableness.

Slavery and whiteness were not the only ways in which able white men's property in themselves was reinforced. Emancipation dissolved property in human chattel without compensation effecting a momentous legal transformation in the right to personhood and the right to property; it did not end white men's dominion over black Americans. Forced labor remained central to the labor system in the American South through at least the mid-twentieth century, embodied in a vast array of laws that criminalized quitting employment or the failure to be employed, and imposed forced labor as penalty. Vagrancy, contract fraud, criminal surety, and other open-ended state statutes facilitated white subordination of and control over African Americans, thereby denying them the control of their labor fundamental to self-ownership.[24]

---

[23] Quoted in Charles A. Lofgren, *The Plessy Case: A Legal-Historical Interpretation* (New York, 1987), 154.

[24] Section 1 of the Thirteenth Amendment barred slavery, but, in its prohibition of "involuntary servitude, except as a punishment for crime whereof the party shall have been duly convicted," left the door open to other forms of coerced labor. Congressional and court action closed off only some of these. In 1867, Congress passed the Peonage Abolition Act of 1867 making peonage unlawful. As Risa Goluboff notes, the U.S.

The law also reinforced men's self-ownership by defining other labor – Chinese contract labor; Indian child indentured labor; married women's sexual, reproductive, household, and productive labor; and paupers and beggars – as unfree or not labor at all and then putting that labor at the disposal of white men. So, for example, California's 1850 indenture act gave "citizens" the right to take custody of an Indian child and place him or her under apprenticeship; the state's vagrancy law authorized law enforcement officials to arrest and hire out to the highest bidder Indians found loitering, drunk, or "guilty" of any number of other offenses. Together the two laws meant that as many as 10,000 Native Americans in California were held in virtual slavery. Peonage laws in Utah and New Mexico (in effect in New Mexico until 1867 when Congress moved to enforce the Thirteenth Amendment's prohibition against servitude) and the importation of thousands of Chinese contract workers in the 1850s similarly assured white men of both their own freedom and a pool of unfree labor.[25]

It would be hard to refute that there was a market for women's sexual labor or that crippled persons could attain

Supreme Court narrowly interpreted peonage to mean "coerced labor in payment of a debt created by a contract between two individuals." The laborer had to prove not only a debt, but also "that attempts to leave the employment would be met with physical force, arrest or imprisonment to make out a peonage claim." *Bailey v. Alabama*, 219 U.S. 219, 242 (1911). Risa L. Goluboff, "The Thirteenth Amendment and the Lost Origins of Civil Rights," *Duke Law Journal* 50 (2000–2001): 1648, 1655. Three years after *Bailey*, the Court struck down criminal surety laws as a violation of the Thirteenth Amendment in *U.S. v. Reynolds*, 235 U.S. 133 (1914). Criminal surety laws facilitated landowners and employers access to labor by allowing them to pay the fine for an indigent convict (most often poor African Americans who had been arrested on questionable grounds to generate a labor pool) in return for which the convict/laborer would pay off the debt through his labor. But these limitations aside, the southern labor system remained one based on the coerced labor of poor African Americans. Laws criminalizing vagrancy (the crime of appearing to be without visible means of support) tracing their origins back to medieval and early modern England, but in the wake of the Civil War reinvigorated and applied against African Americans, were only declared unconstitutional in the 1960s.

[25] Evelyn Nakano Glenn, *Unequal Freedom: How Race and Gender Shaped American Citizenship and Labor* (Cambridge, MA, 2002), 68–9.

some measure of self-support by playing on the sympathy their disability generated on the public street. Indeed, had it been otherwise, there would have been no need to make prostitution illegal or to criminalize begging by the physically disabled. Law privileged the labor of mentally and physically able men in part by marking the boundaries of free labor. The beggar who persisted in refusing to sell his labor, the woman who treated her body as a market commodity, the disabled person who was seen as having no labor to sell, each came to be represented as an economic, or, in the case of the prostitute, a moral and reproductive, drain on the nation. The state's expansive police power coupled with the provisionary language of the Thirteenth Amendment – "except as punishment for crime whereof the party shall have been duly convicted" – offered a constitutional safe haven, as it were, for laws and ordinances criminalizing vagrancy, prostitution, begging, and even public display by the physically disabled (unsightly beggar ordinances), that wrung labor from the unwilling, channeled sexual labor through the marriage contract, and hid from public view those supposed to have no labor to sell.

Near the end of the nineteenth century, philosopher and psychologist William James noted, *"a man's self is the sum, is the sum total of all that he CAN call his,* not only his body and his psychic powers, but his clothes and his house, his wife and children ... his reputation and works, his lands and horses, and yacht and bank-account."[26] But what his statement overlooked was the centrality of law in crafting men's ownership of self and defining it to include the persons and labor of others, including wives, children, slaves, and racialized others more generally. Even as industrialization undermined the meaningfulness of hirelings' ownership of their own labor, laboring men joined their voices to those of political and policy elites decrying the market's incursion on their rights to the labor of a wife, demanding a "family wage," asserting their rights as "free men."

---

[26] William James, *The Principles of Psychology,* 2 vols. (1890, Reprint New York, 1918), 1:291.

Deeply intertwined with and resting on the gendered, raced, and abled conditions for full legal personhood in the new American Republic was a second quality critical to marking the borders of belonging: citizenship. As Jennifer Nedelsky and other scholars have noted, when those who led the Revolution and crafted the constitution "used the term men, they had males (in fact, white males) in mind. They expected only men to participate in government as voters, office holders, or even members of juries."[27] The abled, racialized, and gendered contours of citizenship as able, white, and male, took form in a dye cast by the dependency and subjectness of disabled persons, paupers, women, slaves, free blacks, and Indians. In Revolutionary rhetoric traits defined as female represented the antithesis of the good republican, coded male. So too, Revolutionary elites understood a man's independence – the key qualification of the citizen-voter – to be secured through property ownership, family headship, meeting his obligations of support and military service.

Moreover, although the Constitution did not define citizenship, in any number of particulars it marked the boundaries of citizenship through exclusion. So, for example, Indians were excluded from the constitutional order; slaves were ballast in the delicate balance between North and South, a property right with constitutional sanction.[28] Despite the fact that a few states recognized free blacks as citizens, the compromise over slavery in the U.S. Constitution provided a text from which Chief Justice Roger B. Taney could conclude in *Dred Scott v. Sandford* (1857) that, slave or free, blacks were not "constituent members of the sovereignty;" "they are not

---

[27] Jennifer Nedelsky, *Private Property and the Limits of American Constitutionalism: The Madisonian Framework and Its Legacy* (Chicago, 1990), 4, 279 n. 5.

[28] Commonly referred to by the shorthand of the "3/5th Clause," Art. I, sec. 2 of the U.S. Constitution balanced northern and southern representation in the U.S. House of Representatives by counting slaves as three-fifths persons: "Representatives ... shall be apportioned among the several states ... according to their respective Numbers, which shall be determined by adding to the whole Number of Free Persons, including those bound to Service for a Term of Years, and excluding Indians not taxed, three fifths of all other persons." U.S. Const. Art. 1, sec. 2.

included, and were not intended to be included." Not only could they never be citizens of the United States, they were "so far inferior that they had no rights which the white man was bound to respect."[29] Taney's opinion captured a central fact of citizenship in the pre-Civil War era: citizenship was determined largely at the state level and hence varied from state to state. But it demonstrated equally the limits of that variation and just how quickly the Supreme Court could eviscerate recognitions of citizenship at the state level that could be read, as in *Dred Scott*, as conflicting with the Constitution itself. Moreover, the nation's first Naturalization Law, passed in 1790, limiting naturalization to "free, white persons," and the steadfast resistance to anything more than the symbolic amendment of the law in the wake of the American Civil War, testified to the assumption that the United States was in fact and was determined to remain a white nation.[30]

That the United States was understood to be a republic of free able-bodied white men was fostered from the outset by the connection between citizenship and military service. The Federal Militia Act of 1792 made explicit what elsewhere was left implicit: only "*free able-bodied white male citizens* of the respective States" were subject to service.[31] The obligation of free able-bodied white males, whether actually called on to bear arms or whether they in fact served or hired a substitute, embodied citizenship as abled, racialized, and gendered.

It was also the foundation from which rights flowed. Military service offered immigrant men a fast track to citizenship. In World War I, for example, Congress granted any "alien" who served in the war the right to naturalize without first having made a declaration of intent or having resided five years in the United States. Compensation for military service also took the form of monetary payments and a stake in the

---

[29] *Scott v. Sandford*, 60 U.S. (19 How.) 393, 407 (1857).
[30] 1 U.S. Statutes at Large 103 (1790).
[31] Militia Act of 1792, 2 U.S. Statutes at Large 262 sec. 1 (1792) (emphasis added). Chief Justice Roger Taney used the language of the 1792 act in his opinion in *Dred Scott* as evidence that from the nation's beginning even free blacks could not be citizens. *Dred Scott v. Sandford*, 60 U.S. (19 How.) 393, 409, 416 (1857).

land. Beginning with the Revolutionary War and continuing with the War of 1812 and the Mexican War, the federal government and a number of states compensated military service with land warrants that were readily convertible through sale to cash.[32] By mid-century, the initial impetus for the legislation – securing sufficient troops – was overwhelmed by the demands of veterans. Their demands transformed the bounty land warrants into an entitlement for service of even a matter of days rendered decades earlier and extended the entitlement to every veteran, of every war, including the Indian Wars and Indian Removal. Classes of veterans who were either initially excluded from particular legislation or given smaller land bounties than others successfully mobilized for what they saw as theirs by right. So, for example, following the Mexican War, veterans of the War of 1812 successfully lobbied for legislation increasing their original bounties. A group of Arkansas veterans argued that, "in adding millions of acres [by their service] to the public domain, which have brought also millions of dollars into the national treasury, ... [it would be] a small pittance [to award them] an inconsiderable fraction of the unappropriated portion of the domain thus won by their valor and patriotism."[33] The sense of entitlement and the scale of provision increased with each passing conflict, so that provisions to veterans of earlier wars were dwarfed by pensions provided to northern veterans of the Civil War. By the early twentieth century, Civil War pensions had become a huge social welfare program providing disability, old-age, and survivors' benefits to veterans, however brief the service to the northern cause. Moreover, the mantle of men's citizenship extended over their wives, widows, and

[32] The focus here is less on land than on the fact of compensation. Land was the only currency, so to speak, that the Treasury had in sufficient quantity to meet its commitment. Moreover, while the initial legislation was structured to and rested on the hope that former soldiers would settle the land they received in warrants, few veterans resettled; the vast majority sold their warrants.

[33] "Soldiers of 1812 of Van Buren, Arkansas," quoted in James W. Oberly, *Sixty Million Acres: American Veterans and the Public Lands before the Civil War* (Kent, OH, 1990), 16.

children. Just as widows and children could pursue wrongful death claims following the negligently caused death of a husband or father, wives, widows, and children of veterans were named as beneficiaries in legislation establishing military bounties and pensions.

But men's citizenship extended over their wives and children even more directly than benefiting them as men's dependents from military pensions. In 1855, Congress mandated that any woman who by virtue of marriage to a U.S. citizen and eligible for naturalization under existing laws (in other words, who was free and white) "shall be deemed and taken to be a citizen."[34] The change brought U.S. practice into line with European practice and might be seen as simply an administrative matter except that it completely ignored whether an American woman's citizenship extended over her alien husband. Moreover, until 1934, children born abroad were recognized as U.S. citizens only if their father was a citizen who had lived in the United States before the child's birth.[35]

From its beginnings as a nation, the United States distinguished between territory and its inhabitants. Article I of the U.S. Constitution gave Congress authority to "regulate commerce with the Indian tribes"; Article IV addressed governance of the territory of the United States and the addition of new states. Neither the Constitution nor the Northwest Ordinance envisioned or provided for naturalization or citizenship of the "territory's" native inhabitants.[36] The path of U.S. empire through the long nineteenth century balanced the desire for territorial expansion against the cost of acquiring racialized others who inhabited the land. In drawing the boundaries of the territory that the United States would annex from Mexico under the Treaty of Guadalupe Hidalgo

[34] "Act to Secure the Right of Citizenship to Children of Citizens ..." 10 U.S. Statutes at Large 604, ch. 71 (1855).
[35] Nancy F. Cott, "Marriage and Women's Citizenship in the United States, 1830–1934," *American Historical Review* 103 (1998), 1469.
[36] U.S. Constitution, art. 1, sec. 8, cl. 3; art. 4, sec. 3, cl. 1 and 2; Northwest Ordinance, July 13, 1787, sec. 9, sec. 14, art. 3 (http://avalon.law.yale.edu/18th_century/nworder.asp)(last accessed September 13, 2009).

at the close of the Mexican-American War, the United States trimmed its expansionist designs to maximize the acquisition of land while minimizing the number of Mexican (Catholic) inhabitants seen as undesirable on both racial and religious grounds.

At century's end, as the path of American empire extended to lands separate from the continent – Hawaii (annexed in 1898); the Philippines, Guam, and Puerto Rico (acquired from Spain by the Treaty of Paris in 1898); and Eastern Samoa (through the Berlin Treaty, ratified in 1900) – anxiety to protect the racialized borders of belonging increased. In *Downes v. Bidwell* (1901), one of a group of cases collectively known as the Insular Cases addressing the constitutional status of the territory acquired from Spain that came before the court between 1901 and 1904, the court wiped clean the long history of a continent peopled by diverse races. Writing for the majority, Justice Henry Billings Brown insisted that the contiguous territory of the United States had been "inhabited only by people of the same race, or by scattered bodies of native Indians."[37] By effectively erasing the history of Native Americans, blacks, Mexicans, and Asians, the way was clear for Brown to argue that the territories acquired from Spain were a different case altogether, representing "differences of race, habits, laws and customs." The racial threat, as Brown's words suggested, was compounded by language and religious differences. It was simply inconceivable to most white Americans that the people of Puerto Rico or the Philippines could ever become assimilated, and the risk to American identity, in any case, seemed simply too great. Just as it had early in the nineteenth century in addressing the conundrum of Native Americans – a racial other both within and outside the nation – the Supreme Court provided a constitutional fix to the "problem" of the territories annexed from Spain. Nothing in the treaty with Spain, Justice Edward Douglas White explained in his concurring opinion, provided for the incorporation of the Philippines, Puerto Rico, or Guam. They

37 *Downes v. Bidwell*, 182 U.S. 244, 282 (1900).

were "unincorporated territory" and as such their inhabitants were most certainly not citizens of the United States.
Moreover, it would be for the United States to decide whether
ultimately to retain or release the newly acquired territory.[38]
"Unincorporated territory" was the end of the century analogue to "domestic dependent nation." Both protected the
borders of belonging by rendering the racialized other (in the
one case, Native Americans, in the other Filipinos, Puerto
Ricans, and inhabitants of Guam) subject to, even dependent
upon, white protection and tutelage, and firmly outside the
rights that came with citizenship.

The differences in the immediate and ultimate status of
the territories annexed at the end of the nineteenth century
remind us of the importance of attention to the particulari-
ties of place and the significance of historical context, yet
running through those differences was the persistent thread
of race. In their very differences, the histories of these territories and others annexed at the end of the nineteenth century highlight the multiplicity and complexity of the interests
served by racial hierarchy at the core of the borders of belonging. There were the economic interests of a handful of white
businessmen in Hawaii and national pride in shouldering the
white man's burden in the Philippines and Puerto Rico. But
in both cases the interests served were those of whites and a
nation that perceived itself as assuming a place on an international stage in which empire rested on white hegemony. As
W. E. B. Du Bois expressed it in 1906, "The color line belts
the world."[39]

Laying Claim to the Land and the Space
of the Nation

As the preceding sentences suggest, free white able men
assumed their right to the land and more broadly that they

[38] 182 U.S. 244, 307–15 (J. White, concurring).
[39] W. E. B. Du Bois, "The Color Line Belts the World" (1906, Collier's
Weekly), reprinted in *W. E. B. Du Bois: A Reader*, ed. David Levering
Lewis (New York, 1995), 42–3.

represented the nation. At its founding, the United States was a mere foothold on the eastern edge of a vast continent. Yet, within a matter of decades, the building of what Thomas Jefferson had derided as an oxymoron – "a republican empire" – was set in motion with none other than now President Jefferson's purchase of the Louisiana Territory. By the mid-nineteenth century, the territory of the United States spanned the continent from the Atlantic Ocean in the East to the Pacific Ocean in the West. The nation expanded through law, and through law, in equal parts affirmative and negative, ensured that the United States would be an able white man's nation. It was, in Aristide Zolberg's evocative phrase, "a nation by design."[40]

The story of the steady and relentless white dispossession of Indian land is well-known. What is most important to highlight here is that dispossession was authorized by and legitimated through law. One of the first official acts of the federal government on behalf of the new nation was to claim ownership of all the land east of the Mississippi River. American Indians, who in the main had fought on the side of the British in the Revolutionary War, found their rights and interests sacrificed in the Treaty of Paris of 1783. This treaty, which formally recognized the independence of the United States and to which Native Americans were not parties, ceded to the new American republic all British claims to the land from the Appalachian Mountains to the Mississippi River.[41] In turn, the undefeated tribes were forced into treaties yielding their claim to the land. Article I, Section 8 of the U.S. Constitution, adopted in 1789, which gave Congress the power "[t]o regulate Commerce with foreign Nations, and among the several States, and with the Indian Tribes"[42] affirmed the liminal status of Native Americans vis-à-vis the new nation. And in its first decision defining the legal relationship of Native

[40] Aristide R. Zolberg, *A Nation by Design: Immigration Policy in the Fashioning of America* (Cambridge, MA, 2006), 1.
[41] Article 2, Paris Peace Treaty of September 30, 1783 (http://avalon.law.yale.edu/18th_century/paris.asp) (last accessed September 13, 2009).
[42] U.S. Constitution, art. 1, sec. 8.

Americans to the United States, the U.S. Supreme Court in 1823 affirmed that Native Americans did not have a right to the land. In its unanimous opinion in *Johnson and Graham's Lessee v. McIntosh*, the Court explained that under the Doctrine of Discovery, Europeans held absolute right to the land, rights which in turn the United States had acquired from the British.[43] Native Americans held a right of occupancy only, a right they held at the sufferance of the sovereign and which meant that they could sell the land they occupied only to the sovereign. The tension of Indian nations "outside" the Republic yet within the physical borders of the United States increased with each phase of westward expansion and white settlement. Yet, for a full century, U.S. Indian policy – alternately embodied in treaties, legal decisions, statutes, administrative regulations, wars, massacres, and forced relocations – focused on keeping Native Americans outside the boundaries of the nation. Under this policy, Indians were pushed physically ever farther westward onto increasingly marginal lands until there was literally nowhere else to go.

The other side of dispossession was the seeding, if you will, of the West, with white settlers, what James Madison termed "a free expansion of *our* people."[44] Warrants for veterans numbered in the millions of acres, but they were dwarfed by white settlers who simply acted of their own initiative, so confidant were they that ultimately their industry would be legitimized. James Willard Hurst opens his iconic *Law and the Conditions of Freedom in the Nineteenth-Century United States* with the story of the formation of the Pike River Claimants Union by a group of "settlers," or, as Hurst admits, "squatters; put less sympathetically they were trespassers," at Pike Creek on the southeastern Wisconsin shore of Lake Michigan in 1836. As the preamble to the Pike River Claimants Union constitution expressed it, "as Government has heretofore encouraged emigration by granting pre-emption to actual settlers, we are

---

[43] 21 U. S. (8 Wheat.) 543 (1823).
[44] James Madison to Thomas Jefferson, Aug. 20, 1784, in *The Writings of James Madison*, 9 vols., ed. Gaillard Hunt (New York, 1901), 2:72 (italics added).

assured that our settling and cultivating the public lands is in accordance with the best wishes of Government." They had sacrificed much (friends, society, security) by "advancing into a space beyond the bounds of civilization." They committed themselves in that interval that they hoped would be short as they waited for the public sale day "to render each other our mutual assistance, in the protection of our just rights. ..." As Hurst explains, "settlers all over the central and midwestern states" followed a similar practice. To Hurst, the Pike Creek Claimants Union "tells us some basic things about the working legal philosophy of our nineteenth-century ancestors." He breaks these down into two "working principles" of law in the nineteenth century: the legal order "should protect and promote the release of individual creative energy" and it "should mobilize the resources of the community to help shape an environment which would give men more liberty by increasing the practical range of choices open to them."[45] The story of the Pike River Claimants Union is significant in ways that Hurst did not elaborate: the assurance and sense of right with which white settlers, squatters, able men claimed the land; the naturalness with which they invoked legal forms in defense of their actions; the fact that able white men came to stand in for all "settlers" and "inhabitants" as they engaged in one of the fundamental rites of political manhood and community formation, constitution making; and, finally, the seamless erasure of the Potawatomi Indians who, even as the settlers at Pike Creek settled in, the U.S. government was removing from their Wisconsin lands.[46]

The story of the Pike River Claimants Union provides one telling glimpse into a larger, longer history. From the treaties

[45] James Willard Hurst, *Law and the Conditions of Freedom in the Nineteenth-Century United States* (Madison, 1956), 3–6.
[46] The Potawatomi ceded their land on the southeastern Wisconsin shore of Lake Michigan to the federal government by treaty in 1833. The treaty was ratified in 1835 and removal began later. The treaty documents are reprinted in Milo M. Quaife, "Documents: The Chicago Treaty of 1833," *Wisconsin Magazine of History* 1 (1918): 287–303: Edmunds, *The Potawatomis: Keepers of the Fire* (Norman, OK, 1978), 230–3, 240–50.

with individual tribes following the Treaty of Paris of 1783, to the Indian Removal Act of 1830, to the forced removals to reservations following the Civil War, to the opening of "No-man's land" in western Oklahoma to non-Indian homesteading in 1889, America's native inhabitants were forced to make way for white settlement. One of the most farsighted provisions of the Constitution, as then embodied in the Northwest Ordinance (1787), was the provision that new states would come into the union with the same status as the original thirteen.[47] Yet, from the outset, law provided that statehood rested on settlement by white men. Under the terms of the Northwest Ordinance, settlers could elect their own legislatures only when their numbers reached 5,000 free adult men; admission to statehood depended on the number of settlers – not Indians – growing to 60,000 and adoption of a republican constitution. The Homestead Act (1862) made settlement of the West by white yeoman farmers national policy.[48] Thus, law assured that white men would hold the reins of power as the nation expanded. By the end of the nineteenth century, the addition of new western states had created powerful new constituencies for the erosion of Indian land rights. And, as was true of white Southerners with respect to African Americans in the post-Reconstruction South, whites

---

[47] U.S. Const., art. 4, sec. 3; Northwest Ordinance Art. 5 ("There shall be formed in the said territory, not less than three nor more than five states … And, whenever any of the said States shall have sixty thousand free inhabitants therein, such State shall be admitted, by its delegates, into the Congress of the United States, on an equal footing with the original States in all respects….").

[48] The Act, which took effect January 1, 1863, was titled "An Act to secure homesteads to actual settlers on the public domain." It authorized Congress to grant 160 acres of public land to "any person who is the head of a family, or who has arrived at the age of twenty-one years, and is a citizen of the United States, or who shall have filed his declaration of intention to become such, as required by the naturalization laws of the United States, and who has never borne arms against the United States Government or given aid and comfort to its enemies" as well as to those who "shall have performed service in the U.S. Army or Navy" and who were then required to live on the land for five years to establish title. The Homestead Act, 12 U.S. Statutes at Large 392 (1862) (http://avalon.law. yale.edu/19th_century/homestead_act.asp) (last accessed September 13, 2009).

in the new western states were seen as knowing what was best for Indians.[49]

For almost a century, U.S. policy was predicated on an assumption of separation of white and Indian peoples. That policy changed course in the last quarter of the nineteenth century. The legal foundation for a change in U.S. policy was laid in 1871 with congressional repeal of the treaty system. For almost two centuries, first the English and then the Americans had acknowledged limited Native tribal sovereignty by entering into treaties with various Indian nations for the cession of land. The 1871 law – a rider to the Indian Appropriation Act of 1871 – ended U.S. acknowledgment of Indian tribes as "nations" and thus any collective right to the land.[50] Henceforward, Congress could simply legislate changes in Indian land ownership without securing tribal approval. It did just that in the Dawes Act in 1887.

The 1887 Dawes Act gave the President of the United States authority to divide tribal lands, giving 160 acres to each family and smaller plots to individuals.[51] Many factors and many constituencies, including white "friends" of the Indian, supported passage of the Dawes Act. While the Act did not lead immediately to white dispossession of huge tracts of Indian land, its passage was driven by the tantalizing promise that

[49] With the exception of Texas (1845) and California (1850), states west of the Missouri River, including many with significant Native American populations, entered the Union as states during the second half of the nineteenth century or in the first two decades of the twentieth century. (Minnesota (1858), Oregon (1859), Kansas (1861), Nevada (1864), Nebraska (1867), Colorado (1876), North Dakota (1889), South Dakota (1889), Montana (1889), Washington (1889), Idaho (1890), Wyoming (1890), Utah (1896), Oklahoma (1907), New Mexico (1912), Arizona (1912)).

[50] The rider provided: "No Indian nation or tribe within the territory of the United States shall be acknowledged or recognized as an independent nation, tribe or power with whom the United States may contract by treaty. ..." Although the second half of the rider (not quoted here) acknowledged the validity of earlier treaties, the rider was an important precursor for undermining recognition of earlier treaties as well. 16 U.S. Statutes at Large 544–71 at 566 (1871).

[51] The General Allotment Act of 1887 (known as the Dawes Severalty Act, or simply the Dawes Act, after the author of the bill, Congressman Henry L. Dawes of Massachusetts), 24 U.S. Statutes at Large 388 (1887).

it held out of some 80 million "surplus" acres of land that would be freed for white settlement – a promise that was fulfilled. Later amendments to the law easing "protections" in the Act that had limited Indians' ability to alienate their land allotments further marginalized Indians' claim to the land. Turning its back on its own earlier decisions recognizing Native American land rights and sovereignty, the Supreme Court in *U.S. v. Kagama* (1886) upheld Congress's right to assert federal jurisdiction (Major Crimes Act of 1885) over certain crimes committed by one Indian against another on Indian Territory. And in *Lone Wolf v. Hitchcock* (1903) the Court held that Congress had plenary power over Indian property and with it the authority to unilaterally abrogate the terms of earlier treaties, provided only that its action toward its "wards" was guided by "perfect good faith."[52] The record of that good faith is perhaps best measured by facts on the ground: in less than two decades' time, the flood of white settlers into South Dakota and Oklahoma left Indians a dispossessed minority on lands once wholly theirs. In just over a century's time, from the policy of separation through the policy of "assimilation," and through the wars and massacres to which these policies gave license, the white man had effectively supplanted Native Americans' property right in the land.

Whereas white men used law and the force it legitimated to erase Native Americans' claim to the land through dispossession, they used law and the force it legitimated to prevent women, blacks, and other racialized minorities from making claims to the land through possession. Men's full personhood provided the foundation of their superior claim to the land. Fathers passed land to sons, because only they were fully empowered under law to contract and devise and bequeath, and thereby reap the benefits of the land's riches. The law of coverture protected men's superior claim. Under the law of coverture, at marriage, a husband not only took ownership of all his wife's personal belongings, but upon the birth of a

---

[52] *Kagama*, 118 U.S. 375 (1886); *Lone Wolf*, 187 U.S. 553 (1903).

child, he assumed the status of "tenant by courtesy" over his wife's real estate and with it the right to rent out those lands, cut timber on them, or otherwise collect profits from them until they passed to her heirs. He could not sell the land, but neither could she. Beginning with modifications of lands subject to dower in the years of the Early Republic, states tempered the law of coverture, and by the end of the nineteenth century every state had passed married women's property and earnings laws.

We are long past thinking of these laws as "a silent revolution" pioneered by feminist activists. Although influenced by pressure from women's rights advocates, the principal force leading to change was economic. Industrialization brought the threat of business failure to an emergent middle class and with it a desire on the part of male legislators to protect property inherited by daughters from their husband's losses. Indeed, the first married women's property law was in Mississippi in 1839 and was intended to protect white married women's right of ownership of slaves they acquired through inheritance or gift.[53]

The laws reflected as well the need to clarify the status of new kinds of "paper" property such as stocks that did not fit neatly into established categories of "real" and "personal" property. And, most fundamentally, even before the American Revolution, land had become a commodity with the incumbent pressure to make it freely exchangeable, something that women's inheritance rights ("dower") under coverture impeded. In other words, reform in married women's legal status reflected, in important respects, the need to liberate land and men from the burdens of coverture. The reforms granted families power in the market; they did little to free women from their

---

[53] "An Act for the protection and preservation of the rights of Married Women," Miss. Laws, 1839, ch. 46, p. 72. The New York act provided a template for many states. See "An Act for the more effectual protection of the property of married women," NY Laws, 1848, c. 200, p. 307. Because fathers generally passed real property to sons, what were known as "earnings acts" had the potential for a greater impact on women. See New York Earnings Act, Laws of the State of New York, passed at the Eighty-Third Session of the Legislature... (Albany, 1860), p. 157–9.

dependence on men or to disrupt the importance of women's dependence in the construction of men's independence. Men's self-ownership continued to be defined in law and social theory in terms that included sovereignty over a wife. And, as in the case of states' wrongful death statutes that protected men's status as providers even in death, state court's interpretations of homestead exemption laws in the thousands of suits brought before state courts in the second half of the nineteenth century fell into recognizable patterns: protecting men's homesteads (and hence their role as head of household and provider) from the claims of creditors for nonpayment of debt even after a man's death. While courts' interpretation of the laws provided women and children with homesteads in the face of economic adversity, they benefited as dependents; courts proved far more reluctant to recognize women as heads of household.[54]

The law of slavery in place in every state in the union at the time of the American Revolution constructed blacks as property to be claimed by whites just as whites claimed the land itself. Moreover, as property, blacks were barred under the law from acquiring property themselves. Like the relationship to the Indians, the Nation's founders wrote chattel slavery into the U.S. Constitution.[55] And with abolition, whether

[54] States began passing homestead exemption laws following the Panic of 1837. By the mid-1860s most states and territories in the United States had passed laws protecting the family homestead from creditors even after the death of the family head. As Alison Morantz notes, state appellate courts decided literally thousands of cases involving interpretation of homestead exemption laws in the second half of the nineteenth century with cases concentrated in the post–Civil War years. Alison D. Morantz, "There's No Place Like Home: Homestead Exemption and Judicial Constructions of Family in Nineteenth-Century America," *Law and History Review* 24 (2007): 1–37. On the political forces sparking the movement to pass homestead exemption laws beginning with the Panic of 1837, Paul Goodman, "The Emergence of the Homestead Exemption in the United States: Accommodation and Resistance to the Market Revolution, 1840–1880," *Journal of American History* 80 (1993): 470–98.

[55] The key provisions in this regard are the three-fifths clause (U.S. Const., art. 1, sec 2), protection of the slave trade (U.S. Const., art 1, sec. 9), the fugitive slave clause (U.S. Const., art. 4, sec. 2), and provision that the constitution could not be amended to affect the slave trade (U.S. Const., art. 5).

in the North in the early nineteenth century or the South with the Civil War, came new legal measures safeguarding white claims to the land.

Northern states' abolition of slavery in the early decades of the nineteenth century created a population of free persons of color in the North (and through individual manumissions in the same time frame, in the South). The end of slavery in the North was vigorously coupled with other legal measures, as well as discriminations in employment, place of residence, public accommodations, and other elements related to sustaining daily life against which blacks had no legal recourse, to ensure that the polity remained defined as white. As Leon Litwack notes, "[B]y 1840, some 93 per cent of the northern free Negro population lived in states which completely or practically excluded them from the right to vote."[56] Discrimination in education and employment led to the concentration of free blacks at the bottom of the economic ladder as servants and common laborers. Every northern state considered, and many states, especially border states including Illinois and Indiana, enacted, laws prohibiting the immigration of free blacks from other states. Others, like Ohio, required blacks entering the state to prove their free status and post a bond guaranteeing their good behavior. Newly admitted western states, like Missouri and Oregon, came into the union with state constitutional bans on black immigration. That the laws largely went unenforced did not remove their power or their border-setting message. They testified that in freedom, as under slavery, this was a white polity.

The Civil War did not change this. In the American South following emancipation, laws safeguarding whites' claims to the land and creating a pool of immobile, black agricultural laborers were tools as vital in safeguarding white supremacy as slavery had ever been. The main focus of the Black Codes adopted by states of the former Confederacy in 1865 and 1866 was to ensure that freedmen and freedwomen were bound to plantation labor. Mississippi's Black Code, for example,

[56] Leon F. Litwack, *North of Slavery: The Negro in the Free States, 1790–1860* (Chicago, 1961), 75.

required all freedmen, at the beginning of each year, to have written evidence of their employment contract for the coming year, and, made any freedman leaving that employment subject to arrest. The law went so far as to forbid freedmen from even renting land in rural areas. Other states' Black Codes imposed similar restrictions. Republicans assailed the Black Codes as a return to slavery, and yet, in their place through the Freedmen's Bureau gave freedmen what Eric Foner aptly labeled "a compulsory system of free labor," with no right to opt out and be unemployed, and most certainly, not land.[57] There were important differences between the regime of contract and that of slavery, but at its core there was a fundamental continuity: after the Civil War, as before, whites owned the land. Despite commitments to the freedmen, Reconstruction Era officials turned their backs on land redistribution.

The end of Reconstruction brought a vigorous backlash against even the modest freedoms and economic independence southern blacks had achieved in the years since the Civil War. In any number of particulars these laws consolidated whites' claim to the land and their claim to black labor, at the same time that they worked to undermine the fragile hold on economic independence that some African Americans had gained. Following Redemption, Southern state legislators rolled back the substantial property taxes that landowners had faced for the first time during Reconstruction, coupling these tax reductions with taxes that pointedly targeted types of property owned by blacks. Former slave states enacted laws exempting from taxation machinery and implements used on plantations, at the same time taxing mules and tools used by black sharecroppers. So too, they enacted laws cutting off customary rights such as hunting and fishing on private property that had provided blacks and poor whites with a vital margin of economic independence. These laws borrowed on provisions from state Black Codes passed during Presidential Reconstruction that had defined hunting and fishing on private property as vagrancy and imposed taxes

---

[57] Foner, *Reconstruction: America's Unfinished Revolution* (New York, 1988), 56.

on dogs and guns – essential tools for hunting – owned by blacks. Black Codes provided a template as well for state criminal code revisions following Redemption that sharply increased penalties for petty theft and, in turn, convict labor and vagrancy laws, facilitating white access to and control over the labor of African Americans. Retracing the elements of these laws, Eric Foner notes, "The point is not that the law succeeded fully in its aims, but that the state's intervention altered the balance of economic power between black and white."[58]

Miscegenation and Jim Crow laws passed at century's end were equally critical in reclaiming and safeguarding white property claims. As Peggy Pascoe shows, state miscegenation laws – long a fixture of the American slave-holding nation – reached their full flowering in the years after Reconstruction and amidst western expansion. Newly admitted western states expanded on the original white-black racial binary of southern miscegenation laws – prohibiting intermarriage between whites and a plethora of racialized others, including blacks, Indians, Chinese, and Japanese. There were stunning examples of variation on a theme – in Arizona whites and Hindus could not marry, in South Dakota "Coreans" were added to the list. But the bottom-line remained the same: racialized others could themselves intermarry, but they were not to muddy the white side of the color line. Marriage conferred not only social respectability, but also vital economic benefits, denied to those who could not legally marry, such as legitimacy for children and rights of inheritance. Miscegenation laws proved a vital tool enabling white relatives of deceased white men to claim for themselves property or inheritance that otherwise would have passed out of white hands to the surviving spouses.[59]

Jim Crow too secured white claims to the space of the nation. Jim Crow transit laws included a positive grant, a source of

[58] Eric Foner, *Nothing But Freedom: Emancipation and Its Legacy* (Baton Rouge, LA, 1983), 52–73.
[59] Peggy Pascoe, *What Comes Naturally: Miscegenation Law and the Making of Race in America* (New York, 2008).

new rights: the legal right to occupy space from which blacks, traveling in their own right, were excluded. In every state in the South, beginning with the passage of Jim Crow transit laws and continuing into the 1930s and 1940s, whites brought and won damage suits against common carriers for violating state law by allowing black passengers to ride in the same rail coach or eat in the dining car at the same time as whites. Jim Crow, in essence, granted whites a temporary property claim by virtue of a contract for passage. That right, and with it the power of southern states, whatever the formal restraints of federalism, extended across state boundaries. The separate coach laws – that beginning in the 1940s the U.S. Supreme Court would hold violated the Commerce Clause of the Constitution – were enforced for the preceding half century by states like Mississippi and Tennessee to police segregation in interstate travel.[60]

Despite passage of state antidiscrimination laws following the U.S. Supreme Court's invalidation of the Civil Rights Act of 1875 in *The Civil Rights Cases* (1883), Jim Crow was widely practiced, and in places codified, in the North and West. Jim Crow operated in law and practice in the West and North in everything from public schools to welfare benefits, housing, public swimming pools, restaurants, movie houses, and town and residential property lines. So, for example, local officials in the Southwest and North denied mothers' pensions benefits to black and Mexican mothers. And across the West and Southwest in the late nineteenth and early twentieth centuries, states relied on constitutional precedents like *Plessy* in passing their own laws and ordinances imposing segregated school systems for Mexicans, Asians, and Native Americans. Where law proved a stumbling block – as in the case of Mexicans – school boards could fall back on the segregated landscape; locating schools in "white" or "Mexican" neighborhoods; gerrymandering school district lines where necessary; and, finally, "explaining" segregation not by

---

[60] *Morris v. Alabama & Vicksburg Ry. Co.* 103 Miss. 511 (1912); *Southern Ry. Co. v. Norton*, 112 Miss. 302 (1916); Welke, *Recasting American Liberty: Gender, Race, Law and the Railroad Revolution*, 1865–1920 (New York, 2001), 369–75.

resort to race, but by racially coded criteria, such as language, morals, and disease.

Private property gave license to discriminate. Through the first half of the twentieth century and beyond, the legal right of owners of a broad array of "private" businesses – restaurants, hotels, beauty parlors, bars, theatres, and so on – to discriminate among patrons on the basis of race held firm. "Whites only" signs or their racial negative "No _____ allowed" dotted establishments in towns and cities across the nation. All that differed was the targeted racial other: Indians in Minnesota and the Dakotas; Chinese and Japanese in California, Oregon, and Washington; Mexicans in Arizona, New Mexico, California, and Texas; and blacks throughout the South, Southwest, and even areas in the North. In the eyes of most white Americans, whites were the public.

In cities and suburbs across the nation beginning in the early twentieth century, white property owners entered into "restrictive covenants" barring sales of residential property to an array of racial and religious minorities including blacks, Chinese, Japanese, and Jews. A unanimous U.S. Supreme Court in *Corrigan v. Buckley* (1926) gave white property owners free rein to do what it had held in *Buchanan v. Warley* (1917) that cities could not constitutionally do: protect residential segregation.[61] Essentially expanding whites' rights beyond their own property lines, restrictive covenants compensated for what individual homeowners lost in terms of the right to freely convey their property. Restrictive covenants ran with the land and gave white homeowners a property right in perpetuity to a white neighborhood.

Supreme Court precedents aside, beginning in the 1890s and continuing well past the end of legal segregation, James Loewen argues, the practice of incorporated towns, cities, and suburbs in the Midwest, Northeast, and West barring

[61] *Buchanan v. Warley*, 245 U.S. 60 (1917); *Corrigan v. Buckley*, 271 U.S. 323 (1926). The Court in *Buchanan* held that a city ordinance that required residential segregation by race violated the Fourteenth Amendment.

African Americans (and in some cases other racialized groups including Chinese, Mexicans, Native Americans, and Jews) by law, custom, and violence became commonplace. Known by the shorthand "sundown towns," towns like Niles, Ohio, Appleton, Wisconsin, and Glendale, California, extended the safeguarding of white's superior claim to the land beyond the Jim Crow South, and with it the imagining of America as a white nation, to the nation as a whole.[62]

Through much of the long nineteenth century the focus of nation-building was on internal borders: the erasure of Indian claims to the land, the peopling of that land with white immigrants from Northern and Western Europe, and the transformation of territories into new states. But immigration regulation was by no means nonexistent. Indeed, states and localities were keen not to be dumping grounds for foreign convicts; free and slave states alike regulated the interstate movements of and attempted to protect themselves from settlement by free blacks; and, continuing practices from the English poor laws, states and localities exerted their power to exclude or at least require the removal of ("transportation" of) newcomers whom they considered likely to become public charges whether their origins were other towns, states, or foreign nations. In bringing an end to slavery, the Civil War resolved the major impediment to a truly national vision of the state (the United States) and with it authority over immigration.[63] The U.S. Supreme Court decisions in *Henderson v. Mayor of New York* (1876) and *Chy Lung v. Freeman* (1876)

---

[62] James W. Loewen, *Sundown Towns: A Hidden Dimension of American Racism* (New York, 2005).

[63] As Kunal Parker notes, "as long as slavery remained alive, the U.S. Supreme Court would not definitively rule that states had no constitutional authority to regulate immigration, because to do so would have stripped states – especially southern states – of the power to regulate alien and native free blacks' access to their territories." Kunal M. Parker, "Citizenship and Immigration Law, 1800–1924: Resolutions of Membership and Territory," in *The Cambridge History of Law in America*, 2:176. Pre–Civil War Supreme Court cases relating to immigration include *New York v. Milne*, 36 U.S. (11 Pet.) 102 (1837) and two cases known by the shorthand the *Passenger Cases*, 48 U.S. (7 How.) 283 (1849).

asserted federal authority over immigration and thus paved the way constitutionally for the era of national regulation of immigration.[64]

One of the central objects of federal regulation of immigration was protection of the United States as a white nation. Beginning with the Page Law of 1875 and culminating with the Immigration Act of 1924, the United States – exercising its sovereign authority – limited the flow of immigration by ever-finer sieves. The first targets were the Chinese, lunatics, and idiots, then the Japanese, polygamists, anarchists, and a bevy of others singled out by personal characteristics. Finally, the imposition of a quota limiting annual immigration to two percent of people of each nationality in the United States as of the 1890 national census, with Asian immigrants excluded entirely. But, as Mae Ngai explains, there was no firm basis for determining the "national origins" of the nation's population as of 1890.[65] In fact, the Quota Board effectively "excised all nonwhite, non-European peoples" from the base population; "the 'colored races' were imagined as having no country of origin."[66] And, in this

[64] 92 U.S. 259 (1876); 92 U.S. 275 (1876). Both cases involved state laws imposing head taxes on immigrants, but the California law, in contrast to the New York law, imposed the tax only on particular immigrants, including "lewd and debauched women." The Court struck down both statutes, paving the way for the shift of restrictive legislation directed at the Chinese from the states (particularly California) to the federal government. What is often cited as the first federal regulation of immigration, the Page Act, excluding convicts and prostitutes, was passed in 1875. 18 U. S. Statutes at Large 477 (1875). In the *Chinese Exclusion Cases*, upholding the Chinese Exclusion Act (1882), the Court reinforced the authority of the federal government over immigration. 130 U.S. 581 (1889).

[65] Mae M. Ngai, *Impossible Subjects: Illegal Aliens and the Making of Modern America* (Princeton, NJ, 2004), 25–6. As Ngai explains, "The census did not differentiate the foreign-born until 1850 and did not differentiate the parental nativity of the native-born until 1890. Immigration was unrecorded before 1820, and not classified according to national origin until 1899, when the Immigration Service began designating immigrants by 'race or people.'... To complicate things further, many boundaries in Europe changed after World War I, requiring a translation of political geography to reattribute origins and allocate quotas according to the world in 1920."

[66] Ngai, *Impossible Subjects*, 26.

way, the trickle of continued immigration permitted under the immigration acts of 1920 and 1924 privileged European, especially Northern and Western European, countries, further bolstering the borders of belonging that made America a white nation. In this context, the physical borders of the nation took on a new salience. And to protect whites' claims to the land against the tiny Asian population in the United States, western states, harkening back to an earlier history prohibiting aliens from land ownership, passed alien land laws prohibiting property ownership by those ineligible for naturalized citizenship, which the U.S. Supreme Court, in turn, upheld.[67]

It was not just that the nation was defined as a white man's nation, it was an able white man's nation. Although not always said in so many words, law in the long nineteenth century safeguarded the right of the able, not the disabled, "to live in the world."[68] In personal injury suits, state courts acknowledged that the physically disabled had the same right as the able to assume that streets and sidewalks were in a safe condition and rebuffed attempts by cities, villages, and those with property abutting the public way to escape liability for their own negligence in personal injury suits brought by the blind, crippled, or otherwise disabled. Yet the public way was structured for the able (e.g., think here of stairs, curbs, and intersections) and it was taken for granted that the disabled were the ones who had to adjust to account for their disability. As the New Hampshire Supreme Court explained in an 1872 case, "Although blindness in itself is not negligence, still, in judging the conduct of a blind man, his unfortunate disability must be considered, and he must doubtless

---

[67] *Terrace v. Thompson*, 263 U.S. 197 (1923). For the text of the early twentieth century laws, see Charles F. Curry, *Alien Land Laws and Alien Rights* (Washington, 1921), 35–67. See also William Marion Gibson, *Aliens and the Law: Some Legal Aspects of the National Treatment of Aliens in the United States* (Chapel Hill, 1940), App. B.

[68] The phrase here is from Jacobus tenBroek, "The Right to Live in the World: The Disabled in the Law of Torts," *California Law Review* 54 (1966), 841, who adapted it from Prosser, *Torts*, 3rd ed., sec 32, at 155 (St. Paul, MN, 1964). ("The man who is blind, or deaf, or lame, or is otherwise physically disabled, is entitled to live in the world.")

be held to govern his conduct with a reasonable regard to his situation in that respect."[69] The disabled well understood the evidentiary burden they faced in making their way in public. So, the blind man or woman introduced evidence of his or her long experience with the particular way (route of travel), the development of his or her other senses, the fact of using a cane, or traveling with a companion.[70]

That the disabled were entitled only to the same care offered to the able came through most clearly in cases involving railroads, streetcars, and other common carriers. With a few narrowly defined exceptions, the common law of common carriers required carriers to accept all those who paid their fare and conformed to the carriers' reasonable regulations. But, as courts made clear, carriers were not required to make what we might think of today as "accommodations" for disability. "Regulations are made for the traveling public," explained the Mississippi Supreme Court in 1883. "If persons sick or under any disability which renders them unable to conform to the reasonable regulations for the community generally are inconvenienced by this inability they have no legal cause of complaint against a carrier." "One too sick or from any cause not able to do as travelers usually do in conforming to the usage in running trains for the traveling public," the court continued, "should avoid them or secure the assistance necessary to enable them to accomplish what is required of passengers generally."[71]

Viewing the long nineteenth century as a whole, what stands out in terms of the rights of the able versus the disabled to live in the world is that the law moved not toward greater accommodation over the course of the century, but toward greater restriction. Penitentiaries and asylums – institutions established by law and funded by the state that separated the criminal and the defective from the general population – emerged early in the nineteenth century. The cost of reform,

[69] *Sleeper v. Sandown*, 52 N.H. 244, 251 (1877).
[70] Id. See also *Smith v. Wildes*, 143 Mass. 556 (1887); *Harris v. Uebelhoer*, 75 N.Y. 169 (1878).
[71] *Sevier v. Vicksburg and Meridian R.R. Co.*, 61 Miss. 8, 10 (1883).

the numbers of inmates, dimming prospects of success (defined in terms of educating the disabled to be productive), all too quickly overwhelmed good intentions. Reinforced, even goaded on by scientific and medical "advances," penitentiaries became simply prisons, and schools for the feeble-minded – renamed as in the Rome Developmental Asylum for Unteachable Idiots – state-funded warehouses that permanently (or long term) segregated the unproductive from society, freeing, at the very least, the fit among the working-class for productive labor.[72] And while some cities excepted cripples from ordinances prohibiting begging, others, including San Francisco; New Orleans; Portland, Oregon; Denver, Colorado; Columbus, Ohio; Omaha, Nebraska; and Manila under U.S. occupation, adopted "unsightly beggar" ordinances making it a crime for a cripple to even show himself in the public way.[73] Chicago's 1881 ordinance provided that "Any person who is diseased, maimed, mutilated, or in any way deformed, so as to be an unsightly or disgusting object, or an improper person to be allowed in or on the streets, highways, thoroughfares or public places in this city shall not therein or thereon expose himself or herself to public view."[74] Clearing the street of the maimed, the unsightly, was part management, ordering, and marking of the modern city, part disgust, part imposed care. That the ordinances were unevenly and irregularly enforced – like the state laws prohibiting the immigration of free blacks in border northern states before the Civil War – did not lessen their border-setting message. The able were entitled to use of the public way free of, as the resolution leading up to the Chicago ordinance put it, "unsightly and unseemly objects, which are a reproach to the City, disagreeable to people upon the streets, and an offense to business houses along the streets."[75]

[72] On the history of the Rome Developmental Asylum for Unteachable Idiots in upstate New York, see Philip M. Ferguson, *Abandoned to Their Fate: Social Policy and Practice Toward Severely Retarded People in America, 1820–1920 (Philadelphia, 1994).*

[73] Susan M. Schweik, *The Ugly Laws: Disability in Public* (New York, 2009).

[74] Sec. 1612, Municipal Code of Chicago (1881), p. 377.

[75] Schweik, *The Ugly Laws*, 193.

Unsightly beggar ordinances were one element in the hostility to the disabled in the late nineteenth and early twentieth centuries. Institutionalization had sequestered the disabled who lived in Americans' midst; immigration restriction and sterilization went a step further to a policy of exclusion and eradication. Federal immigration restriction of the disabled at the end of the century built on a long history of hostility to the disabled as likely to become public charges. Many states' poor laws in the early nineteenth century explicitly singled out mentally and physically disabled newcomers as unwelcome. South Carolina's poor law required masters of vessels to give security for any passengers found to be "impotent, lame or otherwise infirm, or likely to be a charge to the parish."[76] Pennsylvania's 1803 act imposed a charge on the importer of any "infant, lunatic, maimed, aged, impotent, or vagrant" persons to pay for their transportation back to wherever they had been brought from.[77] Other states' laws relating to disabled aliens offered variations on a theme, prohibiting the landing of "lunatic, idiot, maimed, aged or infirm persons" and of the "lunatic, idiot, deaf and dumb, blind, or infirm."[78]

Federal law at the end of the century, then, built on a long history of state and local hostility to the disabled, making such exclusions a matter of national policy. The Immigration Act of 1882 – most often associated exclusively with Chinese exclusion – prohibited entry of any "lunatic, idiot, or any person unable to take care of himself or herself without

[76] S.C. Act of Mar. 25, 1738, No. 671, cited in Gerald L. Neuman, "The Lost Century of American Immigration Law (1776–1875)," *Columbia Law Review* 93 (1993), 1857–8. Neuman notes, although the law was adopted before the Revolution, it remained the law of South Carolina through much of the nineteenth century.

[77] Pennsylvania Act of Mar. 29, 1803, ch. 155, sec. 23, cited in Neuman, "The Lost Century of American Immigration Law," 1858.

[78] Laws of the Commonwealth of Massachusetts, Passed ... 1837 (Boston, 1837), ch. 238, p. 270; Laws of the State of New York, First Meeting of the Seventieth Session, 1847, vol. 1, chap. 195, pp. 182 ff. Printed by Charles Van Benthnysen, 1847, both quoted in E. P. Hutchinson, *Legislative History of American Immigration Policy 1798–1965* (Philadelphia, 1981), 398–400.

becoming a public charge."[79] The public charge clause targeted both single women and persons with disabilities. In 1891, the phrase "unable to take care of himself or herself without becoming a public charge" was replaced by the more flexible "likely to become a public charge."[80] In any event, the judgment belonged not to the individual but to the medical inspectors of the Bureau of Immigration. With each new immigration law, came new restrictions targeting disability. The 1903 law added people with epilepsy to the list of the prohibited; the 1907 law added "imbeciles" and "feebleminded" persons; and so on.[81] From the outset, disability was linked to ethnicity. As one 1924 quota advocate explained, referring to immigrants, "in every face there was something wrong.... There were so many sugar-loaf heads, moon-faces, slit mouths, lantern-jaws, and goose-bill noses that one might imagine a malicious jinn had amused himself by casting human beings in a set of skew-molds discarded by the Creator."[82]

Playing on the title of John Higham's classic text of American nativism in the nineteenth century, Douglas Baynton notes, immigration restriction was not driven simply by fear of "strangers in the land," "it was fueled at least as much by a fear of *defectives* in the land."[83] Colonial and early state laws excluding immigrants based on disability expressed a fear that the disabled were likely to become public burdens; federal legislation at the end of the century continued this theme, but also reflected growing concern about the impact of disability on the nation's gene pool. Immigration restriction, in this sense, like institutionalization, marriage prohibitions, and, ultimately,

---

[79] An Act to Regulate Immigration, 22 U.S. Statutes at Large 214 (1883).

[80] An Act in Amendment to the Various Acts Relative to Immigration and the Importation of Aliens under Contract or Agreement to Perform Labor, 26 U.S. Statutes at Large 1084 (1891).

[81] An Act to Regulate the Immigration of Aliens into the United States, 32 U.S. Statutes at Large 1214 (1903); An Act to Regulate the Immigration of Aliens into the United States, 34 U.S. Statutes at Large 898 (1907).

[82] Quoted in Douglas C. Baynton, "Defectives in the Land: Disability and American Immigration Policy, 1882–1924," *Journal of American Ethnic History* 24 (2005), 41.

[83] Ibid.

compulsory sterilization laws moved to protect the nation's genetic future "in order to prevent," in Justice Holmes's memorable words from *Buck v. Bell* (1927), "*our* being swamped by incompetence."[84]

Justice Holmes spoke in *Buck v. Bell* in his capacity as a U.S. Supreme Court justice, but his words echo those of able white men in other contexts across the sweep of the long nineteenth century. They spoke unself-consciously for themselves and for state and nation. They expressed no embarrassment no discomfort with the interdependence of privilege and subordination, but simply superiority and right. We know from the broader contexts in which they wrote, spoke, and lived that the borders of belonging were never complete, never unchallenged. Yet we also cannot deny the reality of the authority law accorded husbands over wives, masters over slaves; that it was able white men who decided the physical boundaries of the nation, the boundaries and conditions of membership, and even, who would not be allowed to contribute to the nation's progeny.

[84] *Buck v. Bell*, 274 U.S. 200, 207 (emphasis added).

"By the laws of the country from whence I came, I was deprived of myself – of my own body, soul, and spirit." (Frederick Douglass, *Narrative of the Life of Frederick Douglass, An American Slave, Written by Himself*, 1845)

****

"A woman has no name! She is Mrs. John or James, Peter or Paul, just as she changes masters; like the Southern slave, she takes the name of her owner." (Elizabeth Cady Stanton, Letter to the National Woman's Rights Convention, 24 November 1856)

****

"The land of the Dakotas was once large and covered with buffalo and grass," Red Cloud began. But then, *"white people poured into our country" and began to "divide up our land and tell us what part they would give us."* (Red Cloud, speaking to members of Stanley Commission, July 1878, in Jeffrey Ostler, *The Plains Sioux and U. S. Colonialism from Lewis and Clark to Wounded Knee*, 2004)

****

"[S]hould a colored person endeavor, for a moment, to lose sight of his disability, these staring signs would remind him continually that between him and the rest of mankind not of his own color, there was by law a great gulf fixed." (Charles H. Chesnutt, *The Marrow of Tradition*, 1901)

****

"Perhaps the bitterest struggles of the handicapped man come when he tackles the business world … The attitude toward me ranged from 'You can't expect us to create a place for you,' to 'How could it enter your head that we should find any use for a man like you.'" (Randolph Bourne, "The Handicapped," *The Atlantic Monthly*, 1911)

****

"I'm not interested in being a citizen because … I would be a citizen in name only – with no privileges or consideration. I would still be a 'dirty Mexican.'" (Special Survey of the Mexican Colony at Hick's Camp, CA, January 1940, in David Gutierrez, *Walls and Mirrors: Mexican Americans, Mexican Immigrants, and the Politics of Ethnicity*, 1995)

****

"I was no longer Charles Choy Leong, but Charles Choy Wong, a tainted person with an illegal family history and a fractured identity. I was not who I thought I was: the fragile wholeness of my desired 'All American' identity was now cracked into pieces, like Humpty Dumpty." (Charles Choy Wong and Kenneth Klein, "False Papers, Lost Lives," in *Origins and Destinations: 41 Essays on Chinese America*, 1994)

2

SUBJECTS OF LAW

Disabled Persons, Racialized Others, and Women

One of the most fundamental and far-reaching consequences of the law's imagining of "people" as able, white, and male was the impoverishment of individual identity for everyone else. Disabled persons, racialized others, and women were "subject" in at least two senses of the word. First, they were quite literally "subject to" able white men's authority and right. Second, whatever their formal citizenship status, they remained subjects rather than full and equal members of the nation in large measure because they were denied full legal personhood.

For disabled persons, racialized others, and women, the borders of belonging meant being denied rights to property in oneself or to property more generally, being constrained to enjoy rights and protections through able white men, being denied citizenship altogether, having citizenship be contingent, incomplete, or imposed and itself effecting subordination and loss of rights. The abled, racialized, and gendered borders of belonging were assured through administrative regimes that exercised control, authority, or oversight over disabled persons, racialized others, and women. Though there were possibilities for some to escape from their subject identity, escape came at the cost of reinforcing the subject status of others, advantaged men over women, and reinforced the abled, racialized, and gendered borders of belonging more generally. Law effectively rendered whole groups alien, took identity as easily as it granted it, and simply erased others from history. Throughout the long nineteenth century, the borders of belonging depended on violence. Moreover, in making conduct illegal that otherwise would have been legal – immigration, earning a livelihood, marriage, control of reproduction, and so on – the borders of belonging produced distortions in the daily lives of those othered in law. Put most simply, the borders of belonging narrowed life's horizons.

Subject Identities

The American Revolution tested the gendered hierarchy ingrained in the common law; the gendered hierarchy held. In one particular after another, the revolutionaries crafted law to uphold the principle that a husband's right to the loyalty of his wife took precedence over her loyalty to the state: loyalty oaths were required only of adult males not females; confiscation acts excluded dower portions from seizure; married women were routinely granted the right to "cross enemy lines" to join husbands; married women who had joined husbands were assumed to have been subject to their husband's will and thus able to reclaim property following the revolution. As Theodore Sedgwick of the Massachusetts Supreme Judicial Court explained in the 1801 case of *Martin v. Massachusetts*, "A wife who left the country in the company of her husband did not withdraw herself; but was, if I may so express it, withdrawn by him. She did not deprive the government of the benefit of her personal services; she had not to render...."[1] The failure or, more aptly, the refusal of the revolutionary generation to adapt married women's legal status, as Linda Kerber notes, was a critical marker of the conservatism of the Revolution itself.[2]

In turn, from the beginning of the new republic, women were constrained to enjoy the rights and protections of self-

---

[1] Quoted in Linda K. Kerber, *No Constitutional Right to be Ladies: Women and the Obligations of Citizenship* (New York, 1998), 30.
[2] Ibid., 33–4.

ownership and citizenship through men. A woman's legal identity was "covered" by her husband's identity at marriage. Women's legal subordination was marked in the first instance by the requirement that at marriage a woman take her husband's surname. Married women exercised legal rights only through their husbands. Captions at the head of legal pleadings and courts' opinions reading "_____ *et ux*" for "and wife" highlighted the submergence of women's individual identity at marriage. In cases of accidental or intentional injury, a woman's husband, not the woman herself, had the right to bring suit. With only the most narrow of exceptions, the injury was to his rights, not hers – his right to her body, his loss in incurring medical bills, his right to her household services and her lost wages. All that the law treated as personal to or belonging to her was her pain and suffering. A married woman's inability to bring suit in her own behalf was more than an inconvenience. A woman separated, but not divorced, from her husband could not bring suit on her own. Men in the same position suffered no similar hindrance.

Even women's citizenship was subject to their husbands' and defined not in terms of individual obligation to the nation (as was men's), but in terms of obligation to one's husband. Men did not risk losing their citizenship through marriage; women did. Under the Expatriation Act of 1907, Congress provided that American women who married aliens lost their citizenship even if they continued to reside in the United States.[3] The Cable Act (1922) safeguarded the citizenship of only those female citizens who married foreigners eligible for citizenship.[4] American-born women who married Chinese or Japanese men lost their citizenship, and those who married men eligible for citizenship but then resided abroad for two years were themselves treated as naturalized citizens who lost their citizenship. In other words, citizenship for women remained contingent.

[3] Expatriation Act of 1907, 34 U.S. Statutes at Large 1228 (1907).
[4] Cable Act, 42 U.S. Statutes at Large 1021 (1923).

Married women's property reform from mid-nineteenth century on meddled at the margins of married women's subject identity. On paper, the laws effected a broad transformation, including granting to a married woman the right to sue in her own name, to enter into contracts, and to inherit property. In practice, state courts interpreting the laws largely eviscerated gains the statutes otherwise might have yielded. Courts narrowly interpreted provisions such as a married woman's right to her earnings to limit these laws' application to wages earned in workplaces outside the home. Married women's egg money, money from boarders or taking in laundry, even wages earned in industrial "homework," and most emphatically a woman's household labor remained her husband's by law. Marital unity, and with it the legal subordination of married women, remained intact. The U.S. Supreme Court's decision in *Thompson v. Thompson* (1910), holding that a woman whose husband had so severely beaten her that she could no longer earn her living as a seamstress could not bring suit against her husband, despite a Washington, D.C. statute that gave married women the legal right to independently pursue legal claims for accidental and intentional injury, was emblematic of the tenacity of long-held assumptions about the nature of marital unity.[5]

Women were subordinated by the terms of the marriage contract, but they could, at least, marry. Others, including the slave and those suffering from various physical and mental disabilities, were disqualified from even that right. Marriage depended on consent, and neither slaves nor those of "unsound mind" were understood in law to have the capacity to consent. "A person of 'unsound mind,' – an idiot, for example," explained the Kentucky Supreme Court in 1834, "is, to all intellectual purposes, dead; and such a thing, destitute of intellectual light and life, is as incapable as a dead

---

[5] *Thompson v. Thompson*, 218 U.S. 611 (1911)(Interpretation of states' married women's property laws was not a matter of constitutional or federal law; the case appeared before the U.S. Supreme Court because it involved interpretation of the District of Columbia's married women's property law).

body of being a husband or a wife, in a legal, rational or moral sense."[6] Marriage prohibitions on account of disability ranged from those like Georgia's, which simply required that "A person must be of sound mind in order to be able to contract marriage," to those that prohibited marriage of the "insane" or "idiots." But many states also included epileptics and the "feebleminded."[7] Even for categories of disability where law did not formally bar marriage, disabled individuals were often generally understood to be unmarriageable, in the case of a man incapacitated from providing for a family and in the case of a woman incapacitated from caring for children and household.

Women entered public life in the nineteenth century not as full-rights-bearing individuals as men were, but as helpmeets of the state through marriage. Under the common law, (free) women in untenable marriages faced a bitter choice: to leave a marriage was to lose their children.[8] Courts' gradual embrace of a new doctrine under which women might gain custody of their children – the "best interests of the child doctrine" – was in this sense an advance for women. Judicial reform of the common law of child custody, like married women's property reform, was more a product of economic forces, the emergence of a new middle class, and, with these, a shift away from a view of children as economic assets, rather than any newfound recognition of "women's rights." The doctrine did not recognize in women the same unequivocal legal right to their children in the case of separation or divorce that men had historically held. As Michael Grossberg captures in the story of Ellen and Gonzalve D'Hauteville, a judicial patriarchy replaced domestic patriarchy. Women like Ellen D'Hauteville and others who gained custody of their

---

[6] *Jenkins v. Jenkins' Heirs*, 32 KY. 102 (1834).
[7] Stevenson Smith, Madge W. Wilkinson, and Lovisa C. Wagoner, *The Bulletin of the University of Washington No. 82, A Summary of the Laws of the Several States Governing I. – Marriage and Divorce of the Feebleminded, the Epileptic and the Insane. II. – Asexualization. III. – Institutional Commitment and Discharge of the Feebleminded and the Epileptic* (Seattle, 1914).
[8] Slaves had no right to the children produced by their union.

children under the "best interests of the child doctrine" raised their children at the sufferance of male judges.[9]

Mothers' custody of their children depended on a set of assumptions about women as mothers and conditioned that right on a woman meeting a male judge's standards of what it meant to be a "good mother" not simply at the moment, but for life. The risk of loss was always there. Women gained new, conditional rights only by incorporating into law a narrow, fixed identity of women as mothers. Moreover, the rights recognized were not so much women's rights as protection of society's interest in children and the family. And while these rights were not explicitly defined in racial terms, women of color and poor and disabled women did not even enjoy this level of security as mothers.

And women – the right kind of women – were to be mothers. Under the common law, abortion before quickening, that is before the mother could first feel movement, was legal. By 1880, the campaign begun by the American Medical Association two decades earlier had made abortion illegal in every state. The law imposed maternity in other ways as well. The federal and state Comstock laws denied women access to information relating to abortion and birth control by banning it from the mails as "obscene" and forcibly closing birth control clinics.[10] Whereas laws criminalizing abortion and birth control imposed motherhood on some women, other laws proscribing marriage, imposing institutionalization, and legalizing sterilization moved to protect the nation's gene pool from further taint by limiting reproduction of the "unfit" (male and female) – the feebleminded, epileptics, those suffering from congenital defects, and so on.[11] Marriage prohibitions

[9] Michael Grossberg, *A Judgment for Solomon: The D'Hauteville Case and Legal Experience in Antebellum America* (New York, 1996); Grossberg, *Governing the Hearth: Law and the Family in Nineteenth-Century America* (Chapel Hill, 1985), 248–53, 281–5.
[10] States began modifying their birth control laws in the 1930s, but, significantly, the liberalization was justified not in the name of women's freedom and right to control their own reproduction, but in the name of "family planning," "child spacing," and population control.
[11] Though the science of eugenics was fundamentally discredited by Nazi policies in World War II, involuntary sterilization continued in many

of the unfit were inscribed in law early in the nineteenth century, providing a template for categories of restriction of the unfit in immigration at the end of the century. Formal legalization of compulsory sterilization began in 1907 with a law in Indiana. By the late 1920s, two dozen states had eugenic sterilization laws. Because the laws in most instances applied only to inmates of state institutions, the poor were the predominant victims. While laws directed at the institutionalization of the "feebleminded" deprived men and women alike of their freedom, from the 1890s onward, women were the special targets of the laws, just as women would become the special target of sterilization laws in the twentieth century.

Denial of access to professions and "protective" labor legislation effectively precluded women from securing economic independence without which they were bound to remain subject to men's will. Judicial decisions incorporated this subject identity into constitutional doctrine: in *Bradwell v. Illinois* (1873), the U.S. Supreme Court held that the right to practice a profession was not protected by the Privileges and Immunities Clause of the Fourteenth Amendment, leaving states free to bar women, as Illinois had, from the practice of law and other professions; in *Muller v. Oregon* (1908), the Court held that state legislation limiting women's working hours did not violate the Fourteenth Amendment.[12] In Alice Kessler-Harris's apt phrase, the "gendered imagination" incorporated into law recognized (white) men as individuals and women as wives and mothers.[13] As the example of women should suggest, subjectivity was structured and guarded as much by inclusion as exclusion. But this tension went beyond gender.

The border of belonging was never just a matter of the distinction between those who could claim citizenship and those

---

states in the United States for several decades after the War, increasing in numbers, in fact, and shifting from the feebleminded to poor, female welfare recipients.

[12] *Bradwell v. Illinois*, 83 U.S. (16 Wall.) 130 (1873); *Muller v. Oregon*, 208 U.S. 412 (1908).

[13] Alice Kessler-Harris, *In Pursuit of Equity: Women, Men, and the Quest for Economic Citizenship in 20th-Century America* (New York, 2001), 5–6, 21–34.

who could not. White women and disabled persons, male and female alike, were citizens from the beginning of the new republic. Mexicans incorporated into the United States under the Treaty of Guadalupe Hidalgo were guaranteed under the treaty's terms the rights of U.S. citizenship. Section 1 of the Fourteenth Amendment recognized the birthright citizenship of freedmen and freedwomen. Chinese and Japanese persons born in the United States also held birthright citizenship under the terms of the Fourteenth Amendment.[14] The Dawes Act established a path to U.S. citizenship for some Native Americans; the Indian Citizenship Act of 1924 declared all Native Americans to be U.S. citizens.[15] Yet none of these groups enjoyed full membership in the nation. Moreover, with the exception of the largely symbolic gesture of amending the naturalization law in 1870 to include "persons of African nativity or African descent," naturalized citizenship remained limited to white persons.[16]

Elaborate administrative regimes were put in place to assert and assure the subject status of women, racialized others, and disabled persons. Over the course of the nineteenth century, states increasingly outlawed common law marriage, increasingly defining the terms of marriage and marital exits. Having relegated Native Americans to reservations, "knowing" the Indian population – in the sense of being able to assign a fixed identity to each Indian – became an essential

---

[14] Despite the clear language of the Fourteenth Amendment, many resisted its application to Chinese born in the United States. In *U.S. v. Wong Kim Ark*, 169 U.S. 649 (1898), the U.S. Supreme Court held that Chinese born in the U.S. were citizens.

[15] Section 6 of the Dawes Act provided, in part, that "every Indian born within the territorial limits of the United States to whom allotments shall have been made ... who has voluntarily taken up, ... his residence separate and apart from any tribe of Indians therein, and has adopted the habits of civilized life, is hereby declared to be a citizen of the United States." (http://avalon.law.yale.edu/19th_century/dawes.asp.) (last accessed September 16, 2009). The Indian Citizenship Act provided, in part, "That all non-citizen Indians born within the territorial limits of the United States be, and they are hereby, declared to be citizens of the United States." 43 U.S. Statutes at Large 253 (1924).

[16] An Act to Amend the Naturalization Laws and to Punish Crimes Against the Same, and for Other Purposes, 16 U.S. Statutes at Large 256 (1871).

prerequisite to the assertion of U.S. sovereignty. Censuses provided a tool that in turn allowed for the imposition of disciplinary and administrative control in matters ranging from food rations and annuity goods to punishment for crime. Similarly, following passage of the Chinese Exclusion Act, white immigration officials' inability to distinguish one Chinese person from another by appearance led to the creation of increasingly elaborate regimes of paper identification. And whether aggregated in state and federal censuses or grouped physically in institutions provided for by state law for the feebleminded, insane, and others seen as "defective" disabled persons were increasingly rendered subjects of study. There was so little recognition for the humanity of the institutionalized that they could be required to give, in a sense, evidence against themselves: their bodies, their behaviors, and their incapacities provided the medical and scientific evidence for the passage of laws further denying them the most fundamental and intimate rights of personhood.

The very creation of categories of illegality through immigration law among racialized others like the Chinese and later Mexicans coupled with whites' inability to distinguish among them led to the labeling of entire groups as outside the borders of belonging; they became, in Mae Ngai's evocative phrasing, "impossible subjects."[17] The Chinese Exclusion Laws rendered all Chinese in the United States at risk of being falsely identified and deported. But the pattern had begun earlier than this: following passage of the Fugitive Slave Act of 1850, and compounded by the act's provisions barring the fugitive from giving testimony, no black in a free state was safe from the allegation of being a fugitive slave.[18]

There was, in fact, no winning. The extension of citizenship and other rights operated as tools for assuring the subject status of racial others. For example, long denied the right to marry under slavery, freedmen and freedwomen found themselves bound to middle-class white norms defining

[17] Mae M. Ngai, *Impossible Subjects: Illegal Aliens and the Making of Modern America* (Princeton, 2004).
[18] Fugitive Slave Act of 1850, 9 U.S. Statutes at Large 463 (1851).

the marital relationship. The Freedmen's Bureau set out "Marriage Rules" defining who was eligible to marry, establishing procedures for solemnizing relationships and prohibiting consensual marital relations that were not legitimated by license or ceremony. The newly reconstituted southern states' legislatures passed their own laws regulating marriage among freedpeople. The short-lived Black Codes passed by a number of southern states in the immediate wake of the war simply recognized ex-slave couples living together at a certain date as legally married regardless of the intentions or desires of the individuals. When these men or women sought out partners who had been sold under slavery, they found themselves charged with bigamy and leased out to whites under convict labor laws. More generally, freedmen and freedwomen who had long lived as husband and wife suddenly discovered that cohabitation without legal marriage was now a crime. Under the Dawes Act, Native Americans found their citizenship dependent on adopting "civilized," that is, white, living practices.[19] Moreover, racial definition – the litmus test for privilege or subordination – did not rest with the individual herself, but was a matter of law. As legal scholar Cheryl Harris explains, "The legal definition of race was the 'objective' test propounded by racist theorists of the day who described race to be immutable, scientific, biologically determined – an unsullied fact of the blood rather than a volatile and violently imposed regime of racial hierarchy."[20] To be a racial other was to be subject.

What escape there was from subject identities under the law privileged men over women regardless of race, the able over the disabled across time. From the British promise of freedom to slaves who joined the British cause in the American Revolution, to slaves' purchase of their own freedom, to the escape from slavery via the underground railroad, to male slaves who enlisted in the Union Army during the Civil War,

---

[19] The General Allotment Act of 1887 (Dawes Act), 24 U.S. Statutes at Large 388 (1887); *Elk v. Wilkins*, 112 U.S. 94 (1884).

[20] Cheryl I. Harris, "Whiteness as Property," *Harvard Law Review* 106 (1993), 1739.

able black men benefited, however marginally, over black women from the privileges of gender. It was manpower in fighting a war that the British, and, in turn in the Civil War that the North, sought. Black men trained in blacksmithing, carpentry, and other skilled men's crafts, far more than black women, had the opportunity to accumulate money to purchase their freedom. So too black men's gendered experience of slavery gave them greater knowledge of the land beyond their own master's property holdings and fewer close ties to children that impeded individual escape.

Access to citizenship and even immigration similarly privileged men over women. In the wake of emancipation, freedmen, not freedwomen, gained the right to vote, to sit on juries, and to hold elective office. It was no accident that the federal agency established to oversee the path to freedom was titled the "Bureau of Refugees, Freedmen, and Abandoned Lands," in shorthand parlance, the "Freedmen's Bureau." As Nancy Cott notes, "Members of Congress and Union agents in the South frequently spoke of and to the emancipated population as though they were all male."[21] The path to citizenship for Native Americans also privileged men. Whereas most Native Americans were effectively excluded from birthright citizenship under the Fourteenth Amendment through the clause "and subject to the jurisdiction thereof," the Dawes Act (1887) opened a limited path to citizenship. Under the Act, an Indian would be recognized as a citizen only if he had taken an allotment. But allotment, as well as citizenship, under the act assumed a white family structure providing one-quarter section "to each head of a family" and granting citizenship to "every Indian ... who has voluntarily taken up ... his residence separate and apart from any tribe of Indians therein, and has adopted the habits of civilized life...."[22] Did Congress even concern itself with the question of how a married Indian

[21] Nancy F. Cott, *Public Vows: A History of Marriage and the Nation* (Cambridge, MA, 2000), 82.
[22] Sec. 6, An Act to Provide for the Allotment of Lands in Severalty to Indians on the Various Reservations, and to Extend the Protection of the Laws of the United States and the Territories over the Indians, and

woman acquired citizenship under the Dawes Act? If her husband met the terms of the act, did his citizenship extend to her? Was her embrace of domesticity – "the habits of civilized life" – a condition for her citizenship? Could she acquire citizenship independent of her husband? The one sure path to citizenship for Native American women – established by Congress in 1888, the year after passage of the Dawes Act – required marrying a white male citizen and living away from tribal lands among white society.[23]

Immigration law also advantaged (able) men over women. In some cases gendered privilege was incorporated into the law by singling out occupations that men or women, but not both, were understood to hold. For example, the first limitations and exemptions on Chinese immigration were fundamentally gendered. The Page Law (1875) prohibited immigration of individuals entering the country for "lewd or immoral purposes" and was intended to prevent the immigration of primarily Chinese women who were presumed to be prostitutes.[24] In the 1903 Immigration Act, this exclusion was broadened to bar all women who were suspected of being

for Other Purposes. ("Dawes Act") (http://avalon.law.yale.edu/19th_century/dawes.asp) (last accessed September 16, 2009). Some earlier treaties had included similar provisions regarding citizenship. The Treaty of New Echota (1835), for example, which provided for the removal of the Cherokee, included an exception for Cherokee who did not want to move west, were willing to be subject to the laws of the state, and could provide for themselves to become citizens of the state in which they resided. Treaty of New Echota, 7 U.S. Statutes at Large 478, art. 12 (1835). See also 59th Congress, 2d Sess., House of Representatives, Doc. No. 326, "Report on the Subject of Citizenship, Expatriation, and Protection Abroad" (Dec. 18, 1906), App. I ("Citizenship of the United States"), 59.

[23] 25 U.S. Statutes at Large 392, ch. 818, sec. 2, "An act in relation to marriage between white men and Indian women": "That every Indian woman, member of any such tribe of Indians, who may hereafter be married to any citizen of the United States, is hereby declared to become by such marriage a citizen of the United States, with all the rights, privileges, and immunities of any such citizen, being a married woman...." Regarding the requirement that they live away from tribal society, see App. I "Citizenship of the United States," in 59th Congress, 2d Sess., House of Representatives, Doc. No. 326, "Report on the Subject of Citizenship, Expatriation, and Protection Abroad," 59.

[24] 18 U.S. Statutes at Large 477 (1878).

prostitutes. The Chinese Exclusion Act of 1882 exempted merchants, students, and teachers – all occupations held by men – from its provisions.[25] Other immigration provisions, such as the exclusion of those "likely to become a public charge," were not on their face gendered, but reflected a larger concern that independent female migration represented a danger and operated in practice to exclude unaccompanied women. Men with mental and physical disabilities were assumed to be incapable of independent support under the law. The "public charge" clause in the first major immigration act (1882) was a catchall phrase that covered individuals (male and female) with disabilities other than those formally enumerated in the law, as well as single women. In later years, the law became more specific. The 1907 act required a medical certificate for anyone judged "mentally or physically defective, such mental or physical defect being of a nature which may affect the ability of such alien to earn a living."[26] In this way, immigration restriction reinforced the gendered hierarchy of able male providers and female dependents.

While escape from subject identities opened opportunities, it exacted a high cost. For Native Americans, the law and the courts' interpretation of the Fourteenth Amendment made renunciation of Indian life and culture the cost of citizenship. Even then Native Americans did not fully shake their subject identity. Under the terms of the Dawes Act, Indians did not hold full title to their allotment. The federal government held the deed in trust; Indians were prohibited from selling or giving away their land for 25 years.[27] Moreover, the decision of whether an Indian had made the necessary transformation in identity rested not in his own determination, but in the hands of white men.[28]

For African Americans and Chinese there was a different path: passing. For African Americans passing was limited to

[25] Chinese Exclusion Act of 1882, 22 U.S. Statutes at Large 58 (1883).
[26] 22 U.S. Statutes at Large 214 (1883); 34 U.S. Statutes at Large 899 (1907).
[27] *Eells v. Ross*, 64 F. 417 (9th Cir. 1894).
[28] *Elk v. Wilkins*, 112 U.S. 94 (1884).

those who by virtue of skin color would not be identified as black. Passing opened the doors that came with property in whiteness. Privately it required a sundering of even family ties and made African Americans something of fugitives from justice in every drink from a "white" water fountain; every journey by rail in the "white" coach; in marriage, sex, and even in illness and burial at death; in every interaction, that is, where racial separation was mandated by law or custom. And with passing came the daily threat of being unmasked. For most Chinese, through what is called the "Exclusion Era" (1882–1943), immigration itself depended on a form of passing: the assumption of "paper lives" – elaborate fictions that included not only assuming a new name, but also memorizing a new past to pose as a member of the exempt classes. Nor could illegal Chinese immigrants drop their paper identities once they had immigrated. Under the Exclusion Act, the Bureau of Immigration (reorganized as the INS – Immigration & Naturalization Service – in 1933) was authorized to deport anyone who entered the country illegally no matter how many years had passed: once illegal, always illegal.

Inclusion within the borders of belonging for a given group often came at the cost of further subordination of others and tended to reinforce the legitimacy of the stunted narrative of personhood, citizenship, and nation with which the century began. In their effort to retain their fragile hold on the land, the Cherokee in early nineteenth century Georgia reshaped their lives according to white governance, law, and custom in matters ranging from gender roles, to the ownership of black slaves, to a constitution. And yet in the 1830s, the Cherokee, nonetheless, were forced west.[29] In the aftermath of the Civil War, many freedmen asserted their freedom and their manhood by claiming property in the person of their wives. Administrative ease and assumptions about male authority

---

[29] Native Americans were not alone in this regard. Japanese, who had taken up farming in the belief that it would provide a foundation for permanent settlement and their assimilation into American society, lost their land when western states passed alien land laws that prohibited those ineligible for citizenship from owning agricultural land.

and female dependence combined to reinforce freedmen's claim in policy and law. The Freedmen's Bureau affirmed freedmen's property in their wives when it gave them the authority to sign labor contracts for their wives. Moreover, in contrast to the handwringing that accompanied the commodification of Northern white hirelings' wives' labor, Freedmen's Bureau staff scorned as idle freedmen's wives who did only housework. Yet ultimately freedmen's property claim in their wives was as incomplete as their property claim in their own labor, for one of the glaring inconsistencies of freedmen's freedom of contract was that they were not free to not contract. Freed slaves who refused to enter labor contracts were vulnerable to being classed as vagrants and punished through compulsory labor.

In the immediate post–Civil War years, women's rights advocates faced one pointed rebuff after another as women's stunted citizenship was incorporated into the U.S. Constitution. As Nancy Cott explains, Congress had no intention of revolutionizing the law of marriage. When some Senators, including Senator Jacob Howard, Republican from Michigan, expressed the fear that the proposed language of the Thirteenth Amendment, which opened with a broad statement that "all persons are equal before the law," would be read to mean that "before the law a woman would be equal to a man, a woman would be as free as a man. A wife would be equal to her husband and as free as her husband before the law," the language was dropped.[30] From the tailoring of the language of the Thirteenth Amendment to avoid interfering with men's privileged authority as heads of household and women's subjection within marriage; to Section 2 of the Fourteenth Amendment, which made only limitations of male suffrage a cause for reducing representation in Congress; to the refusal to include sex in the Fifteenth Amendment's protection of suffrage; and the U.S. Supreme Court's rejection of women's rights advocates' expansive interpretation of the Fourteenth Amendment as embodying women's right to

[30] Cott, *Public Vows*, 80.

vote (*Minor v. Happersett*, 1875),[31] women found the way forward restricted at every turn. Many in the movement responded by turning away from arguments that all individuals should have the vote irrespective of sex, to embrace arguments that women must be given the right to vote because of their fundamental differences from men. In the process, white women were only too quick to distance themselves and the right they claimed from black women. The passage and ratification of the Nineteenth Amendment was a significant gain for women, but its form was a negative right defined by sex – "The right of citizens of the United States to vote shall not be denied or abridged by the United States or by any State on account of sex" – not the affirmative claim that women had originally fought for that suffrage was a right rooted in the shared identity of individuals as citizens and even more expansively of suffrage as a basic human right.

Women and racial and ethnic minorities, resisting their own subjection, whether in debates about voting or immigration, rejected the label "disability" as applied to them without challenging the idea that physical and mental characteristics should be the foundation for exclusion from fundamental rights of personhood and citizenship. In fighting for their own inclusion by distancing themselves from the

---

[31] Section 2 of the Fourteenth Amendment reads: "Representatives shall be apportioned among the several States according to their respective numbers, counting the whole number of persons in each State, excluding Indians not taxed. *But when the right to vote at any election* for the choice of electors for President and vice President of the United States, Representatives in Congress, the Executive and Judicial officers of a State, or the members of the Legislature thereof, *is denied to any of the male inhabitants* of such State, being twenty-one years of age, and citizens of the United States, or in any way abridged, except for participation in rebellion, or other crime, *the basis of representation therein shall be reduced in the proportion which the number of such male citizens shall bear to the whole number of male citizens twenty-one years of age in such State*." U.S. Constitution, amdmt. 14, sec. 2 (emphasis added). Prior to ratification of the 14th Amendment, there was no reference to male in the Constitution. Section 1 of the Fifteenth Amendment reads: The right of citizens of the United States to vote shall not be denied or abridged by the United States or by any State on account of race, color, or previous condition of servitude." U.S. Constitution, amdmt. 15, sec. 1; *Minor v. Happersett*, 88 U.S. (21 Wall.) 162 (1875).

label disability, they gave credence to the idea that disabled persons were justifiably denied equal rights.[32]

Ultimately, the most fundamental expression of disabled persons', racialized others', and women's subjectivity was their erasure, by law's operation, from the historical record. Slaves were denied even the most fundamental expression of personhood: a legal name. The fact of their existence was memorialized only by the thriving market in human chattel that recorded their exchange for a price. Bans that prohibited blacks from testifying against whites not only protected white men's word against contradiction, but denied African Americans in the antebellum South, as well as in many states in the West, any voice at all. The Fugitive Slave Act of 1850 denied the alleged fugitive a voice even in the proceeding that marked the boundary between freedom and bondage. The treatment accorded those labeled insane, idiotic, feeble-minded, epileptic, and otherwise "defective" in institutionalization proceedings in many states was not so very different. Before the 1860s, involuntary commitment laws in any number of states, including Illinois, Iowa, and Massachusetts, denied the individual any say in whether he or she would be institutionalized.[33] Individuals placed in state institutions for the feebleminded all too quickly went from being seen as potentially educable persons to research subjects.

Until 1850, the U.S. Census recorded only heads of household. Coverture erased whole lives. In the closing pages of her account of the life of Martha Ballard, *A Midwife's Tale*, Laurel Thatcher Ulrich reminds us that "[o]utside her own diary Martha has no history.... It is her husband's name,

[32] Douglas C. Baynton, "Disability and Justification of Inequality in American History," in *The New Disability History: American Perspectives*, eds. Paul K. Longmore and Lauri Umansky (New York, 2001), 33–57.

[33] See, for example, General Laws of the State of Illinois, Passed by the Seventeenth General Assembly (Springfield, 1851), 98. For a collection of state commitment laws as of 1914, see Smith, Wilkinson, and Wagoner, *The Bulletin of the University of Washington No.*, 36–81, and The National Committee for Mental Hygiene, *Summaries of Law Relating to the Commitment and Care of the Insane in the United States* (New York, 1913).

not hers, that appears in censuses, tax lists, and merchants' accounts for her town.... Without the diary, even her name would be uncertain."[34] Almost half a century later, speaking at a Woman's Rights Convention, Elizabeth Cady Stanton reminded her audience, "A woman has no name! She is Mrs. John or James, Peter or Paul, just as she changes masters; like the Southern slave, she takes the name of her owner."[35] This taking of a husband's name was not simply a matter of social convention; the doctrine of coverture as embedded in state law required women to take their husband's name in marriage.

Debates over legal rights in and beyond courtrooms easily elided the voices and the interests of those whose claim to belonging was most tenuous. As John Sweet notes, it was a victory of sorts when Rhode Island's attorney general managed to secure indictments in 1824 against at least a handful of the rioters who had destroyed several blacks' homes in a predominantly black part of Providence known as Hard Scrabble following the provocation the day before when a group of blacks had refused to cede the inner-walk to a group of whites on one of the city's main streets. But the black residents of Hard Scrabble were barred from testifying and there were no convictions. In fact, the white men on trial succeeded in making the case that their nighttime lawlessness was a public service in ridding the community of a "sink of vice."[36] Three quarters of a century later and on the other side of the American continent, the major chords in the story Linda Gordon relates of a group of Mexican American families living in two southwestern towns in Arizona who had adopted fifty-seven Irish orphans from New York sounded the same. The legal proceeding that ultimately decided who would have the right

---

[34] Laurel Thatcher Ulrich, *A Midwife's Tale: The Life of Martha Ballard, Based on Her Diary, 1785–1812* (New York, 1991), 343–4.

[35] Elizabeth Cady Stanton, letter to the National Woman's Rights Convention, Cooper Institute, dated Seneca Falls, November 24, 1856; included in the appendixes of *The History of Woman Suffrage*, ed. Elizabeth Cady Stanton, Susan B. Anthony, and Matilda Joslyn Gage (New York, 1881), 1:860.

[36] John Wood Sweet, *Bodies Politic: Negotiating Race in the American North, 1730–1830* (Baltimore, 2003), 353–56, 368–78.

to the children involved only whites: members of the posse who kidnapped the children on a stormy night at gunpoint from their Mexican adoptive families, the white families who "gave" the children "homes," and the New York Foundling Hospital. As Gordon notes, "Th[e] erasure was breathtaking in its audacity: Throughout the trial not one Mexican voice was heard. No Mexican witness was called, no affidavit from a Mexican was introduced, no Mexican sat in the audience, no Mexican was interviewed by a journalist. Since both sides of the case were Anglo, the effect was not only to reinforce the white line encircling citizenship in Arizona but also to place the Mexicans so far outside the circle as to be of, literally, no account."[37] The case, *New York Foundling Hospital v. John C. Gatti*, in this sense reflected larger patterns. No one, after all, argued, in *Buck v. Bell*, the 1927 test case upholding the constitutionality of state sterilization laws, that Carrie Buck, the young single white woman who had been institutionalized by her adoptive family in the Lynchburg State Colony for Epileptics and Feebleminded when she became pregnant (the result of rape by a nephew that the family hoped to cover up) should have a say in whether she was institutionalized or sterilized. Like the thousands of men and women sterilized under state sterilization laws in the twentieth century, others – white male professionals (doctors, lawyers, judges) – decided her reproductive future.

Sites that gave voice could take that voice away. Private and then state-funded schools for the deaf proliferated in the early nineteenth century, providing for many deaf individuals their first experience meeting and mingling with other deaf people and, in time, creating an American deaf community. But the end of the nineteenth century brought a different calculus that would hold through much of the twentieth century: eliminating the teaching of signing in schools for the deaf in favor of oralism. If they did not succeed in eliminating signing as a means of communication in the deaf community,

---

37 Linda Gordon, *The Great Arizona Orphan Abduction* (Cambridge, MA 1999), 276.

they most certainly effectively disabled generations of deaf Americans. Neither manualism nor oralism was mandated by law. But the experience of the deaf community at the end of the nineteenth century was a powerful story of how institutions that gathered communities of the disabled – whether by the promise of education or care as in the case of deaf and "feebleminded" persons, by treaty and force as in the case of reservations for Native Americans and boarding schools for Native American children, or "separate but equal" schools for African Americans – were sites established by law, based on the vision of able white males. These all too often became sites of repression, control, and cultural erasure from the borders of belonging.

Daily Indignities, Daily Lives

One of Frederick Douglass's earliest memories as a child was of his master ordering his Aunt Hester into the kitchen where he stripped her from neck to waist, bound her hands together and stretched her arms high over her head, tied them to a hook in a ceiling beam, and beat her until the blood dripped on the floor.[38] Why begin with violence? Because violence, sanctioned by law, legitimated by law, sanitized by law, and rendered unaddressable by its victims through law was central in the daily lives of racialized others, women, and disabled persons. All slaves did not themselves have to be beaten, as Douglass's story attests, to know that a master could beat them to within an inch of their lives, indeed, kill them without legal penalty. The relation of master and slave was itself an act of violence and depended on the master's unmitigated authority. In Judge Thomas Ruffin's plainspoken words in *State v. Mann* (1829), "The slave to remain a slave, must be made sensible, that there is no appeal from his master. ..."[39] Hearing of a neighbor woman's cruel treatment at the hands of her husband, in June 1792, Martha Ballard

[38] *Narrative of the Life of Frederick Douglass, An American Slave, Written by Himself*, 1845, ed. David W. Blight (Reprint Boston, 1993), 42–43.
[39] 13 N.C. (2 Dev.) 263, 267 (1829).

recorded in her diary, "O the wretch. He Deserves severe punishment."[40] But he was not punished. Neighbor women were left to talk among themselves of the wrong and perhaps celebrate their own good fortune in not having a husband who would ill-use them, but the law offered them no sanction to assist her and little recourse should they find themselves in a similar position. Following the Revolution the home increasingly came to be seen as private, giving license to men's authority as household head to govern household dependents, including wives, with far greater impunity than they had exercised in colonial America.[41] Law effectively placed wives, like slaves, in harm's way. As Elizabeth Cady Stanton would note, the "care and protection" that men gave women was "such as the wolf gives the lamb, the eagle the hare he carries to the eyrie!!"[42]

Nor was violence licensed by law simply accepted because it was private. Colonial laws authorizing the death, whipping, branding, castration, dismemberment, and ear-slitting of runaway slaves were carried over into state law in the Early Republic. Southern slave patrols were funded by states and manned by white men whose names were drawn from militia muster and tax rolls and then served for a designated term. The Fugitive Slave clause of the Constitution and the Fugitive Slave Acts of 1793 and 1850 blurred the line of free and slave state. Rarely are the incentives of law so naked in expression as in the 1850 act: $5.00 to the commissioner if he determined that the black was not a runaway; $10.00 if he awarded the certificate of rendition; rarely are the protections of the accused so nonexistent: owners and agents licensed by law to seize an alleged fugitive with or without legal process and on their word alone rested the fate of the alleged fugitive.[43] Harriet Jacobs's *Incidents in the Life of a Slave*

[40] Ulrich, *A Midwife's Tale*, 130.
[41] Ruth H. Bloch, "The American Revolution, Wife Beating, and the Emergent Value of Privacy," *Early American Studies* 5 (2007), 226.
[42] Elizabeth Cady Stanton "Address at Seneca Falls" in *Elizabeth Cady Stanton, Susan B. Anthony: Correspondence, Writings, Speeches*, ed. Ellen Carol DuBois (Boston, 1992), 33.
[43] 9 U.S. Statutes at Large 462 (1850).

Girl returns again and again to the gross inhumanities to which the act gave license. "When a man is hunted like a wild beast he forgets there is a God, a heaven," Jacobs's brother Benjamin explained on his recapture. "He forgets every thing in his struggle to get beyond the reach of the bloodhounds."[44] Frederick Douglass demanded, "Let him be a fugitive slave in a strange land – a land given up to be the hunting-ground for slaveholders – whose inhabitants are legalized kidnappers – where he is every moment subjected to the terrible liability of being seized upon by his fellowmen.... and not till then, will he fully appreciate the hardships of and know how to sympathize with, the toil-worn and whip-scarred fugitive slave."[45]

"Chinese catchers" – special agents trained to find and arrest Chinese who were in the United States in violation of the Chinese Exclusion laws – mimicked the role of the fugitive slave catcher of slavery days. Immigration raids in "Chinatowns" across the country at the beginning of the twentieth century destroyed property and terrorized legal and illegal Chinese immigrants alike; "all Chinese are treated as suspects, if not as criminals," wrote sociologist Mary Coolidge. Protesting to President Woodrow Wilson in 1918, the Chinese Six Companies explained, "No matter how long their residence or how firm their right to remain, Chinese are being arrested, hunted, and terrorized."[46]

Organized violence at the hands of the state – "military operations" – pervaded the long history of U.S./Indian relations. When the Seventh Cavalry finished its "disarming" operation at Wounded Knee in December of 1890, 170 to 200 of the 270 to 300 dead or mortally wounded were women and children, "almost all of whom," as Jeffrey Ostler notes, "were slaughtered while fleeing or trying to hide."[47] The non-consensual sterilization of thousands of "unfit" women and

---

44 Harriet A. Jacobs, *Incidents in the Life of a Slave Girl, Written by Herself*, 1861, ed. Jean Fagan Yellin (Reprint Cambridge, MA, 1987), 22.
45 Douglass, *Narrative*, 99.
46 Quoted in Erika Lee, *At America's Gates: Chinese Immigration During the Exclusion Era, 1882–1943* (Chapel Hill, 2003), 186.
47 Ostler, *The Plains Sioux and U.S. Colonialism*, 345.

men housed in state institutions in the twentieth century was no less violent for all its legal, medical, and scientific trappings. Legalized violence framed daily life.

In light of lived experience, the idea of law offering protection of property, life, or even dignity rang hollow. When Cornelia Wells Bailey, a young black woman, was assaulted by two drunken white men, the "Hale boys," on a train in Glasgow, Kentucky, in 1894, and brought suit against the railroad, everyone in the courtroom must have enjoyed the legal charade as the railroad's lawyer questioned Bailey's father. "Did you have these boys arrested and prosecuted for mistreating your daughter?" "No sir." "Didn't swear out any warrant against them?" "No sir." "They both lived here close to Glasgow?" "Yes sir." "Never tried to have them prosecuted at all?" "No sir."[48] Anyone sitting in that courtroom who was honest might have laughed at the idea of the criminal law protecting a black woman assaulted by two white men. Suing the railroad was the Baileys' best bet, but even there it was a "colored" woman's word against that of the white conductor and brakeman as to what happened on the train that day. They denied ever seeing Bailey before and insisted that since "the law" had been in effect (requiring separate coaches for white and black passengers) they had never placed a white passenger in or allowed a white passenger to go into the colored compartment.[49] As Ida B. Wells had remembered her experience of being violently ejected from a rail car in Tennessee some eleven years before, "Everybody in the car seemed to sympathise with the conductor, and were against me."[50] Participants in lynch mobs could brag of their exploits,

[48] Testimony of Perry Wells (Cornelia's father, cross-examination), p. 54, Supreme Court Records Case No. 341, Kentucky Department for Libraries and Archives (Frankfort, KY); Barbara Y. Welke, *Recasting American Liberty: Gender, Race, Law and the Railroad Revolution, 1865–1920* (New York, 2001), 319–20.

[49] Testimony of John Gault (conductor), pp. 63, 67, James T. Ray (head brakeman), p. 77, Supreme Court Records Case No. 341, Kentucky Department for Libraries and Archives (Frankfort, KY). The court ruled in the railroad's favor. *Bailey v. Louisville & Nashville R.R. Co.*, 44 S.W. 105 (1898).

[50] Quoted in Welke, *Recasting American Liberty*, 304.

collect lynching "souvenirs," even pose for pictures, so sure were they that the law was with them and not with the black man whose charred body hung from the tree. In W. E. B. Du Bois's words, "lynching became a form of amusement."[51]

The sequestering of racialized others by force of law in public transit, education, and on reservations; the racial exclusivity practiced through restrictive covenants; the exclusion of women from public life; the institutionalization of those labeled defective physically marked women's, racialized others', and disabled persons' lives as outside the borders of belonging. As Charles Chesnutt expressed it: "Should a colored person endeavor for a moment to lose sight of his disability, these staring signs would remind him continually that between him and the rest of mankind not of his own color, there was by law a great gulf fixed."[52] By the terms of state laws, accommodations in public transit were required to be *equal and* separate. Experience taught a different lesson. "Did you ever see a Jim Crow waiting room?" W. E. B. Du Bois began a description of Jim Crow travel in his 1921 *Darkwater: Voices from Within the Veil.* His description took in the lack of heat in winter, the suffocating lack of air in summer, the smell, the dirt, the crowding, the indignity undifferentiated by season.[53] Four years later in an article in *The Nation,* he wrote, "I am in the hot, crowded, and dirty Jim Crow car where I belong ... I am not comfortable."[54]

On reservations, Indians often waited months for treaty rations and annuities to arrive. "Last winter our people all left their Camps and came to the agency expecting every day to get our goods," leaders at Cheyenne River on the Sioux Reservation in South Dakota complained in 1883, "but we

[51] W. E. B. Du Bois, "Georgia, Invisible Empire State," *Nation* 120 (January 21, 1925): 63–7.

[52] Charles W. Chesnutt, *The Marrow of Tradition*, quoted in Grace Elizabeth Hale, *Making Whiteness: The Culture of Segregation in the South, 1890–1940* (New York, 1998), 49.

[53] W. E. B. Du Bois, *Darkwater: Voices from Within the Veil* (1921), 228–9.

[54] Du Bois, "Georgia, Invisible Empire State," *Nation* (January 21, 1925): 63–7.

did not get them for several weeks.... The weather was very cold and many of our people almost perished because they had no clothing and many of them that had poultry and small stock at home found much of it frozen when they got back." When rations and annuities finally arrived they were often of inferior quality, purposely unsuited to Indian life. Indian women stood in long lines only to have treaty rations thrown to them "as if they were dogs."⁵⁵

Institutions for the insane, idiots, the feebleminded, and epileptics were not so very different from reservations. With increasing urgency over the course of the nineteenth century experts portrayed the mentally and physically "defective" as wasteful drains on family and societal resources (emotional, educational, and financial); threats to the health – financial and moral – of the family and the nation. Their arguments justified institutionalization, exclusion from public education, and ultimately sterilization. Those labeled defective became the quintessential nonpersons, not simply outside the borders of belonging, but a burden to be shed. Eugenicist H. H. Goddard, speaking of the "feebleminded" in 1911, captured the thinking that underlay public policy by the beginning of the twentieth century: "It would be better both for him and for society had he never been born."⁵⁶

Making conduct that otherwise would have been legal illegal did not change the need to engage in that conduct or the sense of a right to do so, but it did contribute to the devaluing or loss of respect for law, fed corruption, and increased both costs and hazards. Following the criminalization of abortion between the 1850s and 1880, women continued, in the hundreds of thousands each year, to have abortions even as criminalization of abortion rendered their efforts to control their reproduction more hazardous. So too with Chinese

⁵⁵ Ostler, *The Plains Sioux and U.S. Colonialism*, 130, 132.
⁵⁶ H. H. Goddard, "The Elimination of Feeble-mindedness," *The Annals* (March 1911): 505, quoted in Sharon L. Snyder and David T. Mitchell, "Out of the ashes of eugenics: diagnostic regimes in the United States and the making of a disability minority," *Patterns of Prejudice* 36 (2002), 89.

immigration in the "Exclusion Era." We will never know just
how many Chinese immigrated during the Exclusion Era,
because they were hidden behind a veil of illegality. And, as
in abortion, the widely shared belief in the Chinese American
community that the exclusion laws were unjust and discrimi-
natory made working around them or ignoring them culturally
acceptable. Criminalization of conduct created new hazards.
With ports of entry closed to them, Chinese laborers resorted
to risky border crossings from Mexico and Canada. For the
immigrant (or more often immigrants plural) hidden in a rail-
car, the delay of a train by a snowstorm or a problem on the
track could mean freezing to death or suffocation. In addition
to the costs of transatlantic transportation these immigrants
had to add the costs of buying (and living) paper identities or
otherwise disguising themselves as members of the "exempt
classes" under the Chinese Exclusion Law, or paying smug-
glers, guides, and any number of other charges for stays at
the border, information, and more. Criminalization of immigration, as of abortion, created underground networks and
economies.

Ferreting out criminal conduct licensed its own forms of
violence, physical as well as psychic. Interrogations of Chinese
immigrants at Angel Island in San Francisco Bay could last
hours or days. They ranged from exhaustive searches of lug-
gage, to, for a time, invasive, humiliating physical examina-
tions borrowing on French scientist and criminal detective
Alphonse Bertillon's belief that detailed body measurements
including everything from length and width (or circumfer-
ence) of forearms, feet, fingers, to head, teeth, and genitalia
provided a means for detecting criminal conduct or proclivi-
ties. Detained in the squalid barracks of Angel Island, immigrants poured out their loneliness, anger, frustration, and
homesickness in thousands of poems written and carved into
the station's walls.[57]

As Leslie Reagan has described, the investigative procedures in abortion cases constituted a form of punishment

[57] Lee, *At America's Gates*, 84–5, 76, 219.

and control calibrated to warn doctors and to humiliate women, publicly expose their transgressions, and force them to become, even in death, a witness against their abortionists. In this respect, Carolina Petrovitis's experience fit a larger pattern. Petrovitis was a Lithuanian immigrant to Chicago, married, and the mother of two children; in 1916 she had an illegal abortion which she ultimately paid for with her life. Her friends called in a doctor as she lay in bed, deathly ill and in terrible pain. Before the doctor would treat her he insisted that she must tell him who performed the abortion. Only after she gave him a name – and thus protected him from allegation – was he willing to call an ambulance to take her to the hospital. At the hospital, three police officers arrived to question Mrs. Petrovitis and collect what in legal parlance was known as a "dying declaration." They instructed an intern to "tell her she is going to die." She began to cry. When they were sure she understood that she was about to die, the police got her to admit to all the details of the abortion: price, place, date, abortionist. The state transformed her dying moments into the foundation for a case supporting the legal structure that bore central responsibility for her death.[58]

As the boundaries of legality changed, so too did the nature of or possibility for community. Chronicling his escape from slavery, Frederick Douglass questioned the term "free state," burdened as it was by the Fugitive Slave Act. "I was afraid to speak to any one for fear of speaking to the wrong one, and thereby falling into the hands of money-loving kidnappers, whose business it was to lie in wait for the panting fugitive.... I saw in every white man an enemy, and in almost every colored man cause for distrust."[59] Enforcement of laws often depended on defections within subject communities. Again and again, Native Americans found themselves bound by treaties signed by those acknowledged by U.S. government officials to act on behalf of the tribe, not by the tribes themselves. Following passage of the Chinese Exclusion Act,

---

[58] Leslie J. Reagan, *When Abortion Was a Crime: Women, Medicine, and Law in the United States, 1867–1973* (Berkeley, 1997), 113–14.

[59] Douglass, *Narrative*, 98–9.

Erika Lee notes, "some of the most active government infor-
mants" came from within the Chinese community.[60] They
acted for personal gain, out of spite and individual grievance,
in an effort to rid the community of undesirable elements,
and in fear that "illegals" undermined their own "legal"
status. Moreover, criminalization of conduct rendered those
excluded by the borders of belonging vulnerable to other
abuses in the shadow of the law. Illegal and undocumented
Chinese, for example, like illegal immigrants today, had little
recourse against exploitation by oppressive employers, extor-
tion or blackmail by corrupt government bureaucrats and
other Chinese, or violent crime.

And there was quite simply the narrowing of life's horizons. Writing in her diary in August 1787, Martha Ballard
noted, "At Mr. Richards, His wife Delivered of a Daughter at
10 O Clok morn." In an entry the next month, she recorded,
"Mr. Ballard gone to Mr. James Pages on public business....
I have been at home." And, in October 1789, "I have been at
home. Received ½ Bushel of rie of Captain Hersey as reward
for assisting his Lady."[61] This one woman's life, like those of
the women she was midwife to, spanned momentous changes
in the life of the nation: the American Revolution, the formation of a new nation, the transformation of subjects to citizens. Martha Moore married and became Mrs. Ballard with
all that that entailed under the law of coverture before the
Revolution. Her diary, penned after the Revolution, attests
as nothing else can to the absence of a revolution in women's
legal rights. Her references were unself-conscious, generally unquestioning expressions of life as she knew it. As the
entries and silences in Martha Ballard's diary suggest, hers
was a world in which women had no role in public life, in
which wives, like houses, belonged to men. By the end of the
nineteenth century, with the criminalization of abortion as a
tool for discrediting midwives, male doctors would be well
on their way to supplanting even the niche that had given

---

[60] Lee, *At America's Gates*, 235.
[61] Ulrich, *A Midwife's Tale*, 38, 103.

Martha Ballard's life so much of its meaning, that had provided, in fact, the reason for the diary that allows us to know
of her life at all.

At the end of the long nineteenth century as at its beginning, the daily indignities and daily lives of those beyond
the borders of belonging took shape at times through the
direct force of law, but far more often in its long shadow.
"The deformed man is always conscious that the world
does not expect very much from him," wrote Randolph
Bourne in a 1911 essay titled "The Handicapped."[62] Replace
"deformed man" with woman, black man, or any of those
cast as "other" in law – here and through most of Bourne's
essay – and you see something of the power of the borders of
belonging. Bourne was writing about his own experience of
life as a "deformed man." Born in 1886, a botched forceps
delivery left him with a twisted mouth, face, and ear; child-
hood spinal tuberculosis then stunted his growth and left him
with a severely curved spine. Throughout his short life people
responded to his physical appearance with revulsion. Bourne
grew to adulthood in a world in which many cities barred
the "diseased, maimed, mutilated, or in any way deformed
so as to be an unsightly or disgusting object ... in or on the
public ways." He lived in a world in which had he been an
immigrant, he would have been excluded from the United
States on the ground that he would be "likely to become a
public charge;" in a world in which had he found a woman
who could overlook his physical disability and think of him
as more than friend, he might well have been barred from
marrying; in a world in which the disabled were often institutionalized and excluded from public schools; in a world in
which fear of the plague of disability led states across the
nation to mandate forced sterilization of the disabled unfortunate enough to be institutionalized. Bourne wrote of none
of these laws in his essay "The Handicapped." He was not
forced to make his livelihood by begging; he was born in the

---

[62] Randolph Bourne, "The Handicapped," *The Atlantic Monthly* CVIII
(September 1911): 320–9.

United States and was an American citizen; he, sadly, did not marry before his untimely death at the age of thirty-two of the Spanish Influenza; he was never institutionalized; he was an intellectual giant of his time. So did these laws not matter to his life? Did laws of exclusion, segregation, subjection, control only shape the lives of those who felt their force directly? To assume so is to miss the real power of law for all those law dis-abled. Bourne again might have been speaking of any of those "othered" by law in his reference, "[H]is environment and circumstances call out all sorts of ambitions and energies in him which, from the nature of his case, are bound to be immediately thwarted."

The world was not fitted for the disabled. "No one but the deformed man can realize," Bourne explained, "just what the mere fact of sitting a foot lower than the normal means in discomfort and annoyance. For one cannot carry one's special chair everywhere, to theatre and library and train and schoolroom." But he saved his strongest words for the frustrations he faced in "making his own way in the world." "Perhaps the bitterest struggles of the handicapped man come when he tackles the business world," Bourne wrote. "The attitude toward me ranged from 'You can't expect us to create a place for you,' to 'How could it enter your head that we should find any use for a man like you?'"

Bourne's essay rejected bitterness and hopelessness, Indeed, it embraced life with a power that makes one choke to think of Justice Holmes's words in *Buck v. Bell* of "those who already sap the strength of the State." Was it temporal context, gender, personality, or perhaps only the medium of expression (a published article with a brave face versus a private pouring out of the heart) that separated Randolph Bourne's acceptance of his disability ("But if I am not yet out of the wilderness, at least I think I see the way to happiness") from Elizabeth Cady Stanton's wish – expressed in a letter to her dear friend Susan B. Anthony in December 1859 following two great losses (the death of her father and that of John Brown). "When I pass the gate of the celestial city and good Peter asks me where I would sit," Stanton wrote

Anthony, "I shall say, 'Anywhere, so that I am neither a negro nor a woman. Confer on me, good angel, the glory of white manhood so that henceforth, sitting or standing, rising up or lying down, I may enjoy the most unlimited freedom.'"[63]

But in Elizabeth Cady Stanton's private anguish, Randolph Bourne's public dignity, indeed in almost every story told in these pages, is a tale, not solely of subject lives or daily indignities, but of resistance to the borders of belonging. "[T]he history of any struggle," Walter Johnson notes, "no matter how one-sided in its initial appearance, is incomplete until told from the perspective of all those whose agency shaped the outcome."[64]

---

[63] Elizabeth Cady Stanton, Letter to Susan B. Anthony, 23 December 1859, in DuBois, *The Elizabeth Cady Stanton~Susan B. Anthony Reader*, 69.

[64] Walter Johnson, *Soul by Soul: Life Inside the Antebellum Slave Market* (Cambridge, MA, 1999), 8.

"No person held to Service or Labour in one State, under the Laws thereof, escaping into another, shall, in Consequence of any Law or Regulation therein, be discharged from such Service or Labour, but shall be delivered up on the Claim of the Party to whom such Service or Labour may be due." (U.S. Const. art. 4, sec. 2, 1789)

****

Judge Hunt: "The court must insist – the prisoner has been tried according to the established forms of law."
Susan B. Anthony: "Yes, your honor, but by forms of law made by men, interpreted by men, administered by men, in favor of men, and against women ..." (Remarks at end of trial for illegal voting, 1873)

****

"An Act to Provide for the Allotment of Lands in Severalty to Indians on the Various Reservations, and to Extend the Protection of the Laws of the United States and the Territories over the Indians, and for Other Purposes." (Dawes Act, 1887)

****

"Not all or nearly all of the murders done by white men during the past thirty years in the South have come to light, but the statistics ... show that during these years more than 10,000 Negroes have been killed in cold blood without the formality of judicial trial and execution." (Ida B. Wells, *The Red Record*, 1895)

****

"[T]he child in question is a white, Caucasian child ... abandoned ... to the keeping of a Mexican Indian, whose name is unknown to the respondent, but one ... by reason of his race, mode of living, habits and education, unfit to have the custody, care and education of the child." (*New York Foundling Hospital v. Gatti*, U.S. Supreme Court, 1906)

****

"Gentlemen's Agreement" (agreement between President Theodore Roosevelt and Japanese officials that Japan would "voluntarily" limit immigration to the United States to avoid the humiliation of restrictive immigration legislation similar to the Chinese Exclusion Act, 1907)

****

"AN ACT to prevent the procreation of persons socially inadequate from defective inheritance, by authorizing and providing for the eugenical sterilization of certain potential parents carrying degenerate hereditary qualities." (Model Eugenical Sterilization Law by Harry H. Laughlin, Assistant Director of the Eugenics Record Office, 1922)

3

BORDERS

Resistance, Defense, Structure,
and Ideology

Privilege built upon exclusion, marginalization, and subordination of others is fragile; it produces individual and collective resistance; it requires work to maintain. And so it was and so it did in the long nineteenth century United States. In myriad individual and collective ways, even as new limitations on their personhood and citizenship were incorporated into law, disabled persons, racialized others, and women challenged the borders of belonging. And women and racialized others especially gained greater recognition in law of their personhood and rights as citizens than had been true at the founding. As significantly, the resistance of those excluded from full personhood, citizenship, and nation rendered legible and exposed the flaw at the foundation of American liberalism: their own subjection and exclusion. But resistance also engendered defense of privilege so that what the founding generation of men took for granted in fomenting a revolution, they and subsequent generations defended as right long after the Civil War.

In part, deeply held assumptions relating to ability, race, gender – an abled, racialized, and gendered "imagination," to borrow and expand on Alice Kessler Harris's evocative phrase – led to the replication of the borders of belonging even as context changed.[1] In part, too, the political process meant that privilege reproduced itself. But the resilience of the borders of belonging depended fundamentally on the fact that men who were white and able held the reins of lawmaking. Over the course of the nineteenth century, incredible effort went into preserving law as the domain of able white men. Moreover, the structure of law itself masked the breadth and depth of able white male privilege. It is really only in making the texts of laws, legal opinions, treatises, treaties, and so on, a concrete subject of inquiry that we can see the operation of law, the structures of lawmaking and ideology in establishing, masking, and justifying able white men's privilege, disabled persons', racialized others', and women's subordination, and the interdependence of the two, in the long nineteenth century United States.

In Pursuit of Right

Writing in the wake of emancipation, a South Carolina educator and minister, noted: "The Negroes are to be pitied. They do not understand the liberty which has been conferred upon them."[2] He could not have been more mistaken. His statement ignored, first, that the subject lives that all African Americans, whether free or slave, lived under slavery offered a school like no other in teaching exactly what was at stake in the word "liberty." As Eric Foner notes, "blacks carried out of bondage an understanding of their new condition shaped both by their experience as slaves and by observation of the free society around them."[3] The minister's statement ignored as well freedmen's and freedwomen's agency in

[1] Kessler-Harris uses the term "gendered imagination" to describe the way in which racialized, gendered "habits of mind" framed and shaped individual and business thought and decisions, as well as public policy. Alice Kessler-Harris, *In Pursuit of Equity: Women, Men, and the Quest for Economic Citizenship in 20th-Century America* (New York, 2001).
[2] Quoted in Eric Foner, "Rights and the Constitution in Black Life during the Civil War and Reconstruction," *Journal of American History* 74 (1987), 869.
[3] Foner, "Rights and the Constitution in Black Life, 870.

their own liberation. Yes, President Lincoln had signed the Emancipation Proclamation, but well before he did thousands of slaves had abandoned their masters and headed for Union lines. Their flight undermined slavery as much as their service to the Union buoyed the Northern cause. In turn, their embrace of self-ownership in the wake of emancipation, quite literally, embodied liberty. They were suddenly able to leave the site of their enslavement; walk down a street without stepping aside, lifting a hat, or bowing a head as a white passed; marry and seek out and claim "relations"; dress as they pleased; create their own churches and hold religious services; establish schools and benevolent societies; buy a dog, or a gun, or alcohol; hold meetings. And they did. That their liberty was all too quickly re-constrained by law should not be allowed to eclipse the moment of freedom. For every individual and every group discussed in this essay the pursuit of right, like subjection itself, was shaped by historical contingencies that related to that individual life and that particular group. But this they had in common: what liberty they had was theirs by their demand, their pursuit of right waged against the defense of privilege, and they well understood its meaning. Liberty, by definition in this new American republic, was secured, not conferred.

Most actions in pursuit of right remain invisible to us; they were the "everyday resistances," the "weapons of the weak."[4] In every story of a slave learning to read, fleeing bondage, feigning illness is a story of resistance. Frederick Douglass prefaces the story of the day he fought back when his master set to beat him, with the sentence: "You have seen how a man was made a slave; you shall see how a slave was made a man."[5] For every story that we know of we must apply a multiplier of some unknowable number. In a world that depended on concealing the inhumanity of slavery, the slave narrative represented resistance of the most profound

[4] James C. Scott, *Weapons of the Weak: Everyday Forms of Peasant Resistance* (New Haven, 1985).
[5] *Narrative of the Life of Frederick Douglass, An American Slave, Written by Himself,* 1845, ed. David W. Blight (Reprint Boston, 1993), 75.

sort. The narrative thread of resistance ran through acts as public as Lucy Stone's refusal to take her husband's name upon marriage and as private as married women claiming voluntary motherhood as a right. Elizabeth Cady Stanton reported that women greeted her private talks on "marriage and maternity," which she began in 1869 and continued for several years, with the greatest enthusiasm.[6] In the late nineteenth century, after abortion had been made illegal in every state in the nation, hundreds of thousands of women continued to have abortions every year. As Leslie Reagan notes, "There would be no history of illegal abortion to tell without the continuing demand for abortion from women, regardless of law."[7] The narrative thread of resistance ran through illegal border crossings, the lives of "paper sons." It was a minor chord at least in the tale of the Mexican women who out of personal longing, commitment to their church, the status that motherhood conferred, and concern for the orphans themselves, signed promises to take in fifty-seven Anglo orphans in a mining town in southwestern Arizona in 1904. In a town in which racial segregation was, as Linda Gordon puts it, "under construction," the act of Mexican women taking in Anglo orphans – even Irish Catholic orphans from as foreign a place as New York – was "truly a border action."[8] There are hazards in charting the pursuit of right. Every act of nonconformity was not an act of resistance; the power of those rendered subject in law to effect real change was limited. Yet, mindful of these warnings, it is vital to be watchful for the register of resistance both for the constitutive role it played in shaping the borders of belonging and, as every sentence in Randolph Bourne's essay "The Handicapped" reminds us, for claims to personhood and injustice in its denial.

[6] Quoted in Ellen Carol DuBois, *The Elizabeth Cady Stanton – Susan B. Anthony Reader: Correspondence, Writings, Speeches* (Boston, 1981), 95–7.

[7] Leslie J. Reagan, *When Abortion Was a Crime: Women, Medicine, and Law in the United States, 1867–1973* (Berkeley, 1997), 1.

[8] Linda Gordon, *The Great Arizona Orphan Abduction* (Cambridge, MA, 1999), 119.

There is a synergy between individual resistance and collective resistance and pursuit of right. But unlike individual resistance, the collective pursuit of right requires the coalescence of a whole series of elements: subjection must be understood for what it is; it must be understood as shared, that is, as resting on characteristics that one individual shares with others that have been made into a condition of subjection. There must be a language of right to call on; there must be tools of communication, including literacy or an ability to associate; and, where individuals truly lack ability to act for themselves, there must be someone to speak for them. Regardless of the intent of the founders, the American Revolution had articulated a new language of universal, God-given, unalienable rights, expressed most fully in the Declaration of Independence. Although directed to the relationship of king and subject, and predicated on the rights of Englishmen as men, this language of right opened the way for reconsideration of relationships of domination and subordination more generally. Abolitionism took root in the fertile ideological soil provided by Enlightenment ideas incorporated in the American Revolution. "Is not all oppression vile?" wrote "a Negro" in a Massachusetts paper the *New London Gazette*, "I live a slave, and am inslav'd by those Who yet pretend with reason to oppose All schemes oppressive ... O mighty God! Let conscience seize the mind Of Inconsistent men, who wish to find A partial god to vindicate their cause, And plead their freedom, while they break its laws."[9]

The American Revolution did not, however, immediately spark a broader revolution. Abolitionist sentiment was centered in the North. The vast majority of slaves in the South remained insulated from the rhetoric of the Revolution by geography, illiteracy, bondage, and, in short order, by the U.S. Constitution. Moreover, with the abolition of slavery in the North, the legal bonds of slavery tightened in the South. Among elite white women there were those who understood

---

[9] Quoted in Leon Litwack, *North of Slavery: The Negro in the Free States 1790–1860* (Chicago, 1961), 11.

that the revolution opened questions about women's relationship to government and even more fundamentally that
went to the heart of familial relations. Yet their challenges
remained private, voiced, as in Abigail Adams's famous correspondence with her husband John or in correspondence
within small circles of women. Women's revolutionary-era
petitions to Congress – even when they voiced rights claims
as directly as the New Jersey widow Rachel Wells who
insisted, "I have Don as much to Carrey on the war as maney
that Sett Now at the healm of government" – remained individual supplications.[10] Women's subjection yet remained
jumbled together with any number of other relationships of
inequality and dependence and complicated by the very relationship that underpinned women's subordination: marriage.
Moreover, the act of association so fundamental to identity
formation rested yet in the future to be spawned as much by
forces and institutions tangential to law – the religious revival
of the early decades of the nineteenth century, the Second
Great Awakening; the beginning of the Industrial Revolution
in America; the antislavery movement; even, the press – as
by law itself. Most Native American tribes which saw themselves as part of the revolutionary moment had staked their
independence on defeat of the revolution. Others' inclusion
within the formal boundaries of the nation awaited territorial
expansion and the westward surge of white settlement. This
was true of the tribes of the Great Plains and the Pacific – the
first and perhaps most enduring goal of which was not inclusion at all, but nationhood and sovereignty. The boundaries
of Mexico subsumed territory that would only later become
the American southwest. The beginnings of Chinese immigration remained well in the future, a product itself of western expansion. Even as disability was separated out from the
shadows of the poor law and the taint of crime and vice,
collective resistance by disabled persons was impeded by
the inaccessibility of public space, and the medicalization of

---

[10] Quoted in Linda K. Kerber, *Women of the Republic: Intellect & Ideology
in Revolutionary America* (New York, 1980), 33.

disability that rendered disability a personal condition and the disabled patients or objects of charity.

For each of these groups, however, exclusion fostered identity and community that became critical support structures and training grounds for the pursuit of right. Women's sphere provided the foundation in the 1830s for the development of a subculture among some white women. Women first acted collectively as women not in pursuit of the rights of women, but in moral reform, temperance, and most importantly, abolition. In the antebellum North and West, excluded from white churches, schools, political assemblies, and organizations, black Americans established their own associations. Similarly, in the wake of emancipation, African Americans, long denied by law the freedom to associate, deliberately began the project of association building. During the years of Reconstruction and even more so after, black community organizations provided the foundation for black challenges to the borders of belonging. In the American Southwest, discrimination and exclusion led Mexican Americans to begin to articulate an ethnic consciousness that combined their Mexican heritage and their status as Americans, providing a foundation by the 1920s for challenges to segregated education and discrimination in public accommodations and on juries, and voter registration drives and poll tax campaigns. For subsets of disabled persons, including the deaf and the blind, the building of community began within schools and institutions constructed especially for their education and training.

Across time, it was the denial of rights in the face of rights or entitlements extended to others that rankled. With each successive expansion of suffrage – first to white men and then to African American men – the link between suffrage and citizenship became more fully established; the inequity of the denial of suffrage to women became increasingly hard to bear. Had suffrage been insignificant, the claim underlying the Fifteenth Amendment that freed*men* needed the franchise to protect their rights, even their persons and that this need justified separating the black man's exclusion from women's equal exclusion would not have been made. In the

1880s, the Chinese understood that it was they alone who had been singled out as a race and denied the right to immigrate, while, at least for a time, others continued to immigrate freely. Something as basic as the provision of a single toilet in a railroad car to be shared by black passengers male and female alike whereas in the coach for whites there were separate toilets, became the foundation for a challenge to the guarantee of equal accommodations. Whatever might be said to attempt to explain away, excuse, or minimize the significance of these inequalities, the very fact that they existed attested to their significance.

Perhaps the most striking commonality across time of individual and collective resistance was the consistency with which pursuit of right took form in law. In *Cherokee Nation v. Georgia* (1832), the Cherokee resisted the state of Georgia's incursions on Cherokee sovereignty, bringing suit as a "foreign state" and insisting that individual states had no authority over Indian tribes, and that the Constitution mandated that relations be regulated by federal treaty.[11] How different and yet how alike was the shopping for a legal forum less than ten years later by Ellen D'Hauteville, the unhappily married daughter of a Boston Brahmin, determined to leave her marriage but to keep the only child, a son, of her union with a Swiss count. Unable to resolve their differences short of law, she allowed herself to be "found," legally speaking, and suit instituted for custody in the state that offered the greatest promise of keeping her child.[12] Elizabeth Ware Packard's decade-plus battle beginning in the 1860s for adoption of what were dubbed personal liberty laws began with her own institutionalization in an insane asylum under an Illinois law that gave a husband or father authority to institutionalize his wife or child on nothing more than his own request and the agreement of a medical superintendent.[13] When William

---

[11] *Cherokee Nation v. Georgia*, 30 U.S. (5 Pet.) 1 (1831).
[12] Michael Grossberg, *A Judgment for Solomon: The D'Hauteville Case and Legal Experience in Antebellum America* (New York, 1996), 68–75.
[13] Hendrik Hartog, "Mrs. Packard on Dependency," *Yale Journal of Law & Humanities* 79 (1988–1989): 79–103.

Heard saw the conditions of the portion of a combination car set aside for black passengers on the Georgia Railroad in 1887 in Atlanta, Georgia, he thought in terms of *his* rights under the law: "the law of the land was sufficient to protect its citizens;" "the law of the land provides a remedy."[14] As one southern legislature after another moved toward adoption of Jim Crow transit, leading black men formed statewide committees to lobby against passage of the laws and, once they were passed, planned constitutional challenges in the state courts.

Constitutional challenges reflected the transformation that the Fourteenth Amendment especially worked in the constitutional order, itself a product of the most fundamental nineteenth century acknowledgement of human rights – the abolition of slavery.[15] So, for example, in *Yick Wo v. Hopkins* (1886), the U.S. Supreme Court struck down as a violation of the Fourteenth Amendment's Equal Protection Clause a San Francisco municipal laundry ordinance that pointedly targeted Chinese laundries; and, just over a decade later in *U.S. v. Wong Kim Ark* (1898), the Court upheld birthright citizenship of Chinese Americans born on U.S. soil.[16] African Americans too could celebrate limited victories in cases like *McCabe v. Atchison, Topeka and Santa Fe Railway Company* (1914) in which, although the Court rejected the claim for injunctive relief against enforcement of the Oklahoma Separate Coach law, it spoke out strongly against the state's attempt to pick and choose to which accommodations the Equal Protection clause applied. Writing for the Court, Justice Hughes explained that the Fourteenth Amendment's guarantee of equality cannot "depend upon the number of persons

---

[14] Quoted in Barbara Y. Welke, *Recasting American Liberty: Gender, Race, Law, and the Railroad Revolution, 1865–1920* (New York, 2001), 299.

[15] Fourteenth Amendment Equal Protection claims relating to disability were not articulated until the 1970s. See Marcia Pearce Burgdorf and Robert Burgdorf, Jr., "A History of Unequal Treatment: The Qualifications of Handicapped Persons as a 'Suspect Class' Under the Equal Protection Clause," *Santa Clara Lawyer* 15 (1975): 855–910.

[16] *Yick Wo v. Hopkins*, 118 U.S. 356 (1886); *U.S. v. Wong Kim Ark*, 169 U.S. 649 (1898).

who may be discriminated against"; rather, "the essence of the constitutional right is that it is a personal one."[17]

When constitutional challenges were exhausted or unavailable, women, racialized others, and disabled persons took the tools of their subordination and made them into platforms for the pursuit of right. Relegated to reservations, Native Americans took the goods the U.S. government intended to promote "civilization," and adapted them to their own ways of life. As Jeffrey Ostler notes of life on the Great Sioux Reservation in the 1880s, the Sioux sold annuity goods like clothing, shoes, and flannel to nearby settlers, or transformed goods to their own ends such as cutting up government issue boots to make hunting lariats. They lived in log houses in the winter, but built those houses congregated along rivers to make an elongated village rather than solitary cabins scattered across the prairie as the government envisioned, and moved back to their tipis in the summer. Instead of papering the walls of their houses with wallpaper, they made large wall coverings similar to those on a tipi painted with historic scenes such as hunting, battles, peacemaking, games, and courtship.[18] In the same temporal context, African Americans took separate-coach laws – long seen by historians solely as tools for enforcing black oppression – and wielded them in pursuit of individual right. Separate-coach laws were not civil rights statutes, but they did create statutory duties that could be enforced in courts of law. In lawsuits brought across the South from the 1880s through the modern civil rights movement of the twentieth century, African Americans challenged inequality in accommodations, the failure of railroad employees to keep whites out of black coaches, and assaults by carrier employees against blacks in enforcement of the laws. Decisions intended to put an end to rights claims like the Supreme Court's decisions in *Minor v. Happersett* (1875), rejecting women's claim that as birthright citizens they had a right to vote, or the unsuccessful challenge to Virginia's

---

[17] *McCabe*, 235 U.S. 151, 161–2 (1914).

[18] Jeffrey Ostler, *The Plains Sioux and U.S. Colonialism from Lewis and Clark to Wounded Knee* (New York, 2004), 130–5.

compulsory sterilization law in *Buck v. Bell* (1927), generated broader movements for suffrage and against compulsory sterilization.[19]

Individually and as groups, women, the disabled and racialized others claimed their right to personhood, citizenship, and the space of the nation. In every suit for personal injury in the public way or on public accommodations by a physically disabled individual or by a woman burdened by clothing, pregnancy, or children was not only evidence that they occupied public space, but a claim of their right to do so. And in every challenge by a Chinese immigrant held at Angel Island or immigrant rejected at Ellis Island on grounds of disability was a refusal to accept the assertion written into law that they were unalterably alien, unproductive, a threat or burden to the republic.

Support of their claims was not limited to their number. Abolitionism from the start was supported by men and women, white and black; the Underground Railroad depended on the labor of thousands. Woman suffrage depended at every stage on the votes of men in state legislatures, referendums, and Congress who embraced the justice of their claims. To the contrary of biologists' claims of the hereditary chain of disability, able family members fought for their disabled relatives' rights whether by rejecting the assumption that a family member could be adequately provided for only in an institution or would "threaten" or "burden" a family if allowed to remain at home, by insisting that they would provide support for an immigrating relative, or rejecting the disability label or the assumptions it carried altogether. Black and white women organized to bring an end to lynching. That these movements began and all too often remained divided along racialized, gendered, and abled lines qualifies but does not negate the fact that the call of justice did not speak only to those denied it.

Why turn to law? In part, they turned to law because they had no other choice: as John and Jean Comaroff noted of

---

[19] *Minor v. Happersett*, 88 U.S. 162 (1875); *Buck v. Bell*, 274 U.S. 200 (1927).

black South Africans in nineteenth century colonial South Africa, so too in the nineteenth century United States: "it often seemed to be the *only* real means to hand, since it was part of the technology of rule on which rested the inequalities and disablements from which they suffered."[20] There was also the fact that by the early nineteenth century law was the dominant discourse in America. If Thomas Paine's claim in *Common Sense* that "in America the law is king" was not fully true at the moment he wrote the words, it became so by the early nineteenth century.[21] In this sense, women, racialized others, and disabled persons turned to law because law offered a vehicle for making their claims comprehensible; or put somewhat differently, they spoke in terms of law because law was the idiom of the nation.

There was also the promise of law and the remarkable exhibition of law's power. Historians like Ellen Carol DuBois have argued that for women's rights activists whose own discontent in the inequalities of their sex took concrete form in the heated battles of abolitionism, the rise of the Republican Party and the end of slavery made many things seem possible that before the Civil War might have seemed impossible.[22] The denial of suffrage itself to most of these groups through most of the long nineteenth century routed challenges through the legal process, rather than the political process. There was also the power of the words inscribed in the Declaration of Independence, the ringing phrase "We the people" in the Constitution's preamble, the pregnant promises of Article IV guaranteeing the "citizens of each State ... all privileges and immunities of citizens in the several states," and guaranteeing every state "a republican form of government," and the Fourteenth Amendment to the Constitution

[20] John L. Comaroff and Jean Comaroff, *Of Revelation and Revolution, vol. two, The Dialectics of Modernity on a South African Frontier* (Chicago, 1997), 404.

[21] Thomas Paine, "Common Sense," in *The Complete Writings of Thomas Paine, 2 vols.*, ed. Philip S. Foner (New York, 1969), 1:29.

[22] DuBois, "The Nineteenth-Century Woman Suffrage Movement and the Analysis of Women's Oppression," in *Woman Suffrage & Women's Rights*, ed. Ellen Carol DuBois (New York, 1998), 69.

with its guarantees of birthright citizenship, privileges and immunities of citizenship, equal protection and due process of law. Elizabeth Cady Stanton turned to the Declaration of Independence as a model for her famous Declaration of Sentiments for the first Women's Rights convention, held in Seneca Falls, New York, in July 1848, in part because she recognized the power of its language.[23]

And they – women, racialized others, disabled persons – achieved a measure of success. Dismantling particular structures of exclusion and subordination, particular expressions or manifestations of the borders of belonging, broadened the sphere of freedom for some, under some circumstances, at particular moments.

In Defense of the Borders of Belonging

To say that the borders of belonging were from the outset defined in terms of ability, race, and gender does not mean that all able white men were equals or that either the character or terms of their privilege were static or unchallenged over the course of the long nineteenth century. The English Poor Law found a welcome home in the new nation: paupers – regardless of gender, race, or ableness – forfeited rights to full personhood and citizenship. While the U.S. Constitution did not explicitly incorporate the Articles of Confederation's exclusion of "paupers, vagabonds and fugitives from justice" from the privileges and immunities of citizens, in practice, state and, later federal, law assumed as much.[24] Moreover, the United States was born a nation in which all white men

[23] "Declaration of Sentiments," in *The Concise History of Woman Suffrage: Selections from History of Woman Suffrage*, eds. Mary Jo Buhle and Paul Buhle (Urbana, 2005), 94–7.

[24] On the Articles of Confederation, see Article IV: "The better to secure and perpetuate mutual friendship and intercourse among the people of the different States in this Union, the free inhabitants of each of these States, paupers, vagabonds and fugitives from justice excepted, shall be entitled to all privileges and immunities of free citizens in the several States. ..." Article IV, sec. 2, cl. 2 of the U.S. Constitution provides only that "The Citizens of each State shall be entitled to all Privileges and Immunities of Citizens in the several States."

did not even share political equality under the law. The assumption that republican government depended on an independent citizenry and that independence demanded property ownership meant that every state (with the single exception of Vermont) carried over property qualifications for suffrage from colonial law. The effect, of course, was that for the first thirty to fifty years of the new nation most "citizens," including anywhere from one-quarter to one-half of adult white men, could not vote.

Yet, as an immediate matter, that exclusion was not especially significant for the borders of belonging. First, at the outset, the right to vote was not freighted with the political and social significance it would acquire as the century progressed; the rights of citizens were yet in the making. Second, there were so many other particulars in which the law protected white men's superior rights. The law of domestic relations was brought wholesale into the new nation's legal structure. The name for the law defining the husband/wife relationship – the law of baron and feme or lord and woman – asserted man's headship. The Founders wrote slaves' subordinate status into the Constitution and state laws relating to slavery, in turn, were reenacted in many states in the Revolution's wake. The borders of belonging were reinforced at sales day, court week, militia musters, citizens' meetings. The physical, that is to say national, borders of belonging too seemed secure. Land was plentiful. Native Americans were peoples apart. Naturalization was limited by law to "free white persons."[25]

But the security of the borders of belonging was on the verge of its first fantastic upheaval. The Jacksonian Era, often seen as a moment of contradiction because of the simultaneous expansion and contraction of rights, was not a contradiction at all. It was simply one of the first tests of the borders of belonging. The challenges began, in fact, during the Revolution itself. There was, first, the reading to which the nation's founding principles lent themselves. There was nothing inherent in the principles expressed in the Declaration of

---

[25] Naturalization Act, 1 U.S. Statutes at Large 103 (1790).

Independence – recognition of the basic humanity of every individual; the right to freedom from tyranny; the promise of liberty, justice, and equality – that limited their imagining or their application to propertied white men. The words themselves were pregnant with the promise of law. Nor were Revolutionary elites insensible to the hazards or possibilities to which their revolutionary rhetoric gave rise. In a famous exchange James Sullivan asked John Adams by what authority women were governed without their consent. Adams's reply was unequivocal:

Depend upon it, Sir, it is dangerous to open So fruitfull a Source of Controversy and Altercation, as would be opened by attempting to alter the Qualifications of Voters. There will be no end of it. New Claims will arise; women will demand the vote; lads from twelve to twenty-one will think their rights not enough attended to; and every man who has not a farthing, will demand an equal voice with any other, in all acts of state. It tends to confound and destroy all distinctions, and prostrate all ranks to one common level.[26]

And, in fact, on the heels of the Revolution, able white men who sensed their own subjectivity insisted on their capacity and asserted it in the revolutionary tradition.

Moreover, during the Revolution there was widespread appreciation of the fact that slavery "embarrassed the American cause."[27] In the wake of the Revolution, the pressure for abolition from African Americans, Quakers, and others was intense. There was international pressure as well on the slavery question. The British Parliament moved toward and then in 1833 abolished slavery in the West Indies. And, indeed, by 1830, every northern state had abolished slavery whether through legislative enactment, judicial decision, or constitutional revision. Yet slavery's abolition in the North was not simply the product of principle. Slavery was abolished in the North because principle coincided with an economic transformation that marginalized slavery's economic importance. Moreover, northern states did not give slaves

[26] John Adams to James Sullivan, May 26, 1776, in *Papers of John Adams*, ed. Robert J. Taylor (Cambridge, MA, 1979), 4:211–12.

[27] Litwack, *North of Slavery*, 6–7.

their freedom outright: the end of slavery was structured to be gradual and designed to protect first and foremost existing property rights. Where principle conflicted with economic demands as it did in the South, economic demands prevailed, thinly veiled by rationalization.

Putting aside for a moment the all-important point that secession did not create a hard and fast line between free and slave states – Maryland, Missouri, and Kentucky, all slave states, stayed in the Union – a legacy of the Civil War, nonetheless has been to falsely sharpen in our memories the line between the free North and the slave South. In fact, the end of slavery in the North edged painfully close to the beginning of the Civil War. Slavery did not finally come to an end in Pennsylvania until 1847. In New York and New Jersey, the largest slaveholding states of the North, gradual emancipation left some blacks locked in bondage or other forms of servitude that looked suspiciously like slavery until the mid-nineteenth century and beyond. The abolition of slavery in the North, after all, was directed toward the children of slaves, not slaves themselves and even then laws gave former slaveholders the right to children's labor until adulthood in recompense for the expense of housing and feeding the child. As John Sweet notes, "the everyday realities of race continued to unite the new nation long after the politics of slavery began to divide it."[28] Finally, although slavery lost its sanction under state law in the North, that did not mean the end of the practice of slavery. The slave catcher's lawful pursuit of his quarry – given further sanction at mid-century in the Fugitive Slave Act of 1850 – and, lest we forget the example of Dred Scott, slave owners traveling through, indeed, spending years in the "free" North and West with their slave property blurred the line between free and slave states and territories.

Massive white migration "west" in the 1820s and 1830s brought Americans into direct conflict with Indian tribes at

---

[28] John Wood Sweet, *Bodies Politic: Negotiating Race in the American North, 1730–1830* (Baltimore, 2003), 11.

the same moment that the destabilizing impact of industrialization swept growing numbers of white men into a subordinate wage-earning class. American courts drew the newly
hired labor into the rubric of master-servant doctrine: a
sleight of hand, if you will, in which "free labor" in fact
represented a dramatic extension of a relationship of subordination. Citizens all perhaps, but divided, as Christopher
Tomlins argues, by law and lived experience, into the "asym-
metrical realm of 'masters' and 'servants.'"[29] The fiction
of the hireling's independence provided the foundation for
common law doctrines such as assumption of risk, the fellow
servant rule, and contributory negligence that furthered the
hireling's subordination.[30]

Nor was industrialization's destabilizing force limited to
the wage-earning class. The boom and bust economy of the
early industrial order challenged cherished ideals of independence. Business failures multiplied exponentially. Little wonder was it that women's household labor came to be seen as
not "work" at all and the language of individualism – the
word was first used in English by Tocqueville in *Democracy
in America* in 1832 – became a defining American trope at
the moment when social and economic changes heightened
white men's awareness of their dependence and vulnera-
bility.[31] And more, industrialization freed a growing group
of white women of the emerging middle-class, urged on by
the teachings of the Second Great Awakening, to pursue a
sense of moral obligation beyond the household. A small elite

[29] Christopher L. Tomlins, *Law, Labor, and Ideology in the Early
American Republic* (New York, 1993), 219.
[30] Collectively, assumption of risk, the fellow servant doctrine, and contributory negligence operated to largely insulate employers from liability
for employees' on the job injuries. These three legal doctrines provided
respectively that the employee in taking a job accepted the risks commonly associated with the employment, that the employer was not
responsible for injuries attributable to another employee's carelessness or
for injuries attributable to the employee's own carelessness.
[31] Jeanne Boydston, *Home and Work: Housework, Wages, and the
Ideology of Labor in the Early Republic* (New York, 1991); Linda
K. Kerber, "Can a Woman Be an Individual?" in Kerber, *Toward An
Intellectual History of Women* (Chapel Hill, 1997), 215.

among women began to see the contradiction between their legal and cultural subordination and the principles for which the Revolution had been fought. First privately, then publicly, in part inspired by activism in the abolitionist movement, they began to resist their own subjection.

Reflecting on the forces at play, what stands out about Jacksonian America is that the stakes of gendered, racialized, and abled privilege had just gone up. This was the context in which states moved to repeal common law restrictions barring aliens from land ownership and extended universal white male suffrage. Seen in this light, these reforms were not the first steps in a progressive broadening of land ownership and suffrage – a realization of the liberal ideal – but, rather, were two examples of a collection of legal reforms to parry the first major threat to the borders of belonging. The Indian Removal Act of 1830; the tightening of the law of slavery in the South, and adoption of laws in Northern states barring free blacks from emigrating to these states, from voting, from property ownership; universal white male suffrage and the exclusion from suffrage in New Jersey of even that narrow class of women who before 1807 could vote; married women's property laws; even the emergence of state-funded institutions for the insane and feebleminded all reinforced the borders of belonging that Revolutionary principle, Northern abolition, industrialization, religious revival, and Western expansion had threatened to undermine.

Challenges to the gendered, racialized, and abled contours of the borders of belonging would only increase over the next two decades. In the summer of 1848, women gathered at Seneca Falls, New York, demanding full and equal rights as individuals and citizens, including the right to vote, sparking the first Women's Rights Movement. The Mexican-American War vastly expanded the territory of the United States, imposing U.S. citizenship on the Mexican inhabitants of the land. Political upheaval and economic disaster abroad fed a growing tide of European and for the first time, Chinese, immigration. As Americans' numbers grew, pressures for Western expansion and white access to Indian lands increased. And, finally, northern population growth and the admission of new (free) states unbalanced the carefully calibrated compromise safeguarding slavery written into the Constitution at the founding.[32]

The Civil War has long been recognized as a dividing line in the history of the United States. Why and with what consequences for our understanding of American history? The final collapse of the slavery compromise into civil war in April 1861 divided the nation between those who claimed supremacy for state's rights and those who claimed the supremacy of union. Slavery was the combustible element. In these terms, that is "nationhood," the Civil War was indeed a second American Revolution. Henceforward, it would be *the* United States," not "*these* United States."

But that dividing line has served to obscure a more fundamental continuity in the nature of the American republic. After the Civil War as before, the borders of belonging of person, citizen, and nation continued to be defined fundamentally in abled, racialized, and gendered terms. This is not to deny the significance of freedom for the four million held in chattel slavery. It is intended to suggest that understanding how freedom could be so hemmed in by constraint requires placing the end of slavery in the broader context of the long nineteenth century, as well as grasping the incremental, other-directed path that led to freedom. Freedom for the four million held in slavery in the South began as a byproduct of Northern victories, was fed by enslaved men's and women's pursuit of freedom, was formalized into military strategy by a desperate president – Lincoln's "threat" of emancipation directed to the rebellious South – and was incorporated into the Constitution in the Thirteenth Amendment in the resolve that the nation would not again be torn asunder by slavery. Section 2 of the Fourteenth Amendment was never intended by most as a guarantee of freedmen's right to vote. The end of slavery washed away the critical balance between North

[32] See Mark A. Graber, *Dred Scott and the Problem of Constitutional Evil* (New York, 2006), part II, "The Constitutional Politics of Slavery."

and South embodied in the three-fifths clause of Article I of the Constitution. Section 2 of the Fourteenth Amendment restored that balance: if granted the right to vote, freedmen would no doubt vote Republican; if denied the right to vote, they would at least not count toward the number of representatives Southern states could send to Congress.[33] For most white Americans North and South, the end of slavery was never about equality as we would recognize that term today. There was certainly no expectation that bringing an end to slavery undermined white men's prerogatives as America's first citizens. Indeed to many whites, an end to slavery was vital to safeguarding the borders of belonging that created an able white man's republic.

The path of Reconstruction and with it the formalization of African American political, civil, and social rights in law – think here not only of the Thirteenth, Fourteenth, and Fifteenth Amendments, but also the Civil Rights Acts of 1866 and 1875 – was fundamentally shaped by continued Southern white intransigence inflaming Northern opinion and the reality that Republican political power in Congress depended on Southern blacks. Republicans were determined not to have won the war only to lose political power. Too often we read Section 1 of the Fourteenth Amendment – with its guarantee of birthright citizenship, and its prohibition of state denial of the privileges and immunities of citizenship, due process, and equal protection – as though it stands alone. Section 1 of the Fourteenth Amendment represented a dramatic reconfiguration of state and federal power in protection of civil rights, but for our purposes here it is important to recall the succeeding sections of the Amendment. And more, it is

[33] The relevant language reads as follows: "Representatives shall be apportioned among the several States according to their respective numbers, counting the whole number of persons in each State, excluding Indians not taxed. But when the right to vote ... is denied to any of the male inhabitants of such State, being twenty-one years of age, and citizens of the United States, or in any way abridged, except for participation in rebellion, or other crime, the basis of representation therein shall be reduced in the proportion which the number of such male citizens shall bear to the whole number of male citizens twenty-one years of age in such State." U.S. Constitution, amend. 14, sec. 2.

vital that we not lump the "Reconstruction Amendments" together as though they were passed and ratified as one. The three amendments span five long, politically tumultuous and violent years in time. Each amendment was itself a response to events on the ground. The scope and limits of their protections were fundamentally shaped not simply by events in the South or even North-South relations, but also by fears of the threat they posed of a broader revolution undermining white men's established authority.

The bounds of freedom are not so easily constrained of course. Like the American Revolution a century before, the Civil War unleashed the expectations of those excluded from the borders of belonging. African Americans embraced Lincoln's Emancipation Proclamation, seeing in it and in the Reconstruction Amendments and Civil Rights statutes a commitment to equality and justice for all. Women pressed for inclusion in the Republic as full-rights-bearing individuals and citizens.

Even if the demands for freedom, equality, and full citizenship could have been limited to freedmen and freedwomen and to white women, they represented a fundamental threat to white men's status. But the threat was greater because the demands could not be limited. In 1866, Senator Charles Sumner began what would evolve into a four-year battle to eliminate the racial prerequisite to naturalization by demanding that Congress strike the word "white" as a requirement for naturalization. In that time period, Congress would pass the Civil Rights Act of 1866, and the Fourteenth and Fifteenth Amendments to the Constitution. And, yet, on July 4, 1870, the Senate overwhelmingly rejected Sumner's amendment.[34] The one concession to Sumner – extending the right to naturalize to "persons of African nativity or descent" – reflected the reality, as Oregon Circuit Court Justice Matthew Deady summed it up a few years later, "that the negroes of Africa were not likely to emigrate to this country, and therefore the provision concerning them was merely a piece of legislative

[34] An Act to Amend the Naturalization Laws and to Punish Crimes Against the Same, and for Other Purposes, 16 U.S. Statutes at Large 256 (1871).

buncombe."³⁵ There were a few, led by Sumner and Lyman Trumball, who passionately argued that the inclusion of the "colored" man within the borders of citizenship was one element in a broader policy to eliminate all distinctions of race or color in American citizenship. Others, more numerous, focusing on the Chinese and Native Americans, immediately moved to distinguish the grant of citizenship to African Americans, seeing in recent events not a harbinger but a warning and adopting a sort of "nimby" – not in my backyard – defense.³⁶

Establishing the Civil War and especially the end of slavery as the fundamental dividing line – the terminus of a nation "half slave and half free" – obscures other exclusions from the borders of belonging even then in the making. It obscures, as well, the opportunity the war offered for safeguarding the borders of belonging in which white men held a superior claim to legal personhood, citizenship, and nation. For example, the limited control over reproduction that abortion accorded women was under attack even before the war. The American Medical Association's successful crusade to make abortion illegal at every stage of pregnancy began in 1857, spanned the war years, and achieved success in every state in the nation by 1880. The war provided the opportunity for passage of the Homestead Act (1862), the explicit purpose of which was to seed the west with white settlers, and for adoption of a Reservation Policy (1867) dispossessing Native Americans of all western land except for two areas in the Dakotas and Oklahoma territories. As importantly, bracketing the Civil War and Reconstruction as the end point of an era ignores the ugly continuities between slavery and the stunted freedom enjoyed by the vast majority of African Americans in the South by the century's end. As Michael Perman notes with respect to black disfranchisement, "the newness of the *form*

³⁵ *In re Camille*, 6 F. 256, 258 (Cir. Ct., D. OR 1880).
³⁶ Congressional Globe, 39th Cong., 1st sess., 1866, pp. 497–507, 2938–44; Congressional Globe, 40th Cong., 1st sess., 1867, pp. 728–9; 40th Cong., 2nd sess., 1867, pp. 268–71; 41st Cong., 2nd sess., 1870, pp. 5114–25, 5148–77.

should not be confused with the enduring *substance* of the South's system of racial domination."[37]

By century's end, industrialization brought further threats to white male privilege. Massive immigration, like a flood of currency, devalued hirelings' labor; inadequate wages pulled their wives and children into the labor force. Legal reform made the state rather than the individual man, as husband and father, the arbiter of children's and women's labor. So too, the criminalization of birth control, like the criminalization of abortion, protected the racial and gender hierarchy not by increasing men's traditional patriarchal authority over the women in their households, but by giving the state itself the power to police women's bodies.

The pursuit of border enforcement was so intense in part because the borders themselves were unclear and shifting. Massive new waves of immigration at the end of the nineteenth century added to the pressure that emancipation coupled with industrialization created for embodying in law formal ways of policing the color line. Law could prohibit intermarriage of whites and racialized others, could mandate racial separation in public transit and education, could limit naturalization to white persons, and so on. But even this, as would become clear, was not a sure fix. Variability of racial categories – with white and color depending upon legal context in a given state, and varying as well from state to state – was an administrative necessity. And yet, the myriad definitions of color in a single state's statutes were themselves testament to the constructed quality of race. Law itself destabilized the racial order, for who was white and who colored and what ways of knowing race now counted invited challenge and subversion. As Ray Stannard Baker remarked regarding white and black streetcar travel in the early twentieth century South, "The color line is drawn, but neither race knows just where it is."[38]

---

[37] Michael Perman, *Struggle for Mastery: Disfranchisement in the South 1888–1908* (Chapel Hill, 2001), 8.

[38] Ray Stannard Baker, "Following the Color Line," *American Magazine* 63 (April 1907): 30, 31, quoted in Grace Hale, *Making Whiteness*, 133.

In turn, immigration restriction beginning in the 1880s must be paired with the assault on Native American sovereignty and extra-continental empire. Immigration restriction imposed increasingly fine filters limiting entrance to the nation; dissolution of Native American sovereignty sought to end the contradiction of nations within a nation; the legal construct "unincorporated territories" facilitated control over new territories without the accompanying burden of extending citizenship to racialized others. The first operated by exclusion, the second by inclusion, and the third again by exclusion; all three were calculated to protect and in fact did protect whites' claim to the land and with it the space of the nation.

Added to these threats to the borders of belonging at the end of the nineteenth century was yet another: the fear that a tide of disability threatened to swamp the nation. In 1850, the federal government began to record the incidence of mental and physical disability in the United States through the U.S. Census.[39] Science, reinforced by statistics from federal and state enumeration of the feebleminded, the deaf, the blind, the epileptic, the physically disabled, etc., and the institutions that housed them, presented the portrait of a nation in peril from the unfit. In a population of just 62.5 million, the U.S. Census Bureau reported in 1895, 1.5 million, "1 out of each 42 persons, or over 2 per cent, were mentally or physically defective."[40] The idea that a tide of disability from without and within threatened to swamp the nation at the turn of the century led to increasingly stringent restrictions on immigration of the mentally and physically disabled to protect the nation from without and to the adoption of compulsory sterilization laws to protect the nation from the unfit

[39] 1850 U.S. Census Questions, IPUMS USA, http://usa.ipums.org/usa/voliii/items1850.shtml (last accessed September 9, 2009); 1880 U.S. Census Questions, IPUMS USA, http://usa.ipums.org/usa/voliii/items1880.shtml (last accessed September 9, 2009).

[40] Department of the Interior, Census Office, "Report on the Insane, Feeble-Minded, Deaf and Dumb, and Blind in the United States at the Eleventh Census: 1890" (Washington, 1895), 1.

in its midst. The U.S. Supreme Court's 1927 decision *Buck
v. Bell* upholding the constitutionality of Virginia's sterilization law gave a green light to eugenics and a public policy of
the able. Writing for the Court, Justice Holmes comfortably
reasoned:

> We have seen more than once that the public welfare may call upon
> the best citizens for their lives. It would be strange if it could not call
> upon those who already sap the strength of the State for these lesser
> sacrifices, often not felt to be such by those concerned, in order to
> prevent our being swamped by incompetence. It is better for all
> the world, if instead of waiting to execute degenerate offspring for
> crime, or to let them starve for their imbecility, society can prevent
> those who are manifestly unfit from continuing their kind.... Three
> generations of imbeciles are enough.[41]

Holmes's infamous words powerfully expressed the perceived threat, the right of the able to protect themselves and
their nation against it, and, finally, how easily the able arro-
gated the power to define the "lesser sacrifices" of those they
deemed "unfit." The unsubstantiated assumption that "these
lesser sacrifices" were "often not felt to be such by those
concerned" was a chillingly modern restatement of the view
Thomas Cobb voiced at mid-century in his *Treatise on the
Law of Negro Slavery* that slaves "suffer little by separation
from their children."[42]

The Lawmakers

Justice Holmes's and Thomas Cobb's words, like the words
of other lawmakers quoted here, reflect a simple truth that
is fundamental to understanding the persistence of the borders of belonging across the long nineteenth century: law
was the domain of able white men. Susan B. Anthony's sting-
ing rebuke at the close of her trial for illegal voting in 1873

[41] *Buck v. Bell*, 274 U.S. 200, 207 (1927).
[42] Thomas Reade Cobb, *An Inquiry into The Law of Negro Slavery in the
United States of America* (Philadelphia, 1858), 39.

recognized that white men's racialized and gendered privilege in the law was safeguarded by the vital fact that they, so to speak, held the key to law's inner chamber.

Through the first half of the nineteenth century, their authority largely went unchallenged. As Michael Grossberg notes, "Masculinity was so fundamental to the profession's consciousness that for most of the century it acted as an unarticulated first principle."[43] The right to hold office was limited to those who could vote and, with a few isolated exceptions such as propertied women in New Jersey before 1807 and propertied free black men in a few states, only white men had the suffrage. Jurors were selected from electors; judges from the ranks of lawyers and other prominent men. The entire structure of the legal system was premised upon a reasoning world of white men separate from the world of women, the disabled, and racialized others. "To be an adept in the art of Government," Abigail Adams observed to her husband, "is a prerogative to which your Sex lay almost an exclusive claim."[44]

The formal structure of lawmaking in turn produced a world of white manly interaction that sealed the bonds of men's authority and loyalties. Judge, juror, legislator, lawyer, legal scholar, voter were themselves most times heads of household: they shared the benefits and obligations of the structured dependencies of husband-wife; father-child; and for many master-indentured servant, -apprentice, -slave; guardian-ward. These identities and roles gave white men a shared identity that bridged deep economic inequalities.

Lawyers in the antebellum Deep South were enmeshed in the slave economy. Many lawyers themselves owned slaves and whether they did or not their practices depended heavily on the slave economy. In the course of a lifetime of legal practice, it was common for a lawyer to become slaveholder and

---

[43] Michael Grossberg, "Institutionalizing Masculinity: The Law as a Masculine Profession," in *Meanings for Manhood: Constructions of Masculinity in Victorian America*, eds. Mark C. Carnes and Clyde Griffen (Chicago, 1990), 134.

[44] Quoted in Linda K. Kerber, *Women of the Republic: Intellect & Ideology in Revolutionary America* (New York, 1980), 269.

planter, and in turn judge.[45] Apparent balance barely con-
cealed deep loyalties. For example, the U.S. Supreme Court
that heard Dred Scott's case was "geographically balanced" in
the sense that five justices were from slave states and the other
four were Northerners who had always lived in free states.
Yet the apparent balance was deceptive politically and geographically – all but one of the justices had been appointed by
a Democrat at a time when the Democratic party was domi-
nated by its southern, proslavery wing (only John McLean
had rejected his Democratic roots); all but two of the justices
had been appointed by southern, slaveholding presidents; two
of the four northern justices had well-acknowledged proslavery sympathies. Whichever way you diced it, the *Dred Scott*
Court was a slaveholder's court.[46]

The life of the nineteenth century judge and lawyer was
a world of the physically fit: judges and lawyers spent long
hours riding on horseback from one court to the next; oral
advocacy required not only a strong voice, but a good back,
strong legs, a healthy constitution for standing; the labori-
ous process of handwriting briefs required a good hand. That
one might point to lawyers who had lost a leg, an arm, or an
eye – many while serving in the Civil War – does not negate
the basic point. And it went without question that this was a
world of the mentally able (those with reason and the ability
to exercise it). An unarticulated assumption of ableness was
imbedded in the words describing judges in popular medi-
ums: "wise, skillful, impartial, upright, and venerable."[47]
Indeed, ableness was a crucial element of masculinity in
the nineteenth century rendered more fundamental over the
course of the nineteenth century as fears of the unfit grew.

Judges and lawyers formed deep personal bonds riding circuit together. The circle was broadened to include jurors and

[45] Ariela J. Gross, *Double Character: Slavery and Mastery in the Antebellum Southern Courtroom* (Princeton, 2000), 27.
[46] Paul Finkelman, ed., *Dred Scott, A Brief History with Documents* (Boston, 1997), 29.
[47] Grossberg, "Institutionalizing Masculinity," 140. Grossberg wrote this article in the 1980s before historians had begun to recognize disability as a category of analysis. His evidence though invites such a reading.

witnesses in individual cases as the male legal actors traveled
to accident scenes and shared authority in the courtroom.
Whether it was the charge "Gentlemen of the jury" as the
judge gave his instructions on the law to the jurors in a case,
or the elucidation of legal standards as, for example, Oliver
Wendell Holmes's description of the "reasonable man" in
The Common Law, these relationships bore tangible fruit in
the law.[48]

From early in the nineteenth century, universal white male
suffrage not only cast white men as a group as lawmakers,
but also thereby bridged fundamental economic inequalities
that otherwise might have divided men. Among the many
stories in Mary Boykin Chesnut's diary documenting the
constraints of womanhood and the privileges of white manhood is a story of an evening spent in the company of her
husband, James Chesnut, Jr., and her uncle, state legislator
Alexander Hamilton Boykin, at Boykin's plantation, with a
third man whom Chesnut considered nothing better than a
common laborer, a "well-digger." Mary Boykin Chesnut has
come down to us as one of the most famous chroniclers of the
slave South and the Civil War. Married to James Chesnut, Jr.
(U.S. Senator from 1858 until South Carolina's secession, and
then aid to President Jefferson Davis and brigadier general
of the Confederate Army) and mistress of a South Carolina
plantation of thousands of acres, Mary Chesnut enjoyed both
power and privilege. But she was, nonetheless, a woman and
"Squire McDonald" was a man. McDonald had a vote and
might command the votes of others. Mary Boykin Chesnut
did not and could not.[49] Chesnut's tale powerfully captures
a fundamental fact of nineteenth century America: even the
lowest yeoman in the antebellum South Carolina low country was the equal, in this arena, of the richest planter from

[48] Oliver Wendell Holmes, Jr., *The Common Law*, 1881 (Reprint, Boston, 1909), 108.

[49] Stephanie McCurry, *Masters of Small Worlds: Yeoman Households, Gender Relations, and the Political Culture of the Antebellum South Carolina Low Country* (New York, 1995), 128–29. For Mary Chesnut's telling of the evening, see C. Vann Woodward, ed., *Mary Chesnut's Civil War* (New Haven, 1981), 204–05.

which the yeoman's and planter's wives alike, to say nothing of the planter's slaves, were excluded. Though "thoroughly unequal," as Stephanie McCurry notes, they were "equally independent – men, masters, and citizens."[50]

Law extended able white men's legal authority beyond formal legal institutions, actors, and procedural safeguards. In pre-Civil War America, as Gautham Rao notes, citizens were regularly compelled to join sheriffs and justices of the peace to "execute arrests, level public nuisances, and keep the peace"; this was the common law posse comitatus. So too, the federal posse comitatus imposed on every citizen the obligation, when demanded, to help track down fugitives from justice, including fugitive slaves.[51] The posse comitatus was made up of "citizens." Yet though its burden and power might have extended to women and free blacks, in fact, the posse comitatus in practice was made up of able white men. At mid-century in a number of states, including Illinois, Iowa, and Massachusetts, a husband, with no judicial or other review, could have his wife committed to a state asylum against her will on nothing more than his request, supported by that of a doctor and the asylum superintendent. At century's end, Jim Crow laws imposed on conductors the power, obligation, and protection of the law in making racial determinations and assigning passengers to the appropriate car, and state abortion laws deputized doctors to report cases of women suspected to have had an abortion. State compulsory sterilization laws provided little or no legal process and operated regardless of the consent of the individual. So, for example, Indiana – the first state in 1907 to formally legalize sterilization – mandated that every state institution provide for the examination of every "inmate" by two surgeons, and, on a finding that "procreation is inadvisable and there is no probability of improvement of the mental and physical condition of the inmates," authorized sterilization. Other states, again with little or no legal process

---

[50] McCurry, *Masters of Small Worlds*, 106.
[51] Gautham Rao, "The Federal Posse Comitatus Doctrine: Slavery, Compulsion, and Statecraft in Mid-Nineteenth-Century America," *Law and History Review* 26 (2008): 1–56.

or safeguards for those being sterilized, made sterilization of not just the "incurably feebleminded," but also "epileptics" and other defectives mandatory.[52] The U.S. Supreme Court in *Buck v. Bell* (1927) upheld Virginia's compulsory sterilization law, giving the green light to proponents of compulsory sterilization laws and sweeping to the side questions about due process.

White men jealously guarded their preserve as lawmakers against intrusion. The extension of universal white male suffrage was coupled in the few northern states that had allowed propertied black males to vote with disenfranchisement of free blacks, bars on black testimony in cases against whites, and bans on immigration of free blacks. Thus, the expansion of white male suffrage in Connecticut in 1818 was paired with the complete elimination of black voting rights.[53] The revised 1821 New York constitution made suffrage a right of all white male citizens, simultaneously erecting in the path of black male voting steep property requirements and harsher residency laws.[54] In slave states, white men's words and actions similarly were protected against contradiction by bans on slave testimony. Ex-slaves confirmed the power the bans placed in white men's hands, seeing in the bans the ultimate guarantee of their disempowerment. As Ariela Gross notes, "[a] culture that made a man's word his badge of honor stripped people of honor by denying them words."[55] Laws barring black testimony against whites in states of the antebellum North and West were similarly viewed by African American men as "humiliating to our manhood."[56] So too,

---

[52] Stevenson Smith, Madge W. Wilkinson, and Lovisa C. Wagoner, *The Bulletin of the University of Washington No. 82, A Summary of the Laws of the Several States Governing I. – Marriage and Divorce of the Feebleminded, the Epileptic and the Insane. II. – Asexualization. III. – Institutional Commitment and Discharge of the Feebleminded and the Epileptic* (Seattle, 1914).

[53] Connecticut Constitution of 1818, art. 6, sec. 2.

[54] New York Constitution of 1821, art. 2, sec. 1.

[55] Gross, *Double Character*, 62.

[56] William H. Hall, President, *Proceedings of the Second Annual Convention of Colored Citizens of the State of California* (San Francisco, 1856) quoted in Barbara Y. Welke, "Rights of Passage: Gendered-Rights

Southern whites responded to black suffrage in the wake of the Fifteenth Amendment with violence, and then, beginning in 1890, by legally disfranchising African Americans. The only state that initially allowed propertied women to vote, New Jersey, disfranchised all women in 1807. The language of the Fourteenth Amendment was scripted to preclude the enfranchisement of women. Although some states, predominantly in the West, moved sooner, it would be a half century before women gained the right to vote nationally and not until the second half of the twentieth century that African Americans in the South were effectively re-enfranchised.

Reciting this history, can we wonder that Reconstruction – the one moment in which African American men held substantial voting, legislative, and judicial power in the American South – was villainized through the first half of the twentieth century as pervasively corrupt, as the imposition of "black rule" on the white South? D. W. Griffith's 1915 film *The Birth of a Nation* merely popularized what was "good" history of the time in celebrating the Ku Klux Klan and the Redeemers for returning order and white rule. In fact, the level of corruption in the Reconstruction Era South was no different from patterns of governance in the rest of the country for the same period: there was corruption and there was good governance and, more to the point, "black rule" did not stand for one or the other.

Indeed, those looking for evidence of corruption would do well to consider the systematic, brutal expulsion of black men from positions of elected and appointed office, suffrage, jury service, and lawyering in the wake of Reconstruction. From a pitiful high of 24 black lawyers in Mississippi in 1900, the numbers steadily dwindled, so that by 1935 there were only five black lawyers in the entire state.[57] To say their numbers dwindled inaccurately suggests a process of natural decline;

Consciousness and the Quest for Freedom, San Francisco, California, 1850–1870," in *African-American Women Confront the West, 1600–2000, eds.* Quintard Taylor and Shirley Moore (Norman, OK, 2003), 71

[57] Neil R. McMillen, *Dark Journey: Black Mississippians in the Age of Jim Crow* (Urbana, 1989), 166–9.

in fact, black lawyers were driven out of practice and even out of the state. The tools were many – in some courts, judges (all white) barred black lawyers from approaching the bench or sitting with other counsel. In others, judges simply barred blacks from appearing in the courtroom in any other guise than spectator, custodian, or defendant. The white bar association harassed black lawyers through frivolous disbarment proceedings. Perhaps most damning of all, was that the racism that pervaded the entire legal, social, economic, cultural, and political order, meant that black lawyers could hope for little justice for themselves or their clients. There is something especially embittering about a system that forces any group of people to seek the assistance of their oppressor, and yet, as a practical matter, blacks with resources had little choice but to hire white lawyers.

Nor could African Americans, women, the Chinese, or others hope for justice from a jury of their peers. Despite the Supreme Court's 1880 holding in *Strauder v. West Virginia* that the Fourteenth Amendment's Equal Protection Clause made it unconstitutional for a state to limit jury service to "white male persons," the fact of the matter was that after the end of Reconstruction, and in many places, well before, blacks were systematically barred from juries.[58] Gilbert Thomas Stephenson's *Race Distinctions in American Law* (1910), for the most part limited to statutes and appellate judicial opinions, sought out actual practices in southern courts on the subject of jury service. In a letter sent to every county court clerk in the South, Stephenson asked whether blacks served on juries and how their service was received. The responses offer a lesson in the law. Despite the fact that the right of African Americans to serve on juries was protected by the Fourteenth Amendment and numerous judicial decisions, the consistent response of clerks across the South was that blacks did not serve. County after county, state after state, the story was much the same – an Alabama county with 5,000 whites and 21,000 blacks and never in the clerk's

---

[58] *Strauder v. West Virginia*, 100 U.S. 303 (1880).

memory had there been a black juror; a Florida county with 17,000 whites and 22,000 blacks: "many years since a Negro sat upon a jury"; a Georgia county with 5,000 whites and 24,000 blacks: "No Negroes serve on our jury."

The reasons given were many. An occasional clerk admitted that the absence of blacks was shaped by prejudice. More commonly, Stephenson's white correspondents cited black incompetence, ignorance, illiteracy, immorality, dishonesty, lack of integrity, and failure to qualify under the law. Exclusion could also be cast as privilege: "Negroes never have this burden heaped upon them in this state," in the words of a Missouri clerk; or choice: in the words of a Kentucky clerk, "I am reliably informed that in various parts of the State the Negroes themselves requested to be left off the juries." In the few places where blacks served, if only occasionally, clerks were quick to emphasize, as one Louisiana clerk put it, that only "exceptionally good, honest, sober, and industrious Negroes" were included in the jury pool, and so their numbers were limited. In other words, an outcome – all white, male juries – that was in fact the calculated product of white racist sentiment and legalized racism was explained in terms that placed the burden at the black man's door. In a context in which a black man showing any independence risked his life, little wonder was it that a Louisiana clerk could describe the rare black juror as no trouble – "they always follow the suggestions and advice of the white jurors" – or that a Mississippi clerk in a county with 3,000 whites, 23,000 blacks, and only a rare black juror could explain that blacks did not like to try white men's cases and that they (black jurors) were especially tough on black defendants. More than one clerk noted that blacks themselves did not want a black juror sitting on their cases. In this context as well then, African Americans became further agents of discrimination against their race.[59]

Women fared equally poorly. Through the nineteenth century, access to law's inner-chamber as legislator, judge, even voter or juror was limited not only to whites, but white men.

[59] Stephenson, *Race Distinctions in American Law*, 253–72.

Women were constrained to act as petitioners. As the experience of the Grimke sisters in the 1830s highlights, women had to fight prejudice and social convention even to speak in public. Women seeking licenses to practice law beginning in the 1870s faced ridicule, condescension, and patronization in equal parts. But behind it all was a steadfast commitment to retain the bar as man's domain. Throughout the long nineteenth century and through much of the twentieth, women's enforced dependence and subordination – their denial of full legal personhood – would be safeguarded against constitutional review by federalism. And so it was here. In *Bradwell v. Illinois* (1873), the majority of the U.S. Supreme Court rejected Myra Bradwell's claim that the right to pursue the occupation of lawyer was among the privileges and immunities of national citizenship protected by the Fourteenth Amendment to the Constitution, and insisted that who could practice law came within a state's privileges and immunities. But it was Justice Bradley's paean to woman's place in his concurring opinion that more likely expressed the mind of the men on the court and that formally incorporated women's subordinate status within constitutional doctrine.[60] Left to struggle for the right to practice law state by state, women found piecemeal success. Yet, even in states that allowed women to practice law, women found the doors largely barred by new standards of professionalization making law school the foundation for the practice of law, but legally excluded from them, and once licensed relegated to the margins of legal practice. The right to serve on juries did not, in most states, come with suffrage or follow naturally after ratification of the Nineteenth Amendment. Indeed, through most of the twentieth century, women's exemption from jury service was one of those exclusions masked as privilege.

The record of the long nineteenth century suggests we would do well to be wary of those who arrogate to themselves, whether based on status, expertise, or privileged position, the authority to know and act in the best interests of others. To

[60] 83 U.S. 130 (1873).

focus on a single moment, at the end of the nineteenth century, "Friends of the American Indian" promoted allotment;
social welfare reformers, including many white middle-class
women, worked for protective legislation for women engaged
in industrial wage-work; hearing administrators banned sign
language from schools for the deaf; asylum superintendents
used their positions to override familial wishes to care for family members at home. So, the Supreme Court in *Lone Wolf v.
Hitchcock*, upholding allotment without tribal consent could
say, "We must presume that Congress acted in perfect good
faith in the dealings with the Indians. ..."[61] And responding
to a man's request that his brother might be released from
the Rome Asylum in upstate New York in 1907 to come live
with him on his farm in Nebraska, the superintendent could
quickly close the query: "Your brother is surely in no condition to be outside of an institution of this kind. ... You may
rest assured he is made comfortable entirely in every way."[62]
The authority of the well-intentioned, like that of the not-so-
well-intentioned, rested at bottom on abled, racialized, and
gendered privilege.

A final "lawmaker" operated on the ground so to speak.
Throughout the long nineteenth century violence was the
right-hand man of law. The policing of racial boundaries and
slavery ("law enforcement") was both violent and a community affair. Antiblack race riots swept across the antebellum
North from Providence, Rhode Island, to Cincinnati, Ohio, as
the region's last slaves were becoming free. In the South, slave
patrols funded by the states and manned by white men just
coming to the age of majority through old age and representing
every segment of Southern society first took form in the colonial era, operated through the Civil War, and then regrouped
into vigilante groups like the KKK during Reconstruction.
There were moments when violence and flagrant denial of
basic rights led to an expanded vision of the republic. Indeed,

[61] 187 U.S. 553, 568 (1903).
[62] The case of Otto G. is discussed in Philip M. Ferguson, *Abandoned to
Their Fate: Social Policy and Practice toward Severely Retarded People
in America, 1820–1920* (Philadelphia, 1994), 129–30, 146–7.

the pattern of violence followed by new legal protections dur-
ing Reconstruction was like a sound wave in its regularity.
And yet even here, violence prevailed. White male violence
was a tool. You can make a list: Providence, Rhode Island,
Sand Creek, Colorado, Snake River, Oregon, Wilmington,
Delaware, Rock Springs, Wyoming, Wounded Knee, South
Dakota, the Philippines, Bellingham, Washington, Chicago,
Illinois, and so on. These and hundreds of other less celebrated
acts of terror and violence one might name prepared the
ground for legal sanction – not limiting the sphere of action of
white men, but limiting that of those marked as racial others.

White male violence led other whites to see the necessity
of reinforcing the borders of belonging. It legitimated separation and exclusion of racialized others, whether it was cor-
ralling Native Americans onto reservations away from white
settlement, exclusion of Chinese laborers under the Chinese
Exclusion Act, Jim Crow and black disfranchisement, or
denial of rights of American citizenship to Filipinos. And it
led these groups of racialized others to accept, in some measure, their legally sanctioned separation and exclusion, for
the measure of protection it afforded. Violence was as important in policing gendered boundaries as racialized boundaries. The master/slave relation meant for enslaved girls and
women living with the threat and all too often the reality
of sexual violation, violation that reinforced the message
that they were subject to their master's will in all things. In
the post–Reconstruction South, the lynching of black men
offered a sort of two-for-one guarantee reminding both
African Americans and white women of their place. But violence was neither limited to the public realm nor the policing
of race. Men's domestic authority gave license to all too many
family nightmares.

The Masks of the Law

Where men's status as lawmakers protected the borders of
belonging, the structure of law masked the breadth and depth
of able white male privilege as well as the subordination of

disabled persons, racialized others, and women. The federal system and beyond that the organization and cataloging of laws and ordinances itself operated to mask, at the same time that it assured in a thousand particulars, law's privileging of able white men. There was not only the United States, but also each state's, constitution; not only federal, but as well each state's or territory's, statutes, administrative laws, and common law; treaties; federal and state funding for schools and institutions; and beyond this ordinances of cities, towns, and villages across the full sweep of America. Taking just one of these categories – a state's statutes – laws were not grouped together under a heading "Laws to Ensure the Happiness and Privilege of Able White Men." The evidence, like the experience of privilege and subordination, was scattered among hundreds and thousands of statutory provisions.

Moreover, compilations of these laws of privilege and subordination were not written as such. Treatises on domestic relations, such as Tapping Reeve's *The Law of Baron and Femme, Parent and Child, Guardian and Ward, Master and Servant, and of the Powers of the Courts of Chancery* (1816), put the reader on notice through title alone that they were expressing the proper order of things. Thomas R. R. Cobb's, *An Inquiry into the Law of Negro Slavery* (1858), one of two Southern treatises on slave law, defended slavery as dictated by natural law. In Cobb's articulation, slavery was not created by whites, but rather was dictated by characteristics of Africans including their physical adaptation to slavery, their intellectual inferiority, and their degraded character. He offered the American law of slavery as an amelioration of the absolute subjection of slaves. The only collection of states' laws on race published in the early twentieth century – Gilbert T. Stephenson's, *Race Distinctions in American Law* (1910) – was intended not to expose, but rather to defend, race distinctions in law. Collections of state laws related to marriage, institutional commitment, and sterilization ("asexualization") of the "feebleminded," "epileptic," "insane," and other disabled persons in the early twentieth century and tracts such as *State Laws Limiting Marriage Selection Examined in the Light of Eugenics* (1913) and *Eugenical Sterilization in the United States* (1922) by leading eugenicists like Charles Benedict Davenport and his assistant Harry H. Laughlin at the Eugenic Records Office in Cold Spring Harbor, New York, purported to be nothing more than compilations of state law and mobilized science, backed by law, in pursuit of a better biology.

Even going to common law precedents or individual statutes and related case law, one did not see privilege and subordination baldly cast. In critical respects, the legal construction of able white male privilege was masked because it was achieved through laws and decisions that did not, on their face, positively privilege ableness, whiteness, or manhood. In the first instance, law created the space in which able white men exercised freedom and authority by excluding others from that physical and figurative space.

Any sense that the Civil War marked a radical turning point, a recasting of the borders of belonging, is refuted by considering law itself. Perhaps the most immediate and notorious example was the Black Codes passed by the former slave states in the war's immediate wake. On their face and in a few of their particulars, these codes claimed to outline the legal rights to be enjoyed by the former slaves. But the codes' main focus and true intent was to assure that freedmen and freedwomen remained a dependent agricultural laboring class subject to white authority. Nor did the Black Codes, which were, after all, revoked during the years of Radical Reconstruction, represent simply the last gasp of the Confederacy. State Jim Crow laws providing for segregated public transit had titles like "An Act to promote the comfort of travelers on railroad trains, and for other purposes" (N.C. 1899). Where race was mentioned at all, it was in the guise of protecting the rights of African Americans, such as "An Act requiring all railroad companies in this State to Furnish First Class Cars on receiving First Class Fare for the Separate and Exclusive Use of Colored Persons" (Fla. 1887), or in the guise of neutrality, such as in Kentucky's

1893 law titled "An Act to regulate the travel or transportation of the white and colored passengers on the railroads of this State."[63] State miscegenation laws took up the work that had been done by slavery and made white supremacy a national project.

The state laws and constitutional provisions that effectively disfranchised African American men beginning with Mississippi's new constitution in 1890 were on their face racially neutral. For example, under Mississippi's constitution, to be a "qualified elector" one had to be male, age 21 or older; a resident of the state for two years and of the election district for one year; never convicted of certain crimes including arson, bigamy, and petty theft; had to have paid all taxes, including a poll tax of $2.00 for the last two years; and able to read and "give a reasonable interpretation" of a provision of the constitution to the satisfaction of the registrar.[64] Nowhere was race mentioned, yet almost every particular was carefully calculated to stop black men from voting. Considering these laws in *Race Distinctions in American Law*, Gilbert T. Stephenson acknowledged that provisions such as poll taxes, property ownership requirements, and understanding clauses could have a disproportionate impact on black men. So, for example, he explained, that "if Negroes are more shiftless and less inclined to pay their taxes than white people, more of them will be unable to satisfy this test. Secondly, if they are careless about preserving their tax receipts for one, two, or three successive years, they will be unable to prove the payment of taxes and, thereby, be disqualified to vote." But he defended the provisions both on the grounds that suffrage restrictions like these were "not peculiar to the Southern states," and that any distinction by race in their impact was attributable to the character and habits of African Americans.[65]

[63] Public Laws of North Carolina, 1899, pp. 539–40 (ch. 384); Laws of Florida, 1887, p. 116 (Ch. 3743); Laws of Kentucky, 1891–93, pp. 63–4 (Ch. 40).
[64] The Constitution of the State of Mississippi, adopted Nov. 1, 1890, art. 12 (Franchise), sec. 241–9, pp. 37–8.
[65] Stephenson, *Race Distinctions in American Law*, 300–01.

Similar thinking underlay the titles of major federal enactments relating to other groups. The formal title of the 1887
Dawes Act was "An Act to Provide for the Allotment of Lands
in Severalty to Indians on the Various Reservations, and to
Extend the Protection of the Laws of the United States and
the Territories over the Indians, and for Other Purposes."[66]
The phrases "to provide for" and "to extend the protection
of" are positive. State alien land laws simply provided that
aliens not eligible for citizenship could not own land.[67] They
never mentioned race in their terms, yet in intent and effect
they imposed a racial prerequisite and thus prohibition to
land ownership. The Immigration Act of 1924 never mentioned race.[68] There is no language here of taking or subordination or denial of identity. Amendments to state marriage
laws barring marriage by those deemed defective reflected the
science of eugenics and the assumption that the purpose of
marriage was reproduction. So, for example, Kansas's 1909
law provided that "No woman under the age of 45 years, or
man of any age, except he marry a woman over the age of 45
years, either of whom is epileptic, imbecile, feebleminded or
afflicted with insanity, shall hereafter intermarry or marry
any other person within this state." State sterilization laws
passed in the early twentieth century reflected the persistence
of an age-old association between disability and moral cul-
pability. Indiana, the first state to pass a compulsory sterilization law, began its 1907 law "Whereas: Heredity plays a
most important part in the transmission of crime, idiocy and
imbecility." New Jersey's 1911 law began, "An act to autho-
rize and provide for the sterilization of feebleminded (including idiots, imbeciles and morons), epileptics, rapists, certain

---

[66] 24 U.S. Statutes at Large 388 (1887).
[67] State alien land laws from the early twentieth century are reprinted in
Charles F. Curry, *Alien Land Laws and Alien Rights* (Washington,
1921), 35–67. See also Gibson, *Aliens and the Law*, 177–81.
[68] 43 U. S. Statutes at Large 153 (1924); Mae M. Ngai, "The Architecture
of Race in American Immigration Law: A Re-Examination of
the Immigration Act of 1924," *Journal of American History* 89
(1999): 67–92; Ngai, *Impossible Subjects: Illegal Aliens and the Making
of Modern America* (Princeton, 2004), 21–55.

criminals and other defectives."[69] So framed, these laws were not denials of rights, but expressions of the state's obligation to protect the health, safety, and welfare of the people.

Only much later in the twentieth century would collections be published, the goal of which was to highlight and challenge law's marginalization of racialized others, women, and disabled persons. Not until the 1930s, '40s, and '50s would collections of federal, state, and local laws, ordinances, and judicial decisions charting racial distinctions in law capture the national scope of legal discrimination with a view to eradicating racial privilege and subordination from law.[70] It was later still – the 1960s and 1970s – that legal scholars began to document and challenge the social and legal construction of disability and the legally imposed disabilities under which women labored and lived.[71] With the exception of a small handful of earlier voices, it was only in the 1970s that a new generation of historians, one that included women, African Americans, Native Americans, and Asian Americans, began to systematically unmask the gender and racial bias of legal structures. With the exception of a few solitary voices in the 1960s, it was not until the 1980s and even more so the 1990s that historians and legal scholars, including scholars with disabilities, began to challenge the medical model of disability and document, beginning with particular disabilities and then through disability as a category of analysis, the social and legal construction of disability.

---

[69] These laws, as well as the laws of other states, are included in *The Bulletin of the University of Washington, No. 82, 7, 18, 24.*

[70] Charles S. Mangum, Jr., *The Legal Status of the Negro* (Chapel Hill, 1940); Charles S. Johnson, *Patterns of Negro Segregation* (New York, 1941); Pauli Murray, *States' Laws on Race and Color*, 1951 (Reprint Athens, GA, 1997).

[71] See, e.g., Jacobus tenBroek, "The Right to Live in the World: The Disabled in the Law of Torts," *California Law Review* 54 (1966): 841–919; Marcia Pearce Burgdorf and Robert Burgdorf, Jr., "A History of Unequal Treatment: The Qualifications of Handicapped Persons as a 'Suspect Class' Under the Equal Protection Clause," *Santa Clara Lawyer* 15 (1975): 855–910. For the report of President Kennedy's Commission on the Status of Women, known as "the Peterson Report," see United States, President's Commission on the Status of Women, *American Women* (1963; reprint, Washington, D.C., 1965). California adopted one

Outright privilege too often was masked by inclusive language. The Illinois law regulating admission to the practice of law at issue in the U.S. Supreme Court's 1873 decision in *Bradwell v. Illinois* provided that "The Superior Court may admit and cause to be sworn as attorneys *such persons* as are qualified therefor. ..." But as Justice Bradley explained in his famous concurrence, upholding the reading of "persons" to mean "men," the court was bound to interpret the law as the legislature would have intended. And, most certainly, he insisted, the legislators who framed the law in the eighteenth century had not intended that women should practice law.[72]

Courts and lawmakers dressed subordination in the language of privilege and protection. The asserted public policy of state antiabortion laws passed between 1860 and 1880 was the protection of women. And in his concurrence to the U.S. Supreme Court's 1873 decision in *Bradwell v. Illinois,* Justice Joseph P. Bradley wrote, "Man is or should be woman's protector."[73] Separate-coach laws, like Indian removal before them, were described in terms of offering protection and safety to blacks and Native Americans. Echoing decisions across the decades, Justice Samuel Miller in *U.S. v. Kagama* (1886) invoked Congress's obligation of care and protection of the Indian to uphold the constitutionality of the Major Crimes Act, which asserted federal criminal jurisdiction in cases of Indian-on-Indian crimes on reservations. "These Indian tribes are the wards of the nation," wrote Justice Miller. "They are communities dependent on the United States.... From their very weakness and helplessness ... there arises the duty of protection, and with it the power."[74] The distant echo of these decisions and laws resounds in late twentieth century legislation such as California's "Civil Rights Initiative"; states' "Women's

of the first state level commissions on the status of women. California Government Code, sec. 8240–50.

[72] *Bradwell v. Illinois*, 83 U.S. 130, 140 (1873) (emphasis added).

[73] *Bradwell v. Illinois*, 83 U.S. 130, 141 (1873).

[74] *U.S. v. Kagama*, 118 U.S. 375, 383–4 (1886).

Right to Know" laws; and the federal 1996 "Personal Responsibility and Work Opportunity Act."[75]

They insisted that difference was part of God's ordained order, which law only yielded to, helpless to do otherwise. In *Bradwell*, Justice Bradley's opinion was a paean to motherhood. "[T]he paramount destiny and mission of woman are to fulfill the noble and benign offices of wife and mother," he declared. "This is the law of the Creator. And rules of civil society must be adapted to the general constitution of things...."[76] In a decision two years later, Judge Ryan of the Wisconsin Supreme Court joined the chorus: "The law of nature destines and qualifies the female sex for the bearing and nurture of the children of our race and for the custody of the homes of the world and their maintenance in love and honor."[77] God, Justice Agnew of the Pennsylvania Supreme Court wrote in the 1867 case *West Chester and Philadelphia R. R. v. Miles*, had created the races "dissimilar" to effect his intent that they not "overstep the natural boundaries He has assigned to them." God, he explained had separated the white and black races on the face of the globe. "The natural separation of the races is therefore an undeniable fact, and all social organizations which lead to their amalgamation are repugnant to the law of nature."[78] Anticipating William Graham Sumner's classic argument that "legislation cannot make mores," the U.S. Supreme Court in *Plessy v. Ferguson* concluded, "Legislation is powerless to eradicate or to abolish distinctions based upon physical differences. ..."[79]

Science and medicine rendered distinctions of race, gender, and physical and mental disability as natural, self-evident, given, thereby legitimating legal distinctions of capacity and

---

[75] "Civil Rights Initiative," Proposition 209, West's Ann. Cal. Const. art. 1, sec. 31; Ala. Code 1975 T. 26, ch. 23A; and "Personal Responsibility and Work Opportunity Act," 110 U.S. Statutes at Large 2105 (1996).

[76] *Bradwell v. Illinois*, 83 U.S. 130, 141-2 (1873).

[77] *In re Goodell*, 39 Wis. 232, 245 (1875).

[78] *West Chester and Philadelphia R. R. v. Miles*, 55 Pa. 209, 213 (1867).

[79] *Plessy v. Ferguson*, 163 U.S. 537, 551-2 (1896); William Graham Sumner, *Folkways; A study of the sociological importance of usages, manners, customs, mores, and morals* (Boston, 1906), 77.

incapacity, independence and dependence, reason and idiocy, normality and abnormality. While we today question the ends and reject the science on which they were based, science was in many respects a step forward from earlier foundations for explaining difference – that women, for example, were defective men or that disability was the product of dissolute lives, moral perversion and corruption. Yet it is impossible to escape the way in which science and medicine legitimated power and, its opposite, subordination. The medical model of disability that gained ground over the course of the nineteenth century located social incapacity in the mind and body of the "disabled," ignoring or overlooking the role of law in literally creating and sanctioning definitions and categories of disability, and excluding, marginalizing, and subordinating those with mental and physical differences and the ways in which law in turn sanctioned cultural, social, environmental, and political marginalization of the dis-abled. In the final decades of the nineteenth century and early decades of the twentieth century, the "science" of immutable racial differences and a hierarchy of races, fears of racial pollution and degeneration, evolutionary theory, the concept of normality, the physiological and biological science of women's bodies and reproductive capacities, and the science of genetics and eugenics all coupled to a potent belief in the imperative of "progress" brought social urgency and efficacy to laws banning interracial marriage between whites and racialized others, restricting immigration of racialized others and disabled persons, justifying laws and court decisions regulating women's hours of industrial-wage work, and justifying marriage restrictions and the coerced sterilization of the unfit to prevent them from further degrading the nation's genetic stock.

The mask of equality shielding the deliberate construction of privilege and disability ran deep in American ideals. The "American" ideal of independence, mastery, the self-made man has long had a cherished place in the lexicon of American ideals. In fact, the claim that identity rests outside of law is and always has been a closely guarded, jealously protected fiction.

This mythic ideal gained new, powerful adherents in the context of the late nineteenth century in the wake of emancipation and in the midst of burgeoning industrial capitalism. From Horatio Alger, to Frederick Jackson Turner, to Andrew Carnegie the ideology of individualism cast failure at the feet of the individual. Ignoring the multitude of ways that law privileged all white men above racialized and gendered others, the able over the disabled, judges embraced the ideology of individualism. Writing for the U.S. Supreme Court in *The Civil Rights Cases* (1883), in which the Court struck down the central provision of the Civil Rights Act of 1875, Justice Bradley insisted that, "[w]hen a man has emerged from slavery ... there must be some stage in the progress of his elevation when he takes the rank of a mere citizen, and ceases to be the special favorite of the laws, and when his rights, as a citizen or a man, are to be protected in the ordinary modes by which other men's rights are protected."[80]

The Enlightenment principles embraced in the American Revolution held both the seeds of radical social reordering and the justification for inequality in the new American republic: all human beings were equal, but only those with the capacity to reason could exercise informed consent. In this way, revolutionary ideology provided a foundation for the exclusion of women, racialized others, and disabled persons from participation in political and civic life.[81] Finally, industrialization transformed the boundary not simply between private and public, the home and the workplace, but between the productive and the unproductive, the useful and the useless that lent urgency and legitimacy to new forms of policing the body. As the authors of a 1914 University of Washington Bulletin explained,

... It is evident that something must be done to diminish the number of mental defectives in our population. War among primitive people, poverty, disease, and capital punishment did a fairly thorough if not a very beautiful piece of work before we began to civilize

[80] *The Civil Rights Cases*, 109 U.S. 3, 25 (1883).
[81] Holly Brewer, *By Birth or Consent: Children, Law, and the Anglo-American Revolution in Authority* (Chapel Hill, 2005), 341.

them away. Some substitute has to be found for natural selection. Procreation of the undesirable must be prevented by means which are least cruel and least wasteful. These laws already in force in the several states indicate the growth of this opinion.[82]

It would be yet several more decades before even a minority of scientists first began to question the legitimacy of laws passed in the name of eugenics. As Abraham Myerson, a professor of neurology at Tufts College Medical School, queried in 1935, "Who shall say who is a useful person?"[83]

In all, the erasure of how law created borders was something like an invisible fence that gives the appearance of there being no fence at all: the dog simply stays in the yard by "choice."

---

[82] *The Bulletin of the University of Washington, No. 82,* 86.

[83] Abraham Myerson, "A Critique of Proposed 'Ideal' Sterilization Legislation," *Archives of Neurology and Psychiatry* (1935): 453–466, quoted in Mark A. Largent, *Breeding Contempt: The History of Coerced Sterilization in the United States* (New Brunswick, NJ, 2008), 99.

CONCLUSION

Abled, Racialized, and Gendered Power in the Making of the Twentieth Century American State

It would be more comfortable if we could relegate abled, racialized, and gendered borders of belonging to history – here the history of America's long nineteenth century. We cannot. The founding assumptions that imagined legal personhood and, from it, citizenship and nation as able, white, and male in America's long nineteenth century fundamentally shaped the development of the American legal and constitutional order for the twentieth century and raise deeper questions regarding the relationship between borders of belonging, the liberal state, and modernity.

The mobilization of law in defense of the able white male republic in the nineteenth century fostered a culture of identity politics that would define the twentieth century. This transformation began with the Reconstruction Amendments to the Constitution in the wake of the Civil War. It is largely to white Southerners' racial intransigence – embodied in such things as the enactment of Black Codes, the reelection of confederate leaders to Congress and state legislatures, and the savage repression of freedmen – that we owe the Fourteenth and Fifteenth Amendments to the Constitution. Even here, what might have been the real birth of a nation dedicated to the equality of all was hedged from its conception. Section 1 of the Fourteenth Amendment was carefully crafted to exclude from citizenship the vast majority of Native Americans. Fears of the budding women's rights movement led lawmakers to rephrase wording of the Thirteenth Amendment to avoid its application to other relationships of hierarchy, such as between man and wife, and to likewise limit the suffrage provision in Section 2 of the Fourteenth Amendment regarding denial of "male" suffrage. The Fifteenth Amendment left holes large enough to walk through in its protection of black male suffrage: concessions to northern and western congressmen's own desire to limit the immigrant vote. And it was hedged because the amendments could be interpreted, as the U.S. Supreme Court in fact chose to do, as a response to the plight of the freedmen, not the birth of federal protection of civil rights and a recasting of American citizenship.

The U.S. Supreme Court's narrow, nugatory interpretation of the Thirteenth, Fourteenth, and Fifteenth Amendments thwarted a politics of human rights. The end of slavery and the recognition of birthright citizenship written into the Thirteenth and Fourteenth Amendments were momentous, but their meaning in the day-to-day lives of African Americans was blunted by the Supreme Court's subsequent interpretations of all three Reconstruction Amendments. The denial of constitutional authority to safeguard African Americans against violence, coupled with constitutional sanction for the exclusion of African Americans from juries and disfranchisement in decisions like *U.S. v. Cruikshank* (1876), *U.S. v. Reese* (1876), *Virginia v. Rives* (1880), and *Williams v. Mississippi* (1898) stripped African Americans of political and civil rights.[1] In turn, the Court paved the constitutional way for Jim Crow with its decisions in *Hall v. Decuir* (1877) and *The Civil Rights Cases* (1883), striking down state and federal civil rights statutes, and then provided state Jim Crow laws constitutional cover in *Louisville, New Orleans & Texas Railway Company v. Mississippi*

---

[1] *U.S. v. Cruikshank*, 92 U.S. 542 (1875); *U.S. v. Reese*, 92 U.S. 214 (1875); *Virginia v. Rives*, 100 U.S. 313 (1879); *Williams v. Mississippi*, 170 U.S. 213 (1879).

(1890), *Plessy v. Ferguson* (1896), and other cases.[2] The combination of these cases left African Americans with little recourse but to defend and demand the stunted rights to equal but separate accommodations accorded them under the laws.

Nor did women, Native Americans, Asian immigrants, disabled persons, or the inhabitants of America's new empire fare better. When the U.S. Supreme Court faced its first interpretation of national citizenship in *Slaughterhouse* and *Bradwell*, it narrowly read the Privileges and Immunities clause of the Fourteenth Amendment in part as a way around women's rights advocates' claims that women already had the right to vote by virtue of being citizens (known as the "New Departure"). And in so doing, the Court gave constitutional sanction to inequality, yielding a broadly construed national citizenship to a bifurcated citizenship in which status distinctions imbedded in state law like coverture retained their legal authority, thus denying full legal personhood to women. With the Court's decision in *Minor v. Hapersett* (1874), women recognized that their only hope for suffrage lay not in a politics of human rights or the rights of citizens, but through a politics of gender difference.[3] Similarly, the Supreme Court's decision in *Lochner v. New York* (1905) led protective labor advocates to focus on what was left to them: not protection of workers generally, but protection of women as a sex, as women, and of all women as potential mothers.[4] In case after case, the Supreme Court turned away the constitutional claims of racialized others, disabled persons, and women, and in so doing expanded the power of the state: denying birthright citizenship to Native Americans (*Elk v. Wilkins*); upholding the sovereign power of the nation to define who should be able to immigrate to the

[2] *Hall v. Decuir*, 95 U.S. 485 (1878); *Louisville, New Orleans & Texas Railway Co. v. Mississippi*, 133 U.S. 587 (1890); *Plessy v. Ferguson*, 163 U.S. 537 (1896).
[3] *Minor v. Happersett*, 88 U.S. 162 (1875).
[4] *Lochner v. New York*, 198 U.S. 45 (1905).

United States (*Chinese Exclusion Case [Chae Chan Ping] v. U.S.*); interpreting deportation as a civil sanction, which in turn meant that deportees did not have a right to the constitutional protections applicable to criminal procedures (*Fong Yue Ting v. U.S.*); creating wholly new categories of territory ("unincorporated territories") to distinguish among and selectively grant citizenship to the natives of America's Caribbean and Pacific empire (*Downes v. Bidwell*); defining the boundaries of whiteness under the Naturalization Act (*Ozawa v. U.S.; U.S. v. Thind*); upholding state sterilization statutes (*Buck v. Bell*).[5] In all, it was a sort of constitutional strategic defense initiative (SDI) shielding the abled, racialized, and gendered borders of belonging against the demands of disabled persons, racialized others, and women opened by the Thirteenth, Fourteenth, and Fifteenth Amendments.

In the one kind of case where the law unwittingly produced inclusive arguments – the law limiting naturalization to "white persons" – Asian Indians', Syrians', and others' arguments that they were "white" themselves reinforced the legitimacy of limiting naturalization to those defined as white, and even among birth citizens reinscribed the racial superiority of those who could claim whiteness.

Equally fundamental, the construction of the modern administrative state was ineluctably linked to defense of abled, racialized, and gendered borders of belonging. The favored interpretation of the rise of the modern administrative state has long been tied to burgeoning industrial capitalism. Cherished pride of place as America's first permanent administrative agency has belonged to the Interstate Commerce Commission (ICC), created under the Interstate Commerce Act (1887). In this interpretive scheme, the administrative state emerged as a response to industrialization; an effort to control the leviathan to protect the interests of the individual.

---

5 *Elk v. Wilkins*, 112 U.S. 94 (1884); *Chinese Exclusion Case (Chae Chan Ping) v. U.S.*, 130 U.S. 581 (1889); *Fong Yue Ting v. U.S.*, 149 U.S. 698 (1892); Downes v. Bidwell, 182 U.S. 244 (1901); *Ozawa v. U.S.*, 260 U.S. 178 (1922); *U.S. v. Thind*, 261 U.S. 204 (1922); *Buck v. Bell*, 274 U.S. 200 (1927).

The ICC served as a stepping-stone to other administrative agencies intended to police industry and corporate power and ultimately to the New Deal. Even as new scholarly work pushes the beginnings of the modern state back into the nineteenth century, with considerations of the U.S. Postal Service and the management of government lands, it retains the hallmark of the earlier interpretation. That is, it places race regulation, and more particularly the South, and gender and disability regulation as outside, before, or peripheral to the birth of the modern legal order.

It is less comfortable, but more accurate, to recognize that early in the nineteenth century Americans embraced the apparatus and enforcement mechanisms that characterize the modern administrative state as tools in defense of the borders of belonging. It is a measure of how completely we have defined the Indian as outside the nation that we do not recognize the Indian Office as one of the nation's first administrative agencies. Well before the ICC, the Bureau of Indian Affairs was administering U.S. reservation policy. The class-action lawsuit filed in federal court in 1996 against the Department of the Interior for mismanagement of the "Indian Trust Fund" – the huge fund that grew out of the allotment of tribal land to individual Indians – attests like nothing else can to the "permanence" of this federal regulatory structure.[6] The Fugitive Slave Act of 1850 offered one of the first examples of administrative courts focused on an exclusive subject matter. The Civil War; Congressional Reconstruction; and the Bureau of Refugees, Freedmen, and Abandoned Lands were the first large-scale federal experiments in administrative governance, more generally. The gendered template for state welfare provision – even what counted as "welfare" versus benefits for service provided – and government surveillance of women's sexuality as a qualification for receipt of state benefits was established with land warrants for veterans, Civil War pensions, and mother's aid

[6] On December 8, 2009, the parties to *Cobell v. Salazar* agreed to a settlement in which the federal government would pay $3.4 billion related to its mismanagement of the fund. *New York Times*, 9 Dec. 2009.

programs. That public policy for the good of a group and of society might mean segregating, policing, subordinating, and denying basic human rights, were all practiced in state institutions for "defectives" early in the nineteenth century. The larger point here is that in writing these agencies and institutions out of the history of the administrative state we do not simply sketch an incomplete history, but a history that misses how fundamentally abled, racialized, and gendered borders of belonging are imbedded in state formation and capitalism in U.S. history. The borders of belonging, as I argue here, fundamentally shaped industrial capitalism. Nineteenth-century debates about corporate capital and its personhood, after all, were pitched in the language of liberalism and its inclusions and exclusions.

In significant respects, the modern regulatory state was born out of the demand for belonging. At the state level, had African Americans in the wake of the Civil War simply accepted their "customary" exclusion from public transit, in other words, had they not insisted that freedom by definition included equal access to public transit, there would have been no need for state-mandated Jim Crow. Had prospective Chinese immigrants and existing Chinese residents in the United States responded to the growing hostility to their presence by not immigrating or, if in the United States, by returning to China, there would have been no need for the complex administrative machinery of the Bureau of Immigration (reorganized as the Immigration and Naturalization Service (INS) in 1933). In both cases, formal, statutory law took authority out of the hands of state and federal courts, which had proved susceptible to rights arguments.

A critical component of the new regulatory order included the criminalization of individual conduct that had been legal. One can see it in state laws criminalizing abortion; state and federal laws banning the distribution of birth control literature and devices; state laws and city ordinances making it a crime for white and black passengers to share the same space in a railroad or streetcar. One can find it in laws banning marriage by the "unfit" and the spread of state laws barring marriages between whites and racial others; restrictions making immigration by certain individuals a crime; the restriction of work beyond a certain number of hours or in violation of certain prescribed conditions. Following passage of the Immigration Act of 1924, as Mae Ngai notes, "One's legal status now rested on being in the right place in the queue – if a country has a quota of N, immigrant N is legal but immigrant N + 1 is illegal – and having the proper documentation, the prized 'proper visa.' "[7] Remember, of course, that by 1924, for some categories of prospective immigrants, including disabled persons and the peoples of China, Japan, and India there was no "N."

By no means was every enactment criminalizing conduct in these years calculated to preserve able white men's privilege. Gilded Age and Progressive Era enactments included also public health and safety measures such as prohibiting the sale of illuminating oil that "flashed" below certain temperatures, prohibiting spitting in public to prevent the spread of tuberculosis, requiring the inspection of meat products, and most famously, prohibition. They included, as well, laws that eroded men's patriarchal privileges by criminalizing child labor and providing for birth certificates without which child labor legislation would have been unenforceable. All of these laws rested on state police power to protect the health, safety, and public welfare of its citizens. But the fact that laws protecting able white men's prerogatives were part of a larger regulatory transformation or that white men too found their freedom constrained should not be allowed to distract from the fact that such laws fundamentally defined the era and that the modern state took shape through them. And, as importantly, the authority the state took from white male patriarchs it did not surrender to women, racialized others, or disabled persons; rather, it expanded the arena of state authority that far more often than not reinforced the abled, racialized, and gendered borders of belonging.

7 Mae M. Ngai, *Impossible Subjects: Illegal Aliens and the Making of Modern America* (Princeton, 2004), 61.

The new regulatory regime mobilized individuals and nongovernmental agencies to serve as agents of the state. The newly organized American Medical Association (AMA) itself spearheaded the movement to criminalize abortion and throughout the 100-year history of criminal abortion laws remained a vital organ of the state in securing their enforcement. Doctors at institutions for the "feebleminded, et al" were sought and rewarded in many states with the state's imprimatur, giving them authority to forcibly sterilize certain of their inmates. Others were less willing state agents. Doctors, fearing prosecution themselves, conditioned their treatment of women patients suffering from botched abortions on giving "dying declarations," informing on their abortionists. Railroads fought enactment and enforcement of Jim Crow at every step of the way, not out of any commitment to racial equality, but rather to retain their own autonomy of action. But they too were mobilized by the criminal sanctions provided against both railroads and conductors under separate coach laws to act as state agents in enforcing the laws. Under every state's Jim Crow laws, a railroad conductor who failed to separate white and black passengers faced criminal prosecution, as did railroad companies and their executives for failure to enforce the statutory mandate of Jim Crow. State miscegenation laws and laws banning marriage by those deemed defective imposed criminal penalties not only on the couple, but also on the minister who ratified their union. Government imposed duties and fines on shipping companies that transported immigrants likely to become public charges or who, in later years, violated immigration statutes and forced companies to screen passengers at ports of embarkation. What these laws recognized was that the "state" in its formal institutions and personnel had limited capacity to enforce these laws. The only way to realize the laws' intent was to target "service providers," – railroads, doctors, ministers, ship owners and others as the case may be – and make them agents of the state, through threat of prosecution, monetary penalties, and/or promise of individual gain.

Even as these laws usurped rights, they created new individual rights that through private legal actions legitimated state power and action and reinforced the abled, racialized, and gendered borders of belonging. For example, in suits brought by white and black passengers, courts recognized that separate coach laws gave individual passengers a legal right to occupy space in a railroad car from which intrastate travelers of the opposite race were excluded. Yet, as black women's suits challenging violations of state Jim Crow laws document, this new right simultaneously enforced the racial order. In the years following the Civil War but before the passage of state Jim Crow laws, black women had resisted conductors attempts to force them to ride in colored compartments or smoking cars, insisting that as ladies they had the right to ride in the ladies car. Jim Crow changed the fundamental category of identity on which black women claimed rights. In their lawsuits during the Jim Crow era, in place of the gendered qualifier, "who is a lady," following a woman's name, black women identified themselves by race – "she being a colored woman" – and what they demanded was what they could by law demand: the right only to ride in the colored coach without incursions by drunk or disorderly white men.[8] "The history of miscegenation law," Peggy Pascoe reminds us, "includes men who insisted on racial equality in order to preserve the gender privileges of manhood, women who fought with other women over the spoils of White men's estates, and men and women who used the laws to try to free themselves from partners they decided they had mistakenly wed as well as men and women who linked their own marriages to the freedom of others."[9] So too, relatives of the "unfit" challenged the capacity of those they hoped to inherit from when a will did not recognize them or when a marriage risked cutting them out of an inheritance

[8] Barbara Y. Welke, *Recasting American Liberty: Gender, Race, Law and the Railroad Revolution, 1865–1920* (New York, 2001), 319.
[9] Peggy Pascoe, *What Comes Naturally: Miscegenation Law and the Making of Race in America* (New York, 2009), 311.

altogether by the operation of state inheritance laws. One of the motivations behind the AMA's drive to criminalize abortion was to push midwives (women) out of the practice of medicine so that male doctors could have the field of obstetrics and gynecology free from female competition. Racially restrictive housing covenants gave whites a legally enforceable right to a white neighborhood.

The modern American state was built, in significant measure, on a supreme faith in statistics, yet Americans seemed oblivious to how fundamentally the borders of belonging shaped the numbers. Return immigration to China was higher because Chinese exclusion laws, miscegenation laws, prohibitions on alien land ownership and on naturalization, and a myriad other legal and extralegal discriminations against the Chinese made the United States a hostile land. The number of immigrants excluded "at America's gates" as "likely to become a public charge" on grounds of disability or due to race was smaller because American immigration laws were widely advertised and discouraged immigration by individuals at risk of being turned away, and because ship captains and ticket agents policed the borders of belonging in their own economic self-interest. Ship captains bore the costs of returning rejected immigrants, and ticket agents faced fines from ship captains for selling tickets to individuals who were rejected when they went to board the ship. Black travel was lower because many blacks who could afford to travel stayed home rather than face the dangers and indignities of Jim Crow transit. Deaths from abortion were higher because of criminalization. So too, the death rate for Native Americans because of poverty and inadequate health care on reservations. The statistical portrait of a nation being overrun by physical and mental defectives rested on historically contingent and questionable medical, scientific, and societal definitions of disability. In other words, for the numbers law produced, one might justly conclude: garbage in, garbage out.

The administrative apparatuses and legal rationales mobilized to safeguard the borders of belonging in the nineteenth century lent themselves to the policing of new categories of belonging in the twentieth century, most importantly sexuality. In practice, if not by the name we know it today, law in the nineteenth century privileged heterosexuality through the benefits accorded married men in the law of coverture and as heads of household. In the twentieth century, heterosexuality and homosexuality became marked more formally in law. The state's construction of heterosexuality as a condition of citizenship grew out of, in the first instance, immigration restriction directed at the disabled. In 1917, the Immigration Act added "constitutional psychopathic inferiority" as grounds for exclusion. The provision was described as barring "various unstable individuals on the border line between sanity and insanity, such as ... persons with abnormal sex instincts." Physical "defects" – "lack of sexual development," "poor physique," "undersized," "deficient in muscular development," "physically degenerate" – were the first signposts, as Margot Canaday has shown, on the way to marking more clearly properly embodied and performed heterosexuality as a condition of citizenship later in the twentieth century.[10] The production of heterosexuality as a condition of citizenship paralleled the erosion of coverture in the twentieth century and assumed the work that coverture had done in protecting male patriarchal authority in the nineteenth century.[11] Moreover, the scientific and medicalized discourse of homosexuality paralleled the nineteenth century discourses of gender, race, and disability, providing new avenues for exclusion and marginalization of women, racialized others, and disabled persons.

The emergence of elaborated categories of exclusion in the twentieth century and the speed and sweep of legal restrictions pointedly targeting disabled persons at the end of the nineteenth century and in the early decades of the twentieth century force us to acknowledge that the categories of exclusion

[10] Margot Canaday, *The Straight State: Sexuality and Citizenship in Twentieth-Century America* (Princeton, 2009), 19–54.
[11] Margot Canaday, "Heterosexuality as a Legal Regime," in *The Cambridge History of Law in America*, 3 vols., eds. Michael Grossberg and Christopher Tomlins (New York, 2008), 3:442–71.

were not fixed. However much we may want to believe in the progressive narrative of personhood and citizenship that has long been a part of America's national myth, it is hard to deny the work of privilege and subjection – borders of belonging – in the building and work of the modern American state.

CODA

In November 1869, as the Fifteenth Amendment to the Constitution hung in the balance, *Harper's Weekly* cast itself firmly on the side of ratification with a political cartoon by Thomas Nast titled "Uncle Sam's Thanksgiving Dinner."[1] The cartoon imagined an inclusive America. Seated at a large oval table – a table that by its very shape insisted America was a nation of equals – was a diverse collection of people: a white woman, a black man and his family, a Chinese family, an American Indian, a Russian family, an Irishman, and many more. As a frontiersman-like figure carved the turkey, the others engaged in what appears to be a lively conversation. And should there be

---

[1] Thomas Nast, "Uncle Sam's Thanksgiving Dinner," *Harper's Weekly* (Nov. 20, 1869), 745.

any question of the rights those seated at the table enjoyed, the words on the centerpiece read "Self Government" and "Universal Suffrage," and flanking the table and the main title were the phrases "Come One Come All" and "Free and Equal." Completing the image were portraits of Presidents Lincoln, Washington, and Grant, with statues of justice and liberty between them, a draped American flag, and a landscape scene titled "Welcome." In this idealized imagining of America, all were equals, and all were full members individually and in the collectivity. Americans could be, must be, Nast argued, a nation in which there were no borders of belonging marked by distinctions of race, gender, class, or ethnicity. Nast's Thanksgiving Dinner was an extraordinary image. It embodied ideals of freedom, liberty, and equality – ideals that it had taken a civil war and emancipation to make truly imaginable to at least a few, for at least a time. And, as it suggests, the Civil War was a watershed; as a moment of possibility for reshaping the borders of belonging, its importance is impossible to overstate. And yet it, like Nast's image, has misled us.

Another look at Nast's image reveals that even at this extraordinary moment, the argument for a nation without borders of belonging rested on elisions and stereotype and was itself transitory. The Indian was seated at the table, his claim to the land equal to rather than prior and hence superior to that of the others. The landscape painting hanging on the wall reinforced the erasure of history. It showed ships approaching a developed shoreline. There was nothing here of white settlers being greeted by native inhabitants of the land. The diversity of membership in the nation was captured in racially and ethnically stereotyped caricatures reinscribing characteristics that had provided a foundation for a hierarchy of belonging. It is telling that the only way in which Nast imagined to iconographically embody full personhood in a woman was to picture a racially white woman seated at the table alone. The nation itself was cast in male terms – it is "Uncle Sam's" Thanksgiving dinner. The able white frontiersman remained, in a way, first citizen, with the honor of carving the turkey. The supreme elision, though, was of the disabled. Everyone seated at the table had sight, and, as suggested by the conversation, hearing, and was physically "normal" and mentally capable. The medicalization of disability was so accepted, and the reduction of disabled persons to wardship so complete, that there could be no sense of law denying the disabled equal rights, much less of society losing something of value by doing so.

Nast's image itself is a kind of statement of what might be if only we try hard enough. It encourages us to embrace a progressive narrative in which the space on the other side of the borders is charged negatively and the space within charged positively. The project of liberalism becomes then that of simply expanding the borders to absorb or bring into the space of belonging those who have been excluded. It is a narrative that lends itself to, and indeed renders imperative, dichotomies such as that expressed in Abraham Lincoln's historic words, "I believe that this government cannot endure, permanently, half slave and half free."[2]

As I have argued here, looking at the United States after the Civil War, as before, one sees not a nation half slave and half free but a nation in which a central condition of freedom and belonging for the few was varying levels of unfreedom for the majority of Americans. Freedom was defined by a set of overlapping, binary oppositions – abled/disabled, white/racialized other, man/woman – in which one side of the opposition enjoyed greater freedom in part by virtue of the other's relative unfreedom. Yet, the borders of belonging were never simply a matter of being inside or outside. Manifestations of belonging were often as fundamental to subordination as exclusion. And being outside the borders of belonging – whether by choice or not – could offer possibilities of independence, identity, and difference. The liberal ideal does not imagine either possibility. Nor does it give us the tools for understanding how dramatic,

---

[2] Abraham Lincoln, Speech before Republican Delegates, Republican State Convention (Springfield, IL), June 16, 1858, in *Lincoln on Race and Slavery*, ed. and intro. Henry Louis Gates, Jr., ed. and coed. Donald Yacovone (Princeton, NJ, 2009), 103–06.

historic change could take place without being transformative in the borders of belonging.

I have often been asked as I worked on this project about the recent past and the present. Did the rights movements of the 1950s, 1960s, and 1970s in the United States erase the borders of belonging? Certainly the black freedom movement, women's rights and liberation movement, gay rights and liberation movement, disability rights movement, immigration reform, and Chicano and American Indian movements dramatically expanded the realm of rights. Yet, beneath the dramatic legacies of federal legislation like the Civil Rights Act of 1964, the Voting Rights Act of 1965, the Disability Rights Act of 1990, and equally significant Supreme Court precedents, can we yet trace a certain stubborn continuity in the borders of belonging? In Chapter 3, I noted that legislation such as California's Civil Rights Initiative, various states' Women's Right to Know laws, and the federal 1996 Personal Responsibility and Work Opportunity Act resound like distant echoes of statutes and court decisions in the nineteenth century that dressed subordination in the language of privilege and protection. What are we to make of the U.S. Supreme Court's embrace of color-blindness or of the language of the "ownership" society? How do restrictive immigration laws in a concededly global economy continue the long-established relationship among race, citizenship, and cheap labor?

What happens when we look at not simply a single category – ability, race, gender, or sexuality – but across those categories? Do new categories – sexuality most certainly became a constituent element in the borders of belonging in the twentieth century – simply establish new borders, or do they also reinforce earlier categories? How long can we dismiss persistent exclusions as simply steps yet to be taken in the long road to achieving the liberal ideal? How does the increasingly elaborate policing of sexuality beginning in the early twentieth century challenge that vision? Might we consider whether borders of belonging defined by race, gender, ability, and sexuality condition American acceptance of dramatic levels of economic inequality? In thinking about the question of persistence and continuity, might we want to consider whether borders of belonging promise stability in the face of modernity, in a world where "all that is solid melts into air"?[3] Might we consider the troubling thought that borders of belonging were not simply imbedded in the American state at its birth, as I have argued here, but are a constituent element of the "liberal" state? And, in any case, might we want to consider whether the borders of belonging as I have traced them here reflect similar patterns in other countries, including other liberal democratic states? And if they do not, or if we see in other states different categories marking borders of belonging, what can that tell us? If we believe that the liberal individual was in its origins and has remained patterned in the form of the able, white, heterosexual male, can we imagine a world with the benefits of liberalism without its inherent flaws? In responding to these challenges, might we consider the limits of law and Audre Lord's admonition that "the master's tools will never dismantle the master's house"?[4] And in considering all of these questions, it seems imperative to look not simply at law as it relates to citizenship but at whether individuals enjoy full legal personhood. These are questions that I ponder and share with you so that you can join me, and hopefully others, in a broader conversation.

[3] The phrase here is originally from Marx and has been popularized by Marshall Berman, who incorporates it in his book title. Marshall Berman, *All That Is Solid Melts in Air: The Experience of Modernity* (New York, 1982), 6.

[4] Audre Lorde, "The Master's Tools Will Never Dismantle the Master's House," in *This Bridge Called My Back: Writings by Radical Women of Color*, eds. Cherríe Moraga and Gloria Anzaldúa (New York, 1983), 98, 99.

BIBLIOGRAPHIC ESSAY

In conceptualizing the borders of belonging of personhood, citizenship, and nation in the United States in the long nineteenth century, I found myself drawn to the visual image of a tessellation. A tessellation is formed by the repetition of a shape or set of shapes covering a plane without gaps or overlapping. Whether or not the term or definition is familiar, I suspect that every reader has seen one. The most famous may be those of M. C. Escher. Examples from his work can serve for the uninitiated. Escher's *Reptiles* (1943) features a single repeating image of a lizard in different rotations. His *Mosaic II* (1957) is constructed from (or yields) a series of creatures, statues, and objects.[1] Three features are critical: a figure or figures are repeated, the borders of each figure gives shape to adjacent figures, and collectively the figures cover the plane. Hence, no single shape in a tessellation is self-defining; they are interlocked and interdependent. Equally critically here, tessellations are often visually confusing; some shapes remain in the background, even as they give definition to others.

This essay offers points of access to pursue in the project of tessellating the borders of belonging as the first step in constructing a literature that has not fully acknowledged

---

[1] For examples of Escher tessellations and an introduction to tessellation generally, see http://library.thinkquest.org/16661/escher.html (last accessed September 10, 2009).

itself. Scholars in a range of subfields, including women's, Native American, African American, Asian American, Mexican American, disability history and disability studies, empire, and labor history since at least the 1970s in some cases, in others well before, and in some only since the 1990s, have been mapping the component figures that chart the borders of legal personhood and citizenship. Without that scholarship I could not have written this book. But that said, there is no historiography of legal personhood. A variety of factors meant that the concept of border maintenance in the service of one sector of the population was hidden, cast instead as specific gender, race, ethnic, medical, or temporal exclusions. It is only by reading both across time and across scholarship that has painstakingly charted the legal disabilities rendering some outside the borders of belonging by virtue of skin color and heredity, gender, ethnicity, ableness, and citizenship that the borders themselves become visible, can be seen as purposeful, persistent, and shared, and through them that the character of able white male privilege across the sweep of the long nineteenth century is clear. With that in mind, the underpinning strategy outlined in this essay might be referred to by the shorthand: border-crossing reading.

In this essay, I offer works that I have found especially productive in conceptualizing and charting the borders of belonging. Though the essay focuses primarily on work that is explicitly about law, I have included works of social, political, economic, and cultural history that provide critical insights into legal personhood, the expression and experience of law in everyday life, and the multiple, often competing, contradictory worlds that law creates. I also have included key theoretical works that I have found fundamental in thinking about legal personhood and citizenship. This essay is long as it is, but it could have been far longer. I have read broadly, but I do not claim to have exhausted the many relevant literatures on which this volume touches. As importantly, even as this volume has gone to press so have other books that belong here. As any historian knows, literatures do not stand still.

My hope is that this essay will, nonetheless, provide a useful starting point for and approach to reading.

The essay itself is divided into two parts. Part I features a vertical reading of literature relating to three broad, deeply intertwined topics central to the history of legal personhood in the long nineteenth century: property, race, and citizenship. Part II privileges a horizontal reading of literature addressing four key moments that are traditionally cast as decisive turning points in the long nineteenth century – the Revolutionary Era; the Age of Jackson; the Civil War and Reconstruction; and Redemption, Empire, and the Progressive State – as they relate to legal personhood and citizenship. I have limited full citations to the first reference of a work and have listed multiple works on a given point in reverse chronological order. To avoid undue repetition, I have limited works cited in Part II to a few suggestive works on each point. As a final aid to the reader, I close with an alphabetical bibliography listing the works cited in this essay.

Part I

Property, race, and citizenship were deeply intertwined in the history of legal personhood in the long nineteenth century. As a result, we could argue over where it seems most appropriate to introduce the literature related to any number of topics. I begin with property because rights to and control of property and nation fundamentally shaped both law relating to race and citizenship. I encourage the reader in thinking about the three categories to read the literature cited here with all three categories – property, race, and citizenship – in mind.

Property. To take the measure of property in the history of legal personhood requires thinking about the nature of property in its fullest sense. Property included property in the self (self-ownership) and property in others, both of which were fundamentally related to more traditional understandings of property as land and things (real and personal property) and the right to inherit, contract, own, convey, devise, and so on. It included, as well, spatial ordering, including zoning, segregation in all its manifestations (disability, race, and gender), and exclusion from public space as in so-called "ugly laws." In its most expansive sense, property related to the extent and boundaries of the nation and, in turn, to who had a right to claim and speak in the name of them as citizens.

For a review of the philosophical underpinnings of the liberal self, see C. B. MacPherson, *The Political Theory of Possessive Individualism: Hobbes to Locke* (New York, 1962). Feminist scholars have been especially critical of the asserted inclusiveness of liberalism. See especially in this regard, Nancy Fraser and Linda Gordon. "Civil Citizenship against Social Citizenship?: On the Ideology of Contract-versus-Charity," in Bart van Steenbergen ed., *The Condition of Citizenship* (Thousand Oaks, 1994), 90–107; Linda K. Kerber, *No Constitutional Right to Be Ladies: Women and the Obligations of Citizenship* (New York, 1998); Kerber, "Can a Woman Be an Individual?: The Discourse of Self-Reliance," in Kerber, *Toward an Intellectual History of Women* (Chapel Hill, 1997), 200–23; Nancy Fraser, *Unruly Practices: Power, Discourse and Gender in Contemporary Social Theory* (Minneapolis, 1989); Carole Pateman, *The Sexual Contract* (Stanford, 1988); and Linda K. Kerber, *Women of the Republic: Intellect and Ideology in Revolutionary America* (New York, 1986). The nineteenth century abolitionist and women's movements were critical in asserting a right to self-ownership rooted in the body. See here Elizabeth B. Clark, "'The Sacred Rights of the Weak': Pain, Sympathy, and the Culture of Individual Rights in Antebellum America," *Journal of American History* 82 (1995): 463–93; Karen Sánchez-Eppler, *Touching Liberty: Abolition, Feminism, and the Politics of the Body* (Berkeley, 1993); Clark, "Self-Ownership and the Political Theory of Elizabeth Cady Stanton," *Connecticut Law Review* 21 (1989): 905–41; and Myra C. Glenn, *Campaigns Against Corporal Punishment: Prisoners, Sailors, Women, and Children in Antebellum America* (Albany, 1984).

As feminist critiques suggest, most scholarship that enables us to trace the borders of belonging focuses on those excluded from the borders of belonging and traces privilege through a particular element of exclusion. But there are important exceptions that chart the creation, instantiation, and defense of white male privilege in law from both within and outside what I have called here the borders of belonging. See Laura F. Edwards, *The People and Their Peace: Legal Culture and the Transformation of Inequality in the Post-Revolutionary South* (Chapel Hill, 2009); Bruce Mann, *Republic of Debtors, Bankruptcy in the Age of American Independence* (Cambridge, MA, 2002); Amy Dru Stanley, *From Bondage to Contract: Wage Labor, Marriage, and the Market in the Age of Slave Emancipation* (New York, 1998); and Stephanie McCurry, *Masters of Small Worlds: Yeoman Households, Gender Relations, and the Political Culture of the Antebellum South Carolina Low Country* (New York, 1995). On the Constitution and the protection of property, see Jennifer Nedelsky, *Private Property and the Limits of American Constitutionalism* (Chicago, 1990); Nedelsky, "Law, Boundaries, and the Bounded Self," *Representations* 30 (Spring 1990): 162–189; and Nedelsky, "Reconceiving Autonomy: Sources, Thoughts and Possibilities," *Yale Journal of Law & Feminism* 1 (1989): 7–36.

Also important are works not written with gendered, racial, or able privilege as their focus, but that nonetheless highlight able white men's capacity in law as propertied individuals. A critical starting point here is work documenting the new American states' adoption of the common law. For an early comprehensive overview, see Elizabeth Gaspar Brown, *British Statutes in American Law, 1776–1836* (Ann Arbor, 1964). Key works of American legal history trace the "transformation" of the common law in the nineteenth century United States. Morton J. Horwitz, *The Transformation of American Law, 1780–1860* (Cambridge, MA, 1977); and William E. Nelson, *The Americanization of the Common Law: The Impact of Legal Change on Massachusetts Society, 1760–1830* (Athens, GA, 1975), trace changes in the common law without addressing the underlying continuity of free white male privilege. Work that predates explicit attention to gender, race, and disability can nonetheless be illuminating.

On claiming the land, see in particular James Willard Hurst's classic *Law and the Conditions of Freedom in the Nineteenth-Century United States* (Madison, 1956). Writing this book has led me to see my own earlier work in new ways regarding ability and disability and their relationship to gender and race that other readers may find productive as well. Barbara Y. Welke, *Recasting American Liberty: Gender, Race, Law, and the Railroad Revolution, 1865–1920* (New York, 2001); and Welke, "Unreasonable Women: Gender and the Law of Accidental Injury, 1870–1920," *Law and Social Inquiry* 19 (1994): 369–403. Susanna L. Blumenthal's ongoing work highlights the struggle of nineteenth century courts to define the substance and limits of mental capacity in a number of areas of law. Susanna L. Blumenthal, "The Mind of the Moral Agent: Scottish Common Sense and the Problem of Responsibility in Nineteenth-Century American Law," *Law and History Review* 26 (Spring 2008): 99–159; "The Default Legal Person," *UCLA Law Review* 54 (2007): 1135–1265; and "The Deviance of the Will: Policing the Bounds of Testamentary Freedom in Nineteenth-Century America," *Harvard Law Review* 119 (2006): 959–1035.

It is easier to find work that highlights the propertied self indirectly by its focus on those denied full legal personhood. Slavery represented the quintessential denial of self-ownership. The literature on slavery is vast. I recommend as starting points work that I have found especially helpful in thinking about legal personhood. On the law of slavery, see Thomas D. Morris, *Southern Slavery and the Law, 1619–1860* (Chapel Hill, 1996). On the compromise in the Constitution allowing slavery, see Mark A. Graber, *Dred Scott and the Problem of Constitutional Evil* (New York, 2006). On the slave market in particular, see Walter Johnson, *Soul by Soul: Life Inside the Antebellum Slave Market* (Cambridge, MA, 1999). Ariela J. Gross, *Double Character: Slavery and Mastery in the Antebellum Southern Courtroom* (Princeton, 2000) follows slave market transactions into the courtroom. Dylan C. Penningroth uncovers the history of slaves ownership of property before the Civil War in *The Claims of*

Kinfolk: African American Property and Community in the Nineteenth-Century South (Chapel Hill, 2003), and in doing so offers an important cautionary example against assuming that law represented lived experience. As he shows, masters had incentives to allow slaves to "own" property, despite the law, in a variety of settings. On the slavery to freedom narrative in American history, see Walter Johnson, "Slavery, Reparations, and the Mythic March of Freedom," *Raritan* 27 (2007): 41–67. Essential foundations for the ways that whiteness has functioned as property include George Lipsitz, *The Possessive Investment in Whiteness: How White People Profit from Identity Politics* (Philadelphia, 1998) and Cheryl I. Harris, "Whiteness as Property," *Harvard Law Review* 106 (1993): 1709–91.

The denial of personhood was at the heart of antislavery campaigns. See, in this regard, David Brion Davis, *Inhuman Bondage: The Rise and Fall of Slavery in the New World* (New York, 2006); Davis, *The Problem of Slavery in the Age of Revolution, 1770–1823* (2nd ed., New York, 1999); Clark "The Sacred Rights of the Weak"; and Jean Fagan Yellin, *Women and Sisters: Anti-Slavery Feminists in American Culture* (New Haven, 1990).

On the experience of slavery for African Americans, I recommend beginning with broad surveys: Steven Hahn, *A Nation Under Our Feet: Black Political Struggles in the Rural South From Slavery to the Great Migration* (Cambridge, MA, 2003); Ira Berlin, *Many Thousands Gone: The First Two Centuries of Slavery in North America* (Cambridge, MA, 1998); and Jacqueline Jones, *Labor of Love, Labor of Sorrow: Black Women, Work, and the Family From Slavery to the Present* (New York, 1985); and then turning to slave narratives, with *Narrative of the Life of Frederick Douglass, An American Slave, Written by Himself,* 1845, Reprint, ed. and intro. David W. Blight (Boston, 1993) and *Harriet A. Jacobs, Incidents in the Life of a Slave Girl, Written by Herself,* 1861, Reprint, ed. and intro. Jean Fagan Yellin (Cambridge, MA, 1987) as excellent starting points. On the meaning of emancipation and freedom for African Americans, see Rebecca

J. Scott, *Degrees of Freedom: Louisiana and Cuba after Slavery* (Cambridge, MA, 2005); Eric Foner, "The Meaning of Freedom in the Age of Emancipation," *Journal of American History* 81 (1994): 435–60; Ira Berlin et al., eds., *Freedom: A Documentary History of Emancipation*, 4 vols. (New York, 1982–94); Eric Foner, "Rights and the Constitution in Black Life during the Civil War and Reconstruction," *Journal of American History* 74 (1987): 863–83; Barbara Jeanne Fields, *Slavery and Freedom on the Middle Ground: Maryland During the Nineteenth Century* (New Haven, 1985); and Leon Litwack, *Been in the Storm: The Aftermath of Slavery* (New York, 1979).

Slavery provided the touchstone against which the freedom of all others in the nineteenth century was measured. But, as this book highlights, it was by no means the only example of the denial of self-ownership. As I explain in the introduction and then elaborate on in each chapter, the discourse of disability justified the exclusion not only of those marked as mentally and physically unfit, but of women and racialized others as well. Especially since the 1990s the scholarship developing disability as a category of analysis has taken off. Important starting points in this literature include Catherine J. Kudlick, "Review Essay. Disability History: Why We Need Another 'Other'," *American Historical Review* 108 (2003): 763–93; Paul K. Longmore, *Why I Burned My Book and Other Essays on Disability* (Philadelphia, 2003); Paul K. Longmore and Lauri Umansky, eds., *The New Disability History: American Perspectives* (New York, 2001), including the essay by Douglas C. Baynton, "Disability and the Justification of Inequality in American History," 33–57; David T. Mitchell and Sharon L. Snyder, eds., *Narrative Prosthesis: Disability and the Dependencies of Discourse* (Ann Arbor, 2000); and Rosemarie Garland Thomson, *Extraordinary Bodies: Figuring Physical Disability in American Culture and Literature* (New York, 1997).

One of the ways in which law gave form to white men as self-owning individuals and women as not was through marriage and the law of coverture. The key theoretical

starting point for thinking about coverture and its relation-
ship to liberalism remains Pateman, *The Sexual Contract*.
The best overview of family law in the nineteenth century
more generally remains Michael Grossberg, *Governing the
Hearth: Law and the Family in Nineteenth Century America*
(Chapel Hill, 1985). See also Norma Basch, "Marriage and
Domestic Relations," in *The Cambridge History of Law in
America, 3 vols.*, eds., Michael Grossberg and Christopher
Tomlins (New York, 2008), 2: 245–79 (hereafter I cite the
Cambridge History volumes as CHLA). For treatises on the
law of coverture, see William Blackstone, *Commentaries on
the Laws of England*, 4 vols. (1765–69, Reprint Chicago,
1979) and Tapping Reeve, *The Law of Baron and Femme,
Parent and Child, Guardian and Ward, Master and Servant,
and of the Powers of the Courts of Chancery* (New Haven
1816). On the significance of Blackstone in reshaping the
law of coverture in the wake of the American Revolution,
see Holly Brewer, "The Transformation of Domestic Law,"
in *CHLA*, 1: 288–323. For monographs that address men's
and women's rights within marriage over the full sweep of
the nineteenth century, see Nancy F. Cott, *Public Vows: A
History of Marriage and the Nation* (Cambridge, MA,
2000); and Hendrik Hartog, *Man and Wife in America: A
History* (Cambridge, MA, 2000). On the exercise of "husband's rights," see Hendrik Hartog, "Lawyering, Husbands'
Rights, and 'the Unwritten Law' in Nineteenth Century
America," *Journal of American History* 84 (1997): 67–96;
and Hartog, "Mrs. Packard on Dependency," *Yale Journal of
Law & Humanities* 79 (1988–89): 79–103. On the work that
heterosexuality does in the twentieth century that coverture
had earlier done to reinforce women's subordinate status, see
Margot Canaday, "Heterosexuality as a Legal Regime," in
CHLA, 3: 442–71.

   On married women's legal rights to property before property reform, see Marylynn Salmon, *Women and the Law
of Property in Early America* (Chapel Hill, 1986). Laurel
Thatcher Ulrich, *A Midwife's Tale: The Life of Martha
Ballard, Based on Her Diary, 1785–1812* (New York, 1990);

Stephanie McCurry, *Masters of Small Worlds: Yeoman Households, Gender Relations, and the Political Culture of the Antebellum South Carolina Low Country (New York,* 1995); and Suzanne Lebsock, *The Free Women of Petersburg: Status and Culture in a Southern Town,* 1784–1864 (New York, 1984) offer insight into how legal constraints shaped women's daily lives before the Civil War. On industrialization's role in remaking the home as a site of domesticity rather than "work," see the foundational work of Jeanne Boydston, *Home and Work: Housework, Wages, and the Ideology of Labor in the Early Republic* (New York, 1990).

There is an extensive literature on married women's property reform before and after the Civil War. Important works include Stanley, *From Bondage to Contract;* Reva B. Siegel, "The Modernization of Marital Status Law: Adjudicating Wives' Rights to Earnings, 1860–1930," *Georgetown Law Journal* 82 (1994): 2127–2211; Siegel, "The First Woman's Rights Claims Concerning Wives' Household Labor, 1850–1880," *Yale Law Journal* 103 (1994): 1073–1217; Carole Shammas, "Re-assessing the Married Women's Property Acts," *Journal of Women's History* 6 (1994): 9–30; Dianne Avery and Alfred S. Konefsky, "The Daughters of Job: Property Rights and Women's Lives in Mid-Nineteenth-Century Massachusetts," *Law and History Review* 10 (1992): 323–56; Richard H. Chused, "Late Nineteenth Century Married Women's Property Law: Reception of the Early Married Women's Property Acts by Courts and Legislatures," *American Journal of Legal History* 29 (1985): 3–35; Richard H. Chused, "Married Women's Property Law: 1800–1850," *Georgetown Law Journal* 71 (1983): 1359–1425; Norma Basch, *In the Eyes of the Law: Women, Marriage, and Property in Nineteenth-Century New York* (Ithaca, NY, 1982); and Suzanne Lebsock, "Radical Reconstruction and the Property Rights of Southern Women," *Journal of Southern History* 43 (1977): 195–216. On comparisons between slavery and marriage, see Stanley, *From Bondage to Contract;* Sanchez-Eppler, *Touching Liberty;* and Elizabeth

B. Clark, "Matrimonial Bonds: Slavery and Divorce in Nineteenth-Century America," *Law and History Review* 8 (1990): 25–53. On the impact of coverture on personal injury claims after the Civil War and through the Progressive Era, see Welke, *Recasting American Liberty.*

On divorce, good starting points for reading include Norma Basch, *Framing American Divorce: From the Revolutionary Generation to the Victorians* (Berkeley, 1999); and three works by Robert L. Griswold, "The Evolution of the Doctrine of Mental Cruelty in Victorian American Divorce, 1790–1900," *Journal of Social History* 20 (1986): 127–48; "Law, Sex, Cruelty and Divorce in Victorian America, 1840–1900," *American Quarterly* 38 (1986): 721–45; and *Family and Divorce in California, 1850–1890* (Albany, NY, 1982). On child custody, see chapter 7 in Holly Brewer, *By Birth or Consent: Children, Law, & the Anglo-American Revolution in Authority* (Chapel Hill, 2005); and Michael Grossberg, *A Judgment for Solomon: The D'Hauteville Case and Legal Experience in Antebellum America* (New York, 1996).

Even as married women's property reform gave married women greater, if still limited, rights to property, and divorce and child custody reform gave women greater, though still limited recognition of their personhood, their rights to reproductive independence – and hence property in the self – were narrowed dramatically. On the criminalization of abortion and birth control beginning in the mid-nineteenth century and the enforcement of those laws, see Leslie J. Reagan, *When Abortion Was a Crime: Women, Medicine, and Law in the United States, 1867–1973* (Berkeley, 1997); and Linda Gordon, *Woman's Body, Woman's Rights: Birth Control in America* (rev. ed. New York, 1990). The state policed women's sexuality from the outset in pension and welfare programs, as well as distinguishing women's "service" to the state from men's. See in this regard, Kerber, *No Constitutional Right to Be Ladies,* ch. 1; Megan J. McClintock, "Civil War Pensions and the Reconstruction of Union Families," *Journal of American History* 83 (1996): 456–80; Linda Gordon, *Pitied But Not Entitled: Single Mothers and the History of Welfare*

(New York, 1994); Theda Skocpol, *Protecting Soldiers and Mothers: The Political Origins of Social Policy in the United States* (Cambridge, MA, 1992); and the essay collection Linda Gordon, ed., *Women, the State, and Welfare* (Madison, 1990).

White men's property right in themselves was tested by the dramatic expansion of wage labor in the nineteenth century. As the work of labor historians suggests, what came to be called "free labor" might have been called more accurately "free labor only by comparison" or "*free* labor?" See in this regard, Robert J. Steinfeld, *Coercion, Contract, and Free Labor in the Nineteenth Century* (New York, 2001); Christopher L. Tomlins, *Law, Labor, and Ideology in the Early American Republic* (New York, 1993); Robert J. Steinfeld, *The Invention of Free Labor: The Employment Relation in English and American Law and Culture, 1350–1870* (Chapel Hill, 1991); Karen Orren, *Belated Feudalism: Labor, the Law and Liberal Development in the United States* (New York, 1991); and Christopher L. Tomlins, "A Mysterious Power: Industrial Accidents and the Legal Construction of Employment Relations in Massachusetts, 1800–1850," *Law and History Review* 6 (1988): 375–438. Industrialization and emancipation tested and intensified the importance of the racialized and gendered safeguards of the borders of belonging. See in this regard, Stanley, *From Bondage to Contract*; and David R. Roediger, *The Wages of Whiteness: Race and the Making of the American Working Class* (New York, 1991).

Throughout the long nineteenth century, the law presumed that men were providers, that husbands had the right to their wives' labor and persons, and that married working women's primary identities were those of wife and mother. On men's obligation of support, see Anna R. Igra, *Wives Without Husbands: Marriage, Desertion, & Welfare in New York, 1900–1935* (Chapel Hill, 2007); and Michael Willrich, *City of Courts: Socializing Justice in Progressive Era Chicago* (New York, 2003). Husbands' rights could trump race as is shown by the work of Todd Stevens, "Tender Ties: Husbands' Rights and Racial Exclusion in Chinese Marriage Cases,

1882–1924," *Law & Social Inquiry* 27 (2002): 271–305. On judicial interpretation of homestead exemption laws, see Alison D. Morantz, "There's No Place Like Home: Homestead Exemption and Judicial Constructions of Family in Nineteenth-Century America," *Law and History Review* 24 (2006): 245–96. On wrongful death laws, see John Fabian Witt, "From Loss of Services to Loss of Support: Wrongful Death, the Origins of Modern Tort Law, and the Making of the Nineteenth Century Family," *Law and Social Inquiry* 25 (2000): 717–55. On husbands' right to their wives' labor and persons and reluctance to acknowledge the same rights in African American families in the South following emancipation, see chapter 2 in Kerber, *No Constitutional Right to Be Ladies*; and Stanley, *From Bondage to Contract*. The same assumptions shaped workmen's compensation law, policymakers' assumptions about men's and women's work after the turn of the twentieth century, and the development of the "two-channel" welfare state. On workmen's compensation, see John Fabian Witt, *The Accidental Republic: Crippled Workingmen, Destitute Widows, and the Remaking of American Law* (Cambridge, MA, 2004). On the "gendered imagination" regarding work and home and its operation in law, see Alice Kessler-Harris, *In Pursuit of Equity: Women, Men, and the Quest for Economic Citizenship in 20th-Century America* (New York, 2001). On protective labor legislation more particularly, see also Nancy Woloch, *Muller v. Oregon: A Brief History with Documents* (Boston, 1996); and Judith Baer, *The Chains of Protection: The Judicial Response to Women's Labor Legislation* (Westport, CT, 1978). For an introduction to the two-channel welfare state, in addition to Kessler-Harris noted above, see, among other works, the essays in Gordon, *Women, the State, and Welfare*; and Molly Ladd-Taylor, *Mother-Work: Women, Child Welfare, and the State, 1890–1930* (Urbana, 1994).

On efforts to exclude women and African Americans from professions such as law and medicine and to maintain professions as white men's domain, see Ellen Carol DuBois, "Taking the Law into Our Own Hands: *Bradwell, Minor*, and Suffrage

Militance, in the 1870s," in Ellen Carol DuBois, ed., *Woman Suffrage and Women's Rights* (New York, 1998), 114–38; Michael Grossberg, "Institutionalizing Masculinity: The Law as a Masculine Profession," in Mark C. Carnes and Clyde Griffen, eds., *Meanings for Manhood: Constructions of Masculinity in Victorian America* (Chicago, 1990), 133–51; Neil R. McMillen, *Dark Journey: Black Mississippians in the Age of Jim Crow* (Urbana, 1989); D. Kelly Weisberg, "Barred from the Bar: Women and Legal Education in the United States, 1870–1890," in D. Kelly Weisberg, ed., *Women and the Law: A Social Historical Perspective, vol. II, Property, Family and the Legal Profession* (Cambridge, MA, 1982), 231–58. But also see Mary Jane Mossman, *The First Women Lawyers: A Comparative Study of Gender, Law, and the Legal Professions* (Portland, OR, 2006) on women's entrance to the bar; Eric Foner, *Freedom's Lawmakers: A Directory of Black Officeholders During Reconstruction* (rev. ed., Baton Rouge, 1996) on the extraordinary interlude of Reconstruction, and Kenneth Mack, "Rethinking Civil Rights Lawyering and Politics in the Era Before *Brown*," *Yale Law Journal* 115 (2005): 256–354; and Mack, "A Social History of Everyday Practice: Sadie T. M. Alexander and the Incorporation of Black Women into the American Legal Profession, 1925–60," *Cornell Law Review* 87 (2002): 1405–74.

On the relationship among abortion restriction, the marginalization of women as midwives, and the exclusion of women from the profession of medicine, see Ulrich, *A Midwife's Tale*; Carroll Smith-Rosenberg, *Disorderly Conduct: Visions of Gender in Victorian America* (New York, 1985), 217–44; James C. Mohr, *Abortion in America: The Origins and Evolution of National Policy, 1800–1900* (New York, 1978); Mary Roth Walsh, *"Doctors Wanted, No Women Need Apply": Sexual Barriers in the Medical Profession* (New Haven, 1977).

Emancipation ended the regime of property in persons, but it did not give African Americans full legal personhood or equal access to the land. For excellent work on the slowness of emancipation in the North, see David N. Gellman,

Emancipating New York: The Politics of Slavery and Freedom, 1777–1827 (New York, 2006); David N. Gellman and David Quigley, *Jim Crow New York: A Documentary History of Race and Citizenship, 1777–1877* (New York, 2003); John Wood Sweet, *Bodies Politic: Negotiating Race in the American North, 1730–1830* (Baltimore, 2003); Joanne Pope Melish, *Disowning Slavery: Gradual Emancipation and "Race" in New England, 1780–1860* (Ithaca, 1998); Fields, *Slavery and Freedom in the Middle Ground*; Ira Berlin and Ronald Hoffman, eds., *Slavery and Freedom in the Age of the American Revolution* (Charlottesville, 1983); and Leon F. Litwack, *North of Slavery: The Negro in the Free States, 1790–1860* (Chicago, 1961).

In the South, Reconstruction, for all its promise, fell short of guaranteeing African Americans full legal personhood; post-Reconstruction legal stratagems ensured the pool of black agricultural laborers in the South. The basic text on Reconstruction remains Eric Foner's now classic *Reconstruction: America's Unfinished Revolution* (New York, 1988). Key works on control of African American labor after Reconstruction include Evelyn Nakano Glenn, *Unequal Freedom: How Race and Gender Shaped American Citizenship and Labor* (Cambridge, MA, 2002); Julie Saville, *The Work of Reconstruction: From Slave to Wage Laborer in South Carolina, 1860–1870* (New York, 1994); and Eric Foner, "The Politics of Freedom," in Foner, *Nothing But Freedom: Emancipation and Its Legacy* (Baton Rouge, 1983), 39–73. Sven Beckert, "Emancipation and Empire: Reconstructing the Worldwide Web of Cotton Production in the Age of the American Civil War," *American Historical Review* 109 (2004): 1405–38, places the development of new systems to control land and agricultural labor in the wake of emancipation in global context.

Glenn, *Unequal Freedom,* is also essential reading for placing actions in the post-Reconstruction South in a national context involving Mexican Americans and Mexicans in the Southwest and West, and Japanese and Chinese in the West and Hawaii. See also Gunther Peck, *Reinventing Free Labor:*

Padrones and Immigrant Workers in the North American West, 1880–1930 (New York, 2000); Linda Gordon, *The Great Arizona Orphan Abduction* (Cambridge, MA, 1999); and Neil Foley, *The White Scourge: Mexicans, Blacks, and Poor Whites in Texas Cotton Culture* (Berkeley, 1998). On convict labor, see Rebecca M. McLennan, *The Crisis of Imprisonment: Protest, Politics, and the Making of the American Penal State, 1776–1941* (New York, 2008); Alex Lichtenstein, *Twice the Work of Free Labor: The Political Economy of Convict Labor in the New South* (New York, 1996) and David M. Oshinsky, *"Worse Than Slavery:" Parchman Farm and the Ordeal of Jim Crow Justice* (New York, 1996). On the importance of vagrancy laws in enforcing the labor of racialized others – women, as well as men – at the end of the nineteenth century, see Kerber, *No Constitutional Right to be Ladies*; Stanley, *From Bondage to Contract*; and Glenn, *Unequal Freedom*.

   The literature on Western expansion and the dispossession of Native Americans of land, like other literatures addressed here, is large. For an introduction, see David E. Wilkins, "Federal Policy, Western Movement, and Consequences for Indigenous People, 1790–1920," in *CHLA*, 2: 204–44. Stuart Banner's *How the Indians Lost Their Land: Law and Power on the Frontier* (Cambridge, MA, 2005) fruitfully takes a long view (the early colonial era through the Indian Reorganization Act in 1934) in exploring the balance of law and power in Native Americans' loss of control of the vast majority of their land to whites. Other more focused studies are also important. On the doctrine of discovery as applied in *Johnson and Graham's Lessee v. McIntosh*, see Lindsay G. Robertson, *Conquest by Law: How the Discovery of America Dispossessed Indigenous Peoples of their Land* (New York, 2005). On the justification for removal, see Tim Allen Garrison, *The Legal Ideology of Removal: The Southern Judiciary and the Sovereignty of Native American Nations* (Athens, GA, 2003). On the Dawes Act and allotment, see in particular David A. Chang, *The Color of the Land: Race, Nation, and the Politices of Landownership in Oklahoma, 1866–1929* (Chapel Hill, 2010); Emily Greenwald, *Reconfiguring the Reservation: The Nez Perces, Jicarilla Apaches, and the Dawes Act* (Albuquerque, 2002); Janet A. McDowell, *The Dispossession of the American Indian, 1887–1934* (Bloomington, 1991); and Frederick E. Hoxie, *A Final Promise: The Campaign to Assimilate the Indians, 1880–1920* (Lincoln, NE, 1984). A number of excellent studies trace key Supreme Court decisions; see Rennard Strickland, "The Tribal Struggle for Indian Sovereignty: The Story of the *Cherokee Cases*," in *Race Law Stories*, eds. Rachel F. Moran and Devon W. Carbado (New York, 2008), 37–57; Jill Norgren, *The Cherokee Cases: The Confrontation of Law and Politics* (New York, 1996); Joseph C. Burke, "The Cherokee Cases: A Study in Law, Politics, and Morality," *Stanford Law Review* 21 (1969): 500–31; Sidney L. Harring, *Crow Dog's Case: American Indian Sovereignty, Tribal Law, and United States Law in the Nineteenth Century* (New York, 1994); and Blue Clark, *Lone Wolf v. Hitchcock: Treaty Rights and Indian Law at End of the Nineteenth Century* (Lincoln, NE, 1994). Larry C. Skogen, *Indian Depredation Claims, 1796–1920* (Norman, OK, 1996) details the over 10,000 claims white settlers filed in federal court between 1796 and 1920 under the little-known federal policy offering indemnity to those who claimed to have lost property because of Indian "depredations," with payment coming out of tribal trust funds.

On the intellectual roots of the asserted superiority of western legal traditions vis-à-vis indigenous peoples, see Robert A. Williams, Jr., *The American Indian in Western Legal Thought: The Discourse of Conquest* (1990). Jeffrey Ostler, *The Plains Sioux and U.S. Colonialism from Lewis and Clark to Wounded Knee* (New York, 2004) and Sweet, *Bodies Politic* productively place U.S.-American Indian relations in the broader study of colonialism. Native American people's adaptation of their legal systems in response to Western law is an important part of the story. See Tiya Miles, *Ties that Bind: The Story of an Afro-Cherokee Family in Slavery and Freedom* (Berkeley, 2005); Claudio Saunt, *A New Order of*

Things: Property, Power, and the Transformation of the Creek Indians, 1733–1816 (New York, 1999); and Rennard Strickland, *Fire and the Spirits: Cherokee Law from Clan to Court* (Norman, OK, 1975). For documents and general reference, see Vine Deloria, Jr. and Raymond J. DeMallie, *Documents of Indian Diplomacy: Treaties, Agreements, and Conventions, 1775–1979, 2 vols.* (Norman, OK, 1999); and Felix S. Cohen, *Handbook of Federal Indian Law* (Washington, 1942).

On the dispossession of Mexican (-Americans) of land by and following the Mexican-American war, see María E. Montoya, *Translating Property: The Maxwell Land Grant and the Conflict over Land in the American West, 1840–1900* (Berkeley, 2002); and Gordon, *The Great Arizona Orphan Abduction.*

The work of many scholars highlights the tightening of racial boundaries on land ownership at the end of the nineteenth century in the North and West. On restrictive covenants, see David Delaney, *Race, Place and the Law, 1836–1948* (Austin, 1998). James W. Loewen, *Sundown Towns: A Hidden Dimension of American Racism* (New York, 2005) argues that beginning from 1890 a majority of incorporated places outside the South barred settlement by African Americans. On miscegenation law and land ownership, see Peggy Pascoe, *What Comes Naturally: Miscegenation Law and the Making of Race in America* (New York, 2009). On the adoption of alien land laws in many Western states in the same temporal context, see Mae M. Ngai, *Impossible Subjects: Illegal Aliens and the Making of Modern America* (Princeton, 2004). For the pre–Civil War analogue to limits on settlement by free blacks in the North, see Gerald L. Neuman, "The Lost Century of American Immigration Law (1776–1875)," *Columbia Law Review* 93 (1993): 1833–1901 (esp. 1865–79); Paul Finkelman, "Prelude to the Fourteenth Amendment: Black Legal Rights in the Antebellum North," *Rutgers Law Journal* 17 (1986): 415–82; and Litwack, *North of Slavery*; on African Americans in the West, see Quintard

Taylor, *In Search of the Racial Frontier: African Americans in the American West, 1528–1990* (New York, 1998).

What restrictive covenants, miscegenation laws, and alien land laws did for private property at the end of the nineteenth century, Jim Crow did for public space. Important works to consider include Welke, *Recasting American Liberty*; Charles A. Lofgren, *The Plessy Case: A Legal-Historical Interpretation* (New York, 1987); Howard N. Rabinowitz, *Race Relations in the Urban South, 1865–1890* (Urbana, 1980); and C. Vann Woodward, *The Strange Career of Jim Crow*, 3rd rev. ed. (1955; New York, 1974).

Throughout the long nineteenth century legal and extralegal violence was essential in enforcing the borders of belonging. Violence safeguarded white men's claims to property in themselves, others, the land itself, and the space of the nation. On the South in particular, see Christopher Waldrep, *Roots of Disorder: Race and Criminal Justice in the American South 1817–1880* (Urbana, 1998); Edward L. Ayers, *Vengeance and Justice: Crime and Punishment in the Nineteenth-Century American South* (New York, 1984). On Southern slave patrols, see Sally E. Hadden, *Slave Patrols: Law and Violence in Virginia and the Carolinas* (Cambridge, MA, 2001). On the development of the law of self-defense, see Richard Maxwell Brown, *No Duty to Retreat: Violence and Values in American History* (New York, 1991). The literature on lynching is vast. Most of it focuses on lynchings by whites of African Americans. For an introduction to this literature, see Christopher Waldrep, *The Many Faces of Judge Lynch: Extralegal Violence and Punishment in America* (New York, 2002); James Allen, Hilton Als, Congressman John Lewis, and Leon F. Litwack, *Without Sanctuary: Lynching Photography in America* (Santa Fe, 2000); Grace Elizabeth Hale, *Making Whiteness: The Culture of Segregation in the South, 1890–1940* (New York, 1998); W. Fitzhugh Brundage, *Lynching in the New South, Georgia and Virginia, 1880–1930* (Urbana, 1993); and McMillen, *Dark Journey*. For Ida B. Wells's telling analysis of the underlying purposes of lynching, see Ida B. Wells-Barnett, *On Lynchings: Southern Horrors, A Red Record, Mob Rule in New Orleans* (1892, 1895, 1900, Reprint Salem, NH, 1993). On the antilynching campaign, see Jacquelyn Dowd Hall, *Revolt Against Chivalry: Jessie Daniel Ames and the Women's Campaign Against Lynching* (rev. ed. New York, 1993). As recent work shows, lynching was a tool of control used against racial minorities generally in enforcing the borders of belonging in the long nineteenth century. See William D. Carrigan and Clive Webb, "The Lynching of Persons of Mexican Origin or Descent in the United States, 1848 to 1928," *Journal of Social History* 37 (2003): 411–38.

Violence as a tool of control protecting and extending white property claims was not, of course, limited to lynching. See, in this regard, Glenda E. Gilmore, *Gender and Jim Crow: Women and the Politics of White Supremacy in North Carolina, 1896–1920* (Chapel Hill, 1996) on the Wilmington massacre; and Alfred L. Brophy, *Reconstructing the Dreamland: The Tulsa Riot of 1921: Race, Reparations, and Reconciliation* (New York, 2002). Nor was it a tool of control in black-white relations only. On anti-Chinese violence, see Victor Jew, "'Chinese Demons:' The Violent Articulation of Chinese Otherness and Interracial Sexuality in the U.S. Midwest, 1885–1889," *Journal of Social History* 37 (2003): 389–410; Erika Lee, *At America's Gates*; and John Wunder, "Anti-Chinese Violence in the American West, 1850–1910," in John McLaren, Hamar Foster, and Chet Orloff, eds., *Law for the Elephant, Law for the Beaver: Essays in the Legal History of the North American West* (Regina, Saskatchewan, 1992), 212–36; on violence against Asian Indians and Filipinos in the U.S., see Ngai, *Impossible Subjects*. Much of the history of Anglo-Native American relations has been one of violence. A good starting point for reading in this regard is Patricia Nelson Limerick, *The Legacy of Conquest: The Unbroken Past of the American West* (New York, 1987). On violence and empire more generally, especially focused on the end of the nineteenth century, see Paul A. Kramer, *The Blood of Government: Race,*

Empire, the United States, and the Philippines (Chapel Hill, 2006); Angel Velasco Shaw and Luis H. Francia, eds., *Vestiges of War: The Philippine-American War and the Aftermath of an Imperial Dream, 1899–1999* (New York, 2002); Sally Engle Merry, *Colonizing Hawaii: The Cultural Power of Law* (Princeton, 2000); and Lou Perez, *The War of 1898: The United States and Cuba in History and Historiography* (Chapel Hill, 1998).

The links between race, gender, and violence are long and haunting. On rape and other violence against women see Hannah Rosen, *Terror in the Heart of Freedom: Citizenship, Sexual Violence, and the Meaning of Race in the Postemancipation South* (Chapel Hill, 2009); Lisa Lindquist Dorr, *White Women, Rape, and the Power of Race in Virginia, 1900–1960* (Chapel Hill, 2004); Diane Miller Sommerville, *Rape and Race in the Nineteenth-Century South* (Chapel Hill, 2004); Laura F. Edwards, *Gendered Strife and Confusion: The Political Culture of Reconstruction* (Urbana, 1997); Darlene Clark Hine, "Rape and the Inner Lives of Black Women in the Middle West: Preliminary Thoughts on the Culture of Dissemblance," *Signs: Journal of Women in Culture* 14 (1989): 912–920; and Jacquelyn Dowd Hall, "'The Mind That Burns in Each Body': Women, Rape, and Racial Violence," *Southern Exposure* 12 (1984): 61–71.

Violence was licensed more often than we are comfortable acknowledging within family relations. On domestic violence and the law see Ruth H. Bloch, "The American Revolution, Wife Beating, and the Emergent Value of Privacy," *Early American Studies* 5 (2007): 223–51; Ann Taves, ed., *Religion and Domestic Violence in Early New England: The Memoirs of Abigail Abbot Bailey* (Bloomington, 1989); Linda Gordon, *Heroes of Their Own Lives: The Politics and History of Family Violence* (New York, 1988); and Elizabeth H. Pleck, *Domestic Tyranny: The Making of Social Policy Against Family Violence From Colonial Times to the Present* (New York, 1987).

The medicalized discourse of institutions "for" the feebleminded, the insane, and other disabled persons, papered over the fact that institutionalization was often accomplished

without legal protection of an individual's wishes, for purposes of control, as well as the violence, masked as treatment,
against persons once institutionalized. On these points, see
in particular, Philip M. Ferguson, *Abandoned to Their
Fate: Social Policy and Practice toward Severely Retarded
People in America, 1820–1920* (Philadelphia, 1994); James
W. Trent, Jr., *Inventing the Feeble Mind: A History of
Mental Retardation in the United States* (Berkeley, 1994);
and Hartog, "Mrs. Packard on Dependency." On the medi-
calized scientific discourse of eugenics that provided a
foundation for laws providing for involuntary or coerced
sterilization of the "unfit" beginning in the early decades
of the twentieth century, see Mark A. Largent, *Breeding
Contempt: The History of Coerced Sterilization in the United
States* (New Brunswick, NJ, 2008); Alexandra Minna Stern,
Faults and Frontiers of Better Breeding in Modern America
(Berkeley, 2005); David Mitchell and Sharon Snyder, "The
Eugenic Atlantic: Race, Disability, and the Making of an
International Eugenic Science, 1800–1945," *Disability &
Society* 18 (2003): 843–64; Sharon L. Snyder and David
T. Mitchell, "Out of the Ashes of Eugenics: Diagnostic
Regimes in the United States and the Making of a Disability
Minority," *Patterns of Prejudice* 36 (2002): 79–103;
Wendy Kline, *Building a Better Race: Gender, Sexuality,
and Eugenics from the Turn of the Century to the Baby
Boom* (Berkeley, 2001); and Philip R. Reilly, *The Surgical
Solution: A History of Involuntary Sterilization in the
United States* (Baltimore, 1991).

On law, the construction of the boundaries of the nation,
and empire, see Bartholomew H. Sparrow, *The Insular Cases
and the Emergence of American Empire* (Lawrence, 2006);
Sanford Levinson and Bartholomew H. Sparrow eds., *The
Louisiana Purchase and American Expansion, 1803–1898*
(New York, 2005); Christina Duffy Burnett and Burke
Marshall, eds., *Foreign in a Domestic Sense: Puerto Rico,
American Expansion, and the Constitution* (Durham, 2001);
David E. Wilkins and K. Tsianina Lomawaima, *Uneven
Ground: American Indian Sovereignty and Federal Law*

(Norman, OK, 2001); Merry, *Colonizing Hawaii*; and David Langum, *Law and Community on the Mexican California Frontier: Anglo-American Expatriates and the Class of Legal Traditions, 1821–1846* (Norman, OK, 1987). On the Supreme Court's decision in the key insular case of *Downes v. Bidwell*, in addition to Sparrow above, see Pedro A. Malovet, " 'The Constitution Fellows the Flag...but Doesn't Quite Catch Up wit It": The Story of *Downes v. Bidwell*," in *Race Law Stories*, 175–235. See also the excellent collection of essays, many of which relate to the long nineteenth century, *Legal Borderlands: Law and the Construction of American Borders*, eds. Mary L. Dudziak and Leti Volpp, *American Quarterly* 57 (2005).

In thinking about the boundaries of the nation, it is equally important to bear in mind the way that legal exclusions marked borders of belonging within the territorial boundaries of the nation: coverture, slavery, Indian reservations, etc., operated to limit the claims women, the disabled, and racialized others could make on the community. Kunal Parker perceptively describes this as a matter of being "legally visible subjects of claims." His work focuses specifically on the practice of townships in late eighteenth-century Massachusetts of avoiding economic responsibility for ex-slaves by assigning them foreign geographic origins even though prior to their emancipation they had lived in the state and belonged to Massachusetts' residents. Jacobus tenBroek's argument regarding the right of the disabled "to live in the world" makes a similar point regarding the disabled, as does Susan Schweik's work on "ugly laws." So do Cheryl Harris's, Peggy Pascoe's, Ariela Gross's, and Mae Nagi's works on whiteness as property and on racial exclusion, and Welke's work relating to gender, race, accidental injury, and public accommodations. See Ariela J. Gross, *What Blood Won't Tell: A History of Race on Trial in America* (Cambridge, MA, 2009); Pascoe, *What Comes Naturally*; Susan M. Schweik, *The Ugly Laws: Disability in Public* (New York, 2009); Susan Schweik, "Begging the Question: Disability, Mendicancy, Speech and the Law," *Narrative* 15 (2007): 58–70; Ngai, *Impossible*

Subjects; Kunal Parker, "Making Blacks Foreigners: The Legal Construction of Former Slaves in Post-Revolutionary Massachusetts," *Utah Law Review* (2001): 75–124; Welke, *Recasting American Liberty*; Harris, "Whiteness as Property;" and Jacobus tenBroek, "The Right to Live in the World: The Disabled in the Law of Torts," *California Law Review* 54 (1966): 841–919.

There is a large scholarship on the legal regulation of immigration. Immigration historians have long argued that the 1870s and 1880s mark the starting point for immigration restriction in the United States, but key recent (and even not so recent) works trace the history of control over immigration to the nation's founding. Most important here is Aristide R. Zolberg's, *A Nation by Design: Immigration Policy in the Fashioning of America* (Cambridge, MA, 2006). Zolberg begins with the revolutionary era, but his narrative stretches to the present, and though his focus is on the United States, his analysis productively places U.S. regulation of immigration in global perspective. See also Kunal M. Parker, "Citizenship and Immigration Law, 1800–1924: Resolutions of Membership and Territory," in *CHLA*, 2:168–203 and other work by Parker cited above; Mary Sarah Bilder, "The Struggle Over Immigration: Indentured Servants, Slaves, and Articles of Commerce," *Missouri Law Review* 61 (1996): 743–824; Neuman, "The Lost Century of American Immigration Law (1776–1875); and E. P. Hutchinson, *Legislative History of American Immigration Policy 1798–1965* (Philadelphia, 1981). Other essential works on immigration restriction, include Douglas C. Baynton, "Defectives in the Land: Disability and American Immigration Policy, 1882–1924," *Journal of American Ethnic History* 24 (Spring 2005): 31–44; Ngai, *Impossible Subjects*; Erika Lee, *At America's Gates: Chinese Immigration During the Exclusion Era, 1882–1943* (Chapel Hill, 2003); John C. Torpey, *The Invention of the Passport: Surveillance, Citizenship, and the State* (New York, 2000); Gerald L. Neuman, *Strangers to the Constitution: Immigrants, Borders, and Fundamental Law* (Princeton, 1996); and Lucy E. Salyer, *Laws Harsh as Tigers: Chinese Immigrants and the Shaping of Modern Immigration Law* (Chapel Hill, 1995).

The racial and gender prerogatives that white men enjoyed in the United States in the long nineteenth century had parallels elsewhere. Especially helpful here is the work of Marilyn Lake on Australia. See Lake, "Translating Needs into Rights: The Discursive Imperative of the Australian White Man, 1901–30," in Stefan Dudink, Karen Hagemann, and John Tosh, eds., *Masculinities in Politics and War: Gendering Modern History* (Manchester, UK, 2004), 199–219; and Lake, "On Being a White Man, Australia, Circa 1900," in Hsu-Ming Teo and Richard White, eds., *Cultural History in Australia* (Sydney, Australia, 2003), 98–112.

Race. W. E. B. Du Bois did not use the term "tessellation" in *The Souls of Black Folk* (1903), but he might have. Throughout the long nineteenth century, giving legal definition to and the policing of race and racial boundaries were fundamental to the borders of belonging. Beyond Du Bois, the reading opportunities are rich. Legal scholars working in the field of Critical Race Theory have been especially important in making intelligible the operation of racial privilege and racial exclusions in American law. For an introduction to this scholarship, see Richard Delgado and Jean Stefancic, eds., *Critical Race Theory: The Cutting Edge* (Philadelphia, 2000); Angela P. Harris, "Equality Trouble: Sameness and Difference in Twentieth-Century Race Law," *California Law Review* 88 (2000): 1923–2015; Adrien Katherine Wing, ed., *Critical Race Feminism: A Reader* (New York, 1997); Kimberlé Crenshaw, Neil Gotanda, Gary Peller, and Kendall Thomas, eds., *Critical Race Theory: The Key Writings that Formed the Movement* (New York, 1995); Neil Gotanda, "A Critique of 'Our Constitution is Color-Blind,'" *Stanford Law Review* 44 (1991): 1–68; and Patricia J. Williams, *The Alchemy of Race and Rights* (Cambridge, MA, 1991). Harris, "Whiteness as Property" and Barbara J. Fields, "Ideology and Race in American History" in J. Morgan Kousser and James M. McPherson, eds., *Region, Race, and Reconstruction: Essays in Honor of C. Vann Woodward*

184   *Bibliographic Essay*

(New York, 1982), 143–77, remain foundational works on race in American history. Recent works of particular importance for addressing the role of law in the construction of race and its consequences for personhood, naturalization, citizenship, and belonging include Gross, *What Blood Won't Tell*; Pascoe, *What Comes Naturally* and her earlier article "Miscegenation Law, Court Cases and Ideologies of 'Race' in Twentieth Century America," *Journal of American History* 83 (1996): 44–69; and Ngai, *Impossible Subjects* and her earlier seminal article "The Architecture of Race in American Immigration Law: A Re-Examination of the Immigration Act of 1924," *Journal of American History* 89 (1999): 67–92. All three authors focus on moments (trials of racial determination; the passage and application of laws prohibiting marriage between whites and racialized others; immigration, citizenship, and belonging), of marking whiteness off from other racialized identities (black, Indian, Mexican, Asian, and so on), highlighting the uncertainties and the individual and societal stakes of the racialized borders of belonging. See also Robert S. Chang, *Disoriented: Asian Americans, Law, and the Nation State* (New York, 1999); Charles W. Mills, *The Racial Contract* (Ithaca, 1997); and Stanford M. Lyman, "The Race Question and Liberalism: Casuistries in American Constitutional Law," *International Journal of Politics, Culture, and Society* 5 (1991): 183–247.

There are numerous works outside of legal history that are nonetheless important for understanding the assumptions behind and justifications for race-related legislation in the long nineteenth century. On the creation and importance of racialized boundaries generally in the nineteenth century, see Ronald Takaki, *Iron Cages: Race and Culture in 19th Century America* (New York, 1979). On creating and enforcing the color line in black-white relations, see Rebecca J. Scott, *Degrees of Freedom: Louisiana and Cuba after Slavery* (Cambridge, MA, 2005); Jane Dailey, *Before Jim Crow: The Politics of Race in Postemancipation Virginia* (Chapel Hill, 2000); Joel Williamson, *The Crucible of Race: Black-White Relations in the American South Since*

Emancipation (New York, 1984); George M. Frederickson, *The Black Image in the White Mind: The Debate on Afro-American Character and Destiny, 1817–1914* (New York, 1971); Alexander Saxton, *The Indispensable Enemy: Labor and the Anti-Chinese Movement* (Berkeley, 1971); and Winthrop D. Jordan, *White over Black: American Attitudes Toward the Negro, 1550–1812* (Chapel Hill, 1968). On Native Americans, see Williams, *The American Indian in Western Legal Thought.* On race, immigration, and empire, see Laura Briggs, *Reproducing Empire: Race, Sex, Science, and U.S. Imperialism in Puerto Rico* (Berkeley, 2003); Matthew Frye Jacobson, *Barbarian Virtues: The United States Encounters Foreign Peoples at Home and Abroad, 1876–1917* (New York, 2000); and John Higham, *Strangers in the Land: Patterns of American Nativism, 1860–1925* (New York, 1969), supplemented by Higham's thoughtful historiographic review of his classic work, "Instead of a Sequel, or How I Lost My Subject," *Reviews in American History* 28 (2000): 327–39 (also included as an Epilogue in the 2002 ACLS Humanities E-book republication of *Strangers in the Land*). Relating to Mexicans and Mexican Americans in this regard, see David Gutiérrez, *Walls and Mirrors: Mexican Americans, Mexican Immigrants, and the Politics of Ethnicity* (Berkeley, 1995).

Because of slavery, the legal history of race relating to black-white relations dwarfs all others. In addition to the work cited in the preceding section, see also Gary B. Nash, *The Forgotten Fifth: African Americans in the Age of Revolution* (Cambridge, MA, 2006); and Ira Berlin, *Slaves Without Masters: The Free Negro in the Antebellum South* (1976, Reprint New York, 1992). Henry Louis Gates, Jr., restores complexity and contradiction to Abraham Lincoln's views on race in his introduction to a volume of Lincoln's speeches, debates, and correspondence. Gates's introduction, coupled with the main text of the volume, is important not simply for understanding Lincoln, but also for reentering the nineteenth century world of racial hierarchy and its significance for American life. Henry Louis Gates, Jr., ed. and intro., and Donald Yacovone, coed., *Lincoln on Race and Slavery*

(Princeton, 2009). For collections of race laws in the United States beginning in the late nineteenth century, see Gilbert Thomas Stephenson, *Race Distinctions in American Law* (New York, 1910); Charles S. Mangum, Jr., *The Legal Status of the Negro* (Chapel Hill, 1940); and Pauli Murray, comp. and ed., *States' Laws on Race and Color* (1951; Athens, GA, 1997). Stephenson's work, it should be noted, is an elaborate justification of "race distinctions" in law which he contrasts with unjustified "race discrimination." His work is usefully read as an early twentieth century defense of race legislation; it is also, though, a useful collation of statutes and institutional practices. Both Stephenson and Murray include laws related to racial groups other than African Americans.

As Stephenson's and Murray's collections highlight, race as a foundation for the borders of belonging was not limited to the law discriminating between black and white. It was fundamental to Euro-Indian relations, defined naturalization from the first naturalization law in 1790 through the long nineteenth century, underlay immigration restriction, and fundamentally shaped both law and actions taken in the shadow of the law for all racial minorities. John Wood Sweet's study of race in Rhode Island productively uses postcolonialism to chart the continuities from the colonial era of white supremacy and Native and African American subordination and exclusion from citizenship in the Revolutionary Era and Early Republic even as slavery was abolished in the antebellum North. Sweet, *Bodies Politic*. On race and Native Americans, see also N. C. Carter, "Race and Power Politics as Aspects of Federal Guardianship over American Indians: Land-Related Cases, 1887–1924," *American Indian Law Journal* 4 (1976): 197–248. On the impact of allotment on racially mixed Native Americans, see Gross, *What Blood Won't Tell*; Miles, *Ties That Bind*; and Claudio Saunt, *Black, White, and Indian: Race and the Unmaking of an American Family* (New York 2005). On the role of race in immigration restriction and enforcement, see Martha Gardner, *The Qualities of a Citizen: Women, Immigration, and Citizenship, 1870–1965* (Princeton, 2005); Kitty Calavita, "Law, Citizenship, and the

Construction of (Some) Immigrant 'Others,'" *Law & Social Inquiry* 30 (2005): 401–20; Ngai, *Impossible Subjects;* Lee, *At America's Gates;* Leti Volpp, "'Obnoxious to Their Very Nature:' Asian Americans and Constitutional Citizenship," *Asian Law Journal* 8 (2001): 71–87; Richard P. Cole and Gabriel Chin, "Emerging from the Margins of Historical Consciousness: Chinese Immigrants and the History of American Law," *Law and History Review* 17 (1999): 325–64; Salyer, *Laws Harsh as Tigers;* and Bill Ong Hing, *Making and Remaking Asian America Through Immigration Policy, 1850–1990* (Stanford, 1990). On naturalization see Ian Haney Lopez, *White By Law: The Construction of Race* (New York, 1996). On the racialization of Mexican Americans, see Glenn, *Unequal Freedom;* Gordon, *The Great Arizona Orphan Abduction;* and although much of the author's focus is on later in the twentieth century, George A. Martinez, "The Legal Construction of Race: Mexican-Americans and Whiteness," *Harvard Latino Law Review* 2 (1997): 321–38; and "Forum. Whiteness and Others: Mexican Americans and American Law," *Law and History Review* 21 (2003): 109–213. Articles on a number of important nineteenth century U.S. Supreme Court cases relating to race, including the *Cherokee Cases, Prigg v. Pennsylvania, Wong Kim Ark, Downes v. Bidwell,* and *Ozawa v. United States,* are collected in *Race Law Stories.*

One part of the project of understanding the role of race in American law is marking the normative, here whiteness. A critical starting point for reading is Harris, "Whiteness as Property." Other key works include, Gross, *What Blood Won't Tell;* Pascoe, *What Comes Naturally;* Ngai, *Impossible Subjects;* Gordon, *The Great Arizona Orphan Abduction;* Lopez, *White By Law;* and Peggy Pascoe, "Miscegenation Law, Court Cases and Ideologies of 'Race' in Twentieth Century America," *Journal of American History* 83 (1996): 44–69. Whereas white privilege in law has been a focus of Critical Race Theorists, theoretical work on whiteness has not focused as squarely on law. One important exception is Lipsitz, *The Possessive Investment in Whiteness.*

See also Devon W. Carbado, "Racial Naturalization," in
Legal Borderlands, 633–58. For review essays surveying the
field of whiteness studies, see the symposium, "Scholarly
Controversy: Whiteness and the Historians' Imagination,"
International Labor and Working Class History 60
(2001): 1–92; Peter Kolchin, "Whiteness Studies: The New
History of Race in America," *Journal of American History*
89 (2002): 154–73; and Daniel Wickberg, "Heterosexual
White Male: Some Recent Inversions in American Cultural
History," *Journal of American History* 92 (2005): 136–57.
Works of cultural and political history that chart the construction of whiteness and manliness through the lenses
of European immigration, the white working class, nation
building, and empire, although explicitly not legal history and
only rarely, if at all, even referring to law, nonetheless provide
important contextualization for understanding the boundaries of legal personhood. See Thomas A. Guglielmo, *White on
Arrival: Italians, Race, Color, and Power in Chicago, 1890–
1945* (New York, 2003); Matthew Frye Jacobson, *Whiteness
of a Different Color: European Immigrants and the
Alchemy of Race* (Cambridge, MA, 1998); Gail Bederman,
*Manliness & Civilization: A Cultural History of Gender
and Race in the United States, 1880–1917* (Chicago, 1995);
Roediger, *The Wages of Whiteness*; Alexander Saxton, *The
Rise and Fall of the White Republic: Class Politics and Mass
Culture in Nineteenth-Century America* (New York, 1990);
and Reginald Horsman, *Race and Manifest Destiny: The
Origins of American Racial Anglo-Saxonism* (Cambridge,
MA, 1981).

The privileges that inhered in whiteness created incentives
to pass as white. Equally important, the legal and administrative structures created to protect the color line provided
a social foundation for breeching those boundaries. Gunnar
Myrdal laid out the incentives and discussed the practice of
passing in the post–Civil War era in his classic *An American
Dilemma* (1944), 683–86. Critical Race theorists Cheryl
Harris and Patricia Williams both relate stories of family
members passing that speak powerfully to its incentives, costs,

and centrality for understanding the property interest at stake in being able to claim whiteness. See Harris, "Whiteness as Property" and Patricia J. Williams, "On Being the Object of Property," in *The Alchemy of Race and Rights* (1991). For accounts by historians of passing and racial indeterminacy before as well as after the Civil War see, Earl Lewis and Heidi Ardizzone, *Love on Trial: An American Scandal in Black and White* (New York, 2001); and Berlin, *Slaves without Masters*. For a sophisticated consideration of passing applied to illegal Chinese immigrants, see Kitty Calavita, "The Paradoxes of Race, Class, Identity, and 'Passing': Enforcing the Chinese Exclusion Acts, 1882–1910," *Law and Social Inquiry* 25 (2000): 1–40.

There is an extensive literature on the legal regulation of interracial sex and marriage. Peggy Pascoe's work convincingly shows that these laws and the enforcement of them were, in important respects, about protecting white men's property claims. But miscegenation laws, as Pascoe and others recognize, were also about asserting and maintaining racial boundaries or, more accurately, about constructing and maintaining the boundary between those considered white and racialized others, reflecting and reinforcing white supremacy. See Pascoe, *What Comes Naturally*; Joshua D. Rothman, *Notorious in the Neighborhood: Sex and Families Across the Color Line in Virginia, 1787–1861* (Chapel Hill, 2003); Martha Hodes, ed., *Sex, Love, Race: Crossing Boundaries in North American History* (New York, 1999); and Martha Hodes, *White Women, Black Men: Illicit Sex in the 19th-Century South* (New Haven, 1997). A great deal of the work cited here is part of a move toward a more complex understanding of race, and race relations and the law both under slavery and in its aftermath.

Citizenship. It seems obvious to say that U.S. citizenship took shape in the long nineteenth century, but it is a point worth considering. Citizenship was not after all defined in the U.S. Constitution. Only over the course of the nineteenth century did citizenship acquire the weight we ascribe to it today. Since the late 1980s there has been a surge in scholarly interest in the history of citizenship. The sources of this renewed interest are many, but include such factors as the U.S. bicentennial, the end of the Cold War, the impending (and now past) end of a century in which the nation-state became the acknowledged foundation for rights, heightened anxiety over immigration in a postindustrial economy, and a focus on globalization. The outpouring of excellent work has come from virtually every field. For an introduction to citizenship studies, see Gershon Shafir, ed., *The Citizenship Debates: A Reader* (Minneapolis, 1998); and Bart van Steenbergen, ed., *The Condition of Citizenship* (Thousand Oaks, CA, 1994).

Key foundational considerations of citizenship that take in much or all of the long nineteenth century include Kerber, *No Constitutional Right to be Ladies*; Rogers M. Smith, *Civic Ideals: Conflicting Visions of Citizenship in U.S. History* (New Haven, 1997); Neuman, *Strangers to the Constitution*; and James H. Kettner, *The Development of American Citizenship, 1608–1870* (Chapel Hill, 1978). On the history of suffrage, see Alexander Keyssar, *The Right to Vote: The Contested History of Democracy in the United States* (New York, 2000) and Robert J. Steinfeld, "Property and Suffrage in the Early American Republic," *Stanford Law Review* 41 (1988–89): 335–76. (I note works relating to African American and woman suffrage later.) See also Linda Kerber's OAH Presidential Address, "The Meanings of American Citizenship," *Journal of American History* 94 (1997): 833–54. On the constitution and rights aspiration, see Hendrik Hartog, "The Constitution of Aspiration and 'The Rights That Belong to Us All,'" *Journal of American History* 74 (1987): 1013–34.

Military service was linked to citizenship from the nation's beginning. On this relationship, its implications for men as citizens, and the entitlements accorded to veterans from the Revolutionary War on, see Mark R. Wilson, "Law and the American State, from the Revolution to the Civil War: Institutional Growth and Structural Change," in *CHLA*, 2: 1–35; John Resch and Walter Sargent, eds., *War and Society in the American Revolution* (DeKalb, IL, 2007); Laura Jensen, *Patriots, Settlers, and the Origins of American Social Policy* (New York, 2003); Kerber, *No Constitutional Right to be Ladies*; Skocpol, *Protecting Soldiers and Mothers*; and James W. Oberly, *Sixty Million Acres: American Veterans and the Public Lands before the Civil War* (Kent, Ohio, 1990). Able white men's authority and shared identity as citizens was also critically shaped by other forms of compelled service to the community, including the posse comitatus, state militias, and, in the pre–Civil War South, slave patrols. On the posse comitatus, see Gautham Rao, "The Federal Posse Comitatus Doctrine: Slavery, Compulsion, and Statecraft in Mid-Nineteenth-Century America," *Law and History Review* 26 (2008): 1–56. On slave patrols see Sally E. Hadden, *Slave Patrols: Law and Violence in Virginia and the Carolinas* (Cambridge, MA, 2001).

Although "citizenship" is, as Linda Kerber notes, "an equalizing term," on closer inspection of the long nineteenth century it was not a guarantee of equal rights to even most of those who could claim its mantle; it served equally as a tool of exclusion and subordination. Up to the Civil War, the citizenship of free African Americans was at best questioned, at worst denied, and mostly irrelevant in providing protection against denials of employment, freedom of movement, or protecting basic civil rights such as jury service or voting. See Parker, "Making Blacks Foreign"; Smith, *Civic Ideals*; Kettner, *The Development of American Citizenship*; Litwack, *North of Slavery*; and Berlin, *Slaves Without Masters*. While those held in slavery could not hope to make claims based on citizenship, until the Supreme Court's decision in *Dred Scott*, the question of national citizenship for free blacks was not clear. On the *Dred Scott* case, in addition to Kettner and Smith, see Lea Vandervelde, *Mrs. Dred Scott: A Life on Slavery's Frontier* (New York, 2009) and her earlier article with Sandhya Subramanian, "Mrs. Dred Scott," *Yale Law Journal* 106 (1997): 1033–122; Graber, *Dred Scott and the Problem of Constitutional Evil*; Paul Finkelman, *Dred Scott v. Sandford: A Brief History with*

Documents (Boston, 1997); and Don E. Fehrenbacher, *The Dred Scott Case, Its Significance in American Law and Politics* (New York, 1978).

For women, the equation was different. No one questioned that they were citizens, but citizenship simply did not mean for them what it meant for men. Linda K. Kerber's pioneering study, *No Constitutional Rights to Be Ladies*, traces the gendered history of obligation in U.S. citizenship from the Revolutionary era through the twentieth century. On the gendered character of citizenship as conceived in the Revolutionary era, see also Carroll Smith-Rosenberg, "Discovering the Subject of the 'Great Constitutional Discussion,' 1786–1789," *Journal of American History* 79 (1992): 841–73; and Joan R. Gunderson, "Independence, Citizenship and the American Revolution," and Ruth Bloch, "The Gendered Meanings of Virtue in Revolutionary America," both in *Signs: Journal of Women in Culture and Society* 13 (1987): 37–58, 59–77. Critical theoretical considerations that similarly highlight the subordinate character of women's citizenship include Fraser and Gordon, "Civil Citizenship against Social Citizenship"; and Pateman, *The Sexual Contract*.

Whereas men did not risk losing their citizenship through marriage, women did. On this point, in addition to Kerber, *No Constitutional Right to be Ladies*, see Gardner, *The Qualities of a Citizen*; Leti Volpp, "Divesting Citizenship: On Asian American History and the Loss of Citizenship Through Marriage," *UCLA Law Review* 53 (2005): 405–83; Cott, *Public Vows*; Candace Lewis Bredbenner, *A Nationality of Her Own: Women, Marriage, and the Law of Citizenship* (Berkeley, 1998); Nancy F. Cott, "Marriage and Women's Citizenship in the United States, 1830–1934," *American Historical Review* 103 (1998): 1440–74; and Nancy Isenberg, *Sex and Citizenship in Antebellum America* (Chapel Hill, 1998).

The Civil War transformed the equation, if not ultimately the substance, of citizenship for women, African Americans, and Americans more generally. Beginning with antislavery and the Constitution, see William M. Wiecek,

The Sources of Anti-Slavery Constitutionalism in America, 1760–1848 (Ithaca, 1977). On the constitutional impact of the Civil War, emancipation, the Civil Rights Act of 1866, and what are collectively referred to the Reconstruction Amendments (Thirteenth, Fourteenth, and Fifteenth Amendments), see Michael Vorenberg, *Final Freedom: The Civil War, the Abolition of Slavery, and the Thirteenth Amendment* (New York, 2001); William E. Nelson, *The Fourteenth Amendment: From Political Principle to Judicial Doctrine* (Cambridge, MA, 1988); Foner, "Rights and the Constitution in Black Life"; and Robert J. Kaczorowski, "To Begin the Nation Anew: Congress, Citizenship, and Civil Rights After the Civil War," *American Historical Review* 92 (1987): 45–68. Kaczorowski more fully elaborates this argument in *The Nationalization of Civil Rights: Constitutional Theory and Practice in a Racist Society, 1866–1883* (New York, 1987); and Harold M. Hyman and William M. Wiecek, *Equal Justice Under the Law: Constitutional Development 1835–1875* (New York, 1982). Bill Novak argues that it is only with the Fourteenth Amendment that citizenship became the "primary constitutional marker of access, status, privilege, and obligation." While I share Novak's sense of the importance of the Reconstruction Amendments and especially the Fourteenth Amendment in shaping citizenship in the twentieth century, understanding the very real limitations of the Fourteenth Amendment in its language and in practice through much of the twentieth century requires giving greater consideration to the Revolutionary Era framing of citizenship, the significance of citizenship for property ownership before and after the Civil War, and, most importantly, state and local law relating to personhood. See William J. Novak, "The Legal Transformation of Citizenship in Nineteenth-Century America," in Meg Jacobs, William J. Novak, and Julian Zelizer, eds., *The Democratic Experiment: New Directions in American Political History* (Princeton, 2003), 85–119.

Whatever their promise, the Supreme Court's interpretation of the Thirteenth, Fourteenth, and Fifteenth Amendments in the quarter century following their adoption rendered their promise largely hollow for racialized others, including African Americans, as well as for women and disabled persons. For work discussing specific cases, see the following: On the Slaughterhouse cases, see Ronald M. Labbé and Jonathan Lurie, *The Slaughterhouse Cases: Regulation, Reconstruction, and the Fourteenth Amendment* (Lawrence, 2003); and Michael A. Ross, *Justice of Shattered Dreams: Samuel Freeman Miller and the Supreme Court During the Civil War Era* (Baton Rouge, 2003). On *Plessy*, Rebecca J. Scott, "Public Rights, Social Equality, and the Conceptual Roots of the *Plessy* Challenge," *Michigan Law Review* 106 (2008): 777–804; Welke, *Recasting American Liberty*; and Lofgren, *The Plessy Case* offer good starting points. On black disfranchisement despite the Fifteenth Amendment, see Keyssar, *The Right to Vote*; Michael Perman, *Struggle for Mastery: Disfranchisement in the South, 1888–1908* (Chapel Hill, 2001); and J. Morgan Kousser, *The Shaping of Southern Politics: Suffrage Restriction and the Establishment of the One-Party South, 1880–1910* (New Haven, 1974). Only for Chinese Americans did the birthright citizenship clause of the Fourteenth Amendment assure the limited protection of citizenship and only for those Chinese born in the United States. On the Supreme Court's decision in Wong Kim Ark, see Erika Lee, "Birthright Citizenship, Immigration, and the U.S. Constitution: The Story of *United States v. Wong Kim Ark*," in *Race Law Stories*; and Salyer, *Laws Harsh as Tigers*. On the limits of that protection, in addition to the above, see Ngai, *Impossible Subjects*; Volpp, "'Obnoxious to Their very Nature': Asian Americans and Constitutional Citizenship"; and Lisa Lowe, *Immigrant Acts: On Asian American Cultural Politics* (Durham, 1996).

On the Fourteenth Amendment's failure as a source of protection for the rights of disabled persons, including legalized sterilization, see Largent, *Breeding Contempt*; Stern, *Faults and Frontiers of Better Breeding in Modern America*; Kline, *Building a Better Race*; Edward J. Larson, *Sex, Race, and Science: Eugenics in the Deep South* (Baltimore, 1995); Reilly, *The Surgical Solution*; and Marcia Pearce Burgdorf and

Robert Burgdorf, Jr., "A History of Unequal Treatment: The Qualifications of Handicapped Persons As A 'Suspect Class' Under the Equal Protection Clause," *Santa Clara Lawyer* 15 (1975): 855–910.

On the Reconstruction Amendments and women's suffrage, see Gretchen Ritter, *The Constitution as Social Design: Gender and Civic Membership in the American Constitutional Order* (Stanford, 2006); Ellen Carol DuBois, "Outgrowing the Compact of the Fathers: Equal Rights, Woman Suffrage, and the United States Constitution, 1820–1878"; and "Taking the Law into Our Own Hands: *Bradwell, Minor,* and Suffrage Militance in the 1870s," both reprinted in DuBois, *Woman Suffrage and Women's Rights,* 81–113, 114–138. Ritter's principle focus is on the relationship between gender and civic membership from the adoption of the Nineteenth Amendment through the 1960s and 1970s. But she opens the book with Reconstruction and offers a compelling interpretation of the Supreme Court's simultaneous consideration of *Slaughterhouse* and *Bradwell* – the first two cases interpreting the Privileges and Immunities Clause of the Fourteenth Amendment. One of the important elements of her argument is tracing the significance of federalism as a vehicle for sustaining coverture, thus perpetuating women's subordinate status even as they acquired some elements of legal personhood over the course of the twentieth century. On the movement to secure woman suffrage more generally, see DuBois, *The Elizabeth Cady Stanton ~ Susan B. Anthony Reader: Correspondence, Writings, Speeches* (Boston, 1992); Paula Baker, "The Domestication of Politics: Women and American Political Society, 1789–1920," *American Historical Review* 89 (1984): 620–47; Ellen Carol DuBois, *Feminism and Suffrage: The Emergence of an Independent Women's Movement in America, 1848–1869* (Ithaca, 1978); Eleanor Flexnor, *Century of Struggle: The Woman's Rights Movement in the United States,* rev. ed. (Cambridge, MA, 1975). On the independent battle women had to wage to secure the right to serve on juries on the same basis as men, see Gretchen Ritter, "Jury Service and Women's Citizenship Before and After the Nineteenth Amendment," *Law and History Review* 20 (2002): 479–516; and Kerber, *No Constitutional Right to be Ladies.* The Nineteenth Amendment granted women a voice in the polity; it did not accord them full legal personhood – recognition that even today remains incomplete. On this point, see Ritter, *The Constitution as Social Design*; Reva B. Siegel, "She The People: The Nineteenth Amendment, Sex Equality, Federalism, and the Family," *Harvard Law Review* 115 (2001–2002): 947–1046; and Kerber, *No Constitutional Right to Be Ladies.*

Mexican American, African American, and Native American women who suddenly found themselves citizens through territorial incorporation, emancipation, or allotment learned that U.S. citizenship could mean a loss of rights as they became subject to coverture, the primary determinant of women's legal status. See Montoya, *Translating Property*; Cott, *Public Vows*; Stanley, *From Bondage to Contract*; Katherine Franke, "Becoming a Citizen: Reconstruction Era Regulation of African American Marriages," *Yale Journal of Law and Humanities* 11 (1999): 251–309; and Wendy Wall, "Gender and the Citizen Indian," in *Writing the Range: Race, Class, and Culture in the Women's West*, Eds. Elizabeth Jameson and Susan Armitage (Norman, OK, 1997), 202–29.

In the shadow of Reconstruction the limits on who had an opportunity to become a citizen tightened, through interpretation of the naturalization law and through new and increasingly stringent restrictions on immigration beginning with the Page Act (1875) and continuing through the National Origins Act (1924). Again, I recommend Zolberg, *A Nation by Design*, as the starting point for any consideration of immigration control in the United States. On the pre-Reconstruction era regulation of immigration and its relevance for thinking about immigration restriction in the long nineteenth century in particular, see Parker "Citizenship and Immigration Law, 1800–1924," as well as Forum: "Citizenship as Refusal. 'Outing' the Nation of Immigrants," *Law and History Review* 19 (2001): 583–660;

Neuman, *Strangers to the Constitution* and the article in which he first traced these arguments: Neuman, "The Lost Century of American Immigration Law, 1776–1875."

Especially important work for tracing the broad arc of immigration restriction in the late nineteenth and twentieth century and its contributions to the development of the administrative state are Ngai, *Impossible Subjects*; Torpey, *The Invention of the Passport*; and Salyer, *Laws Harsh as Tigers*. Other key works to consider focusing on restrictions on Chinese, Japanese, and other Asian immigration, include Lee, *At America's Gates*; Robert Chang, *Disoriented: Asian Americans, Law, and the Nation State* (New York, 1999); and Sucheng Chan, ed., *Entry Denied: Exclusion and the Chinese Community in America, 1882–1943* (Philadelphia, 1994). Higham's *Strangers in the Land* addressing American nativism remains an important account. On restriction of immigration on grounds of disability, see Baynton, "Defectives in the Land." As Baynton argues, the discourses of disability and ethnicity were deeply intertwined. See also in this regard Amy L. Fairchild, *Science at the Borders: Immigrant Medical Inspection and the Shaping of the Modern Industrial Labor Force* (Baltimore, 2003); Nayan Shah, *Contagious Divides: Epidemics and Race in San Francisco's Chinatown* (Berkeley, 2001); and Alan M. Kraut, *Silent Travelers: Germs, Genes, and the Immigrant Menace* (Baltimore, 1994). Baynton's article was published in a Forum titled "Disability and Immigration Policy," 24 *Journal of American Ethnic History* (2005): 31–69. On naturalization, see Lopez, *White by Law* and John Tehranian, "Performing Whiteness: Naturalization Litigation and the Construction of Racial Identity in America," *Yale Law Journal* 109 (2000): 817–48. On the Supreme Court's decision in *Ozawa v. United States*, see Devon W. Carbado's, "Yellow by Law: The Story of *Ozawa v. United States*," in *Race Law Stories*.

Native Americans' relationship to the United States is productively thought of in a long-term context of nation and empire that includes the overseas expansion at the end of the nineteenth century. Through the long nineteenth century, sovereignty, not U.S. citizenship, was the first goal of most American Indian tribes. On borders and sovereignty good starting points for reading include Ostler, *The Plains Sioux and U.S. Colonialism*; Wilkins and Lomawaima, *Uneven Ground*; and Vine Deloria, Jr. and David E. Wilkins, *Tribes, Treaties, and Constitutional Tribulations* (Austin, 1999). On Native Americans and citizenship, see Bartholomew H. Sparrow, "Empires External and Internal: Territories, Government Lands, and Federalism in the United States," in *The Louisiana Purchase and American Expansion*, 231–49; and Kevin Bruyneel, "Challenging American Boundaries: Indigenous People and the 'Gift' of U.S. Citizenship," *Studies in American Political Development* 18 (2004): 130–43. On empire, citizenship, and state-building at the end of the nineteenth century, see the essays in Alfred W. McCoy and Francisco A. Scarano, eds., *Colonial Crucible: Empire in the Making of the Modern American State* (Madison, 2009), including Burnett, "Empire and the Transformation of Citizenship," 332–41; Sam Erman, "Meanings of Citizenship in the U.S. Empire: Puerto Rico, Isabel Gonzalez, and the Supreme Court, 1898–1905," *Journal of American Ethnic History* 27 (2008): 5–33; Christina Duffy Burnett, "'They say I am not an American ...': The Noncitizen National and the Law of American Empire," *Virginia Journal of International Law* 48 (2007–2008): 659–718; Ngai, *Impossible Subjects*; Burnett and Marshall, eds., *Foreign in a Domestic Sense*; Merry, *Colonizing Hawaii*; Smith, *Civic Values*; Juan R. Torruella, *The Supreme Court and Puerto Rico: The Doctrine of Separate and Unequal* (Rio Piedras, P.R., 1988); and José A. Cabranes, *Citizenship and the American Empire* (New Haven, 1979).

Finally, on the census, belonging, and citizenship, see Naomi Mezey, "Erasure and Recognition: The Census, Race, and the National Imagination," *Northwestern Law Review* 97 (2003): 1701–68; Melissa Nobles, *Shades of Citizenship: Race and the Census in Modern Politics* (Stanford, 2000); and Margo J. Anderson, *The American Census: A Social History* (New Haven, 1988).

Part II

At least since Joan Kelly's pioneering essay, "Did Women Have a Renaissance?", reprinted in Joan Kelly, *Women, History, and Theory: The Essays of Joan Kelly* (Chicago, 1984), we have known to be wary of unquestioning acceptance of the historical turning points we inherit. Kelly's work directly inspired U.S. women's historians to question whether the American Revolution was a revolution for women. Applying Kelly's observation to the question of legal personhood in the long nineteenth century makes work that chronologically bridges acknowledged/accepted turning points especially important. Equally important is juxtaposing topics that share a historical moment, but that are generally written about by historians working in different subfields. I provide recommendations for both kinds of reading, focusing on four chronological moments: the Revolutionary Era; the Age of Jackson; the Civil War and Reconstruction; and Redemption, Empire, and the Progressive State. I have limited myself to a few suggested readings in each case, most of which are also included in Part I of this essay – my focus here is primarily to capture an approach to reading.

Revolutionary Era. Works that take as their specific focus the preservation of white male privilege in the Revolution and the Constitutional framework are less common than works that mark that privilege by highlighting the exclusion or subordination of a particular category of other. For work in the first category, see Mann, *Republic of Debtors*; and Nedelsky, *Private Property and the Limits of American Constitutionalism*. Willi Paul Adams, *The First American Constitutions: Republican Ideology and the Making of the State Constitutions in the Revolutionary Era* (New York, 2001), originally written in German and translated into English in 1973, is especially useful in analyzing the state constitutions that were written immediately preceding or following the Declaration of Independence and that served in key respects as a template for the U.S. Constitution. Among other topics, Adams specifically addresses revolutionary understandings of property, property requirements for suffrage and their impact on the scope of the electorate, and slavery. For the texts of the original state constitutions, see Francis Newton Thorpe, ed. and comp., *The Federal and State Constitutions, Colonial Charters, and Other Organic Laws of the States, Territories, and Colonies Now or Heretofore Forming the United States of America*, 7 vols. (Washington, 1909).

The following are especially helpful in exploring the way in which gendered assumptions of women's dependence provided a critical foundation for situating men as independent: Kerber, *No Constitutional Right to Be Ladies* (ch 1); Kerber, *Women of the Republic*; Smith-Rosenberg, "Discovering the Subject of the 'Great Constitutional Discussion'"; Gunderson, "Independence, Citizenship and the American Revolution"; and Bloch, "The Gendered Meanings of Virtue in Revolutionary America." Ulrich, *A Midwife's Tale*, although not a work of legal history, captures the continuities in women's legal status and lives across the Revolutionary era. On what Ruth Bloch calls the Revolution's "delegitimation of government intervention" in the "'private' family," and its effect in giving husbands greater legal license to beat their wives, see Bloch, "The American Revolution, Wife Beating, and the Emergent Value of Privacy."

Nor was the Revolution the revolution that historians once thought it to be for African Americans. As Mark Graber argues in *Dred Scott and the Problem of Constitutional Evil*, slavery was not just present at, but fundamental to, the creation and constitutional structure of the new nation. On African Americans and the Revolution, see, for example, Nash, *The Forgotten Fifth*; and Ira Berlin and Ronald Hoffman, eds., *Slavery and Freedom in the Age of the American Revolution* (Charlottesville, 1983). Work on the Revolutionary Era and the period after that reevaluates the economic role of slavery in northern states, highlights the slow pace of emancipation there, and considers the consequences of both factors for African Americans and for whites' conceptions of African Americans as rights-bearing people, and is essential for seeing the borders of belonging. See, in particular, Gellman,

Emancipating New York; Gellman and Quigley, *Jim Crow New York*; Berlin, *Many Thousands Gone*; Melish, *Disowning Slavery*; and Fields, *Slavery and Freedom in the Middle Ground*. On the law of slavery in the South and the impact of the Revolution, see Morris, *Southern Slavery and the Law*. Robin L. Einhorn's *American Taxation, American Slavery* (Chicago, 2006) traces the origins of limited government or antigovernment rhetoric to slaveholders and highlights its operation in fundamentally shaping tax policy from the colonial era through the Revolution and Civil War, with a lasting legacy to the present. John Sweet's rich study of Rhode Island, *Bodies Politic*, from the 1730s through the years of the Early Republic is rare in incorporating both Native Americans and African Americans to highlight how men in each group were excluded from citizenship and belonging in the new nation.

The shift to reason as the foundation for consent, the centrality of children to this rethinking, and then the use of children as an example to exclude others, including women and African Americans, on the grounds that they too lacked the capacity to reason required in a government based on reasoned consent is powerfully traced in Brewer, *By Birth or Consent*.

Age of Jackson. The "Age of Jackson" is not, as Robin Einhorn puts it so succinctly in *American Taxation, American Slavery*, "what it used to be" (201). The expansion of white male suffrage takes on a less democratic cast when read against Indian removal and the narrowing of suffrage for women and African Americans in the North, and the creation of the asylum, removing the feebleminded and other unproductive individuals from society. On African Americans in the Jacksonian era, see Morris, *The Southern Law of Slavery*; Litwack, *North of Slavery*; and Berlin, *Slaves Without Masters*. On the legal contest over and ramifications of Indian removal, see Miles, *Ties that Bind*; Garrison, *The Legal Ideology of Removal*; and Norgren, *The Cherokee Cases*. On the expansion of suffrage in the Jacksonian era and its very real limits, see Keyssar, *The Right to Vote*; and Steinfeld, "Property and Suffrage in the Early

American Republic." On the creation of the asylum and the
speed with which asylums became institutions for segregating the fit from the unfit, see Ferguson, *Abandoned to Their
Fate*; Trent, *Inventing the Feeble Mind*; and Rothman, *The
Discovery of the Asylum.*

On women's activism in the abolitionist and other social
movements of the early nineteenth century and their foundation for the first women's movement, see Sánchez-Eppler,
Touching Liberty; Yellin, *Women and Sisters*; DuBois, *The
Elizabeth Cady Stanton ~ Susan B. Anthony Reader*; Nancy
Hewitt, *Women's Activism and Social Change: Rochester,
New York, 1822–1872* (Ithaca, 1984); and DuBois, *Feminism
and Suffrage*. On women's pursuit of child custody and the
creation of a judicial patriarchy, see Grossberg, *A Judgment
for Solomon*; and Grossberg, *Governing the Hearth.*

The threat to mastery though was not just from women
and racialized others; industrial transformation played a key
role in limiting white men's independence even as it was pro-
claimed by the doctrine of "free labor." Key works on the legal
construction of "free labor" include Tomlins, *Law, Labor and
Ideology*; and Steinfeld, *The Invention of Free Labor.*

The Civil War and Reconstruction. In reconsidering the
Civil War as a turning point, it is important to look beyond
the South and slavery to other subject groups, including,
among others, women generally and Native Americans.
The Civil War does not merit an index entry in Michael
Grossberg's path-breaking study of family law, *Governing the
Hearth*. Grossberg's carefully crafted heading, "Americans
Fashion Racial Restrictions," in a chapter on "Matrimonial
Limitations" is broad enough to take in antebellum prohi-
bitions on slave marriage and postbellum miscegenation
laws. See also in this regard Cott, *Public Vows*; Ostler, *The
Plains Sioux and U.S. Colonialism*; and Peter W. Bardaglio,
*Reconstructing the Household: Families, Sex, and the Law
in the Nineteenth-Century South* (Chapel Hill, 1995).

Emancipation itself reads differently paired with the
Homestead Act and the criminalization of abortion. The literatures here are uneven, from the overwhelming scholarship

on the Civil War and emancipation, to the smaller but sophisticated literature on the history of abortion regulation, to
a relative dearth of scholarship on the Homestead Act. As
starting points on emancipation and Reconstruction, see
Hahn, *A Nation Under Our Feet*; Foner, *Reconstruction*;
and Litwack, *Been in the Storm So Long*. On the limits of
free labor for freedmen and freedwomen, in addition to the
above, see Glenn, *Unequal Freedom*; Stanley, *From Bondage
to Contract*; and Kerber, *No Constitutional Right to be
Ladies*. And on the mixed freedom of marriage for freedmen and freedwomen, see especially Franke, "Becoming a
Citizen"; Stanley, *From Bondage to Contract*; and Cott,
Public Vows. On abortion, see Reagan, *When Abortion Was a
Crime*; Gordon, *Woman's Body, Woman's Right*; and Mohr,
Abortion in America. And on the Homestead Act, see the
brief coverage of the Act provided in Lawrence M. Friedman,
A History of American Law, 2ⁿᵈ ed. (New York, 1985).

On the Civil War as a catalyst in the transformation
of global capitalism and the role of the imperial state in
extracting labor in its service, see Beckert, "Emancipation
and Empire: Reconstructing the Worldwide Web of Cotton
Production in the Age of the American Civil War."

Redemption, Empire, and the Progressive State. Possibly
no historical moment has undergone more dramatic historical recent reinterpretation than the final quarter of the
nineteenth century and the dawning of the twentieth. From
a time when respectable historians could and did portray
Redemption, Jim Crow, and black disfranchisement as positive developments – routing out corruption (Redemption),
restoring the proper balance of things (disfranchisement), and
protecting the rights of all (separate but equal), the southern
solution to the race question came to be seen as distinctly
undemocratic, a turning away from the promise of the Civil
War and Reconstruction. Even in this interpretation though
the South remained cut off from the nation; the North's only
responsibility was in losing interest. Yet even Woodward's
Strange Career of Jim Crow argued that the Southern solution to the race question was made possible by a broader

rethinking of race in the context of western expansion and empire. Added to this, more recent work has suggested that the southern solution to the race question was not backward looking, but in fact was distinctly modern. Yet even here race remains separate. And, as importantly, the literature of the Progressive Era has remained largely separate from literature on the South and on Western expansion. Incorporating race into a broader picture and reading across a periodization that divides at the Progressive Era to include topics ranging from Redemption, Jim Crow, and black disfranchisement; to the proliferation of miscegenation laws; to allotment and consolidation of white land ownership in the West more generally; to immigration restriction on grounds of race and disability; to the criminalization of birth control and adoption of protective labor legislation; to empire; to forced sterilization of the unfit; is critical not simply for seeing the terms of legal personhood and citizenship at the end of the nineteenth century and the beginning of the twentieth but also for seeing how the safeguarding of the borders of belonging fundamentally gave shape to the twentieth century American state.

On the legal aspects of Redemption and their implications for African American freedom in the South, see Foner, "The Politics of Freedom," in Foner, *Nothing But Freedom*, 39–73. On Jim Crow, see Welke, *Recasting American Liberty*; Rabinowitz, *Race Relations in the Urban South, 1865–1890*; and Woodward, *The Strange Career of Jim Crow*. On disfranchisement, see Keyssar, *The Right to Vote*; Perman, *Struggle for Mastery*; Gilmore, *Gender and Jim Crow*; and Kousser, *The Shaping of Southern Politics*. On the central role miscegenation laws played in reinforcing white supremacy, not simply in the South but throughout the nation, see Pascoe, *What Comes Naturally*. On the criminalization of birth control, see Mohr, *Abortion in America*; Gordon, *Woman's Body, Woman's Right*; and Smith-Rosenberg, *Disorderly Conduct*, 217–44.

Incursions on working-class white men's independence at the end of the nineteenth and early twentieth centuries, as in the Jacksonian era, made the borders of legal personhood relating to race and gender all the more fundamental. See Frank Tobias Higbie, *Indispensable Outcasts: Hobo Workers and Community in the American Midwest, 1880–1930* (Champaign, 2003); Willrich, *City of Courts*; Michael Willrich, "Home Slackers: Men, the State, and Welfare in Modern America," *Journal of American History* 87 (2000): 460–89; and Stanley, *From Bondage to Contract*. On the development of the two-channel welfare state, see Igra, *Wives without Husbands*; Witt, *The Accidental Republic*; Gordon, *Pitied But Not Entitled*; and Gordon, ed., *Women, the State, and Welfare*. For her argument on how white women were imagined as wives and mothers and white men imagined as workers and the imbedding of this "gendered imagination" in American law and policy from the Progressive Era on, see Kessler-Harris, *In Pursuit of Equity*. On protective labor legislation more generally, see Woloch, *Muller v. Oregon*; Baer, *Justice in Chains*; William E. Forbath, *Law and the Shaping of the American Labor Movement* (Cambridge, MA, 1989).

On spatial boundaries, belonging, and the nation, see Zolberg, *A Nation by Design*; Ngai, *Impossible Subjects*; Lee, *At America's Gates*; Salyer, *Laws Harsh as Tigers*; and Sucheng Chan, "Exclusion of Chinese Women," in Chan, ed., *Entry Denied* on the Chinese Exclusion Act and related legislation. On allotment, see Chang, *The Color of the Land*; Miles, *Ties that Bind*; Emily Greenwald, *Reconfiguring the Reservation*; McDowell, *The Dispossession of the American Indian*; and Hoxie, *A Final Promise*. On the consolidation of white land ownership in the West more generally, see Peck, *Reinventing Free Labor*; Glenn, *Unequal Freedom*; Montoya, *Translating Property*; and Gordon, *The Great Arizona Orphan Abduction*. On property exclusions based on race, see Loewen, *Sundown Towns*; and Delaney, *Race, Place, and the Law*. Paralleling these exclusions was yet another: the legal marking of the mentally and physically disabled as so unremedially beyond the borders of belonging, so dangerous to the body politic that they could be excluded from immigrating, segregated from society, barred from marrying, and surgically prevented from reproducing.

The legal crackdown on the disabled at the turn of the century was breathtaking in its severity and haunting in its implications. See in this regard, Schweik, *The Ugly Laws*; Largent, *Breeding Contempt*; Bayton, "Defectives in the Land"; Ferguson, *Abandoned to Their Fate*; and Douglas C. Baynton, *Forbidden Signs: American Culture and the Campaign Against Sign Language* (Chicago, 1996). On legal aspects of empire, see Sparrow, *The Insular Cases*; Levinson and Sparrow eds., *The Louisiana Purchase and American Expansion*; Ngai, *Impossible Subjects*; Merry, *Colonizing Hawaii*; Burnett and Marshall, eds., *Foreign in a Domestic Sense*; Smith, *Civic Ideals*; and Cabranes, *Citizenship and the American Empire*.

It is also important to think across key "expansions" of citizenship in this period for the more complicated understanding of "inclusion" that reading them collectively presents, including the Jones Act (Puerto Rican citizenship), the Nineteenth Amendment (1920, woman suffrage), and the Indian Citizenship Act (1924). On woman suffrage, consider Gilmore, *Gender and Jim Crow*; DuBois, *Woman Suffrage and Women's Rights*; Baker, "The Domestication of Politics"; and Flexnor, *Century of Struggle*. On the impact of the Nineteenth Amendment on jury service, coverture and voting for women, see Ritter, *The Constitution as Social Design*; Ritter, "Jury Service and Women's Citizenship"; and Kerber, *No Constitutional Right to Be Ladies*. On the Indian Citizenship Act and the Jones Act, see Bruyneel, "Challenging American Boundaries"; and Smith, *Civic Ideals*; and David Healy, *Drive to Hegemony: The United States in the Caribbean, 1898–1917* (Madison, 1988). Finally, on key naturalization cases that narrowed the meaning of the word "white" in the act and the tightening of immigration restriction both in the 1920s, see Ngai, *Impossible Subjects*; and Lopez, *White By Law*.

ALPHABETICAL BIBLIOGRAPHY

Adams, Willi Paul. *The First American Constitutions: Republican Ideology and the Making of the State Constitutions in the Revolutionary Era.* New York, 2001.

Allen, James, Hilton Als, Congressman John Lewis, and Leon F. Litwack. *Without Sanctuary: Lynching Photography in America.* Santa Fe, 2000.

Anderson, Margo J. *The American Census: A Social History.* New Haven, 1988.

Avery, Dianne and Alfred S. Konefsky. "The Daughters of Job: Property Rights and Women's Lives in Mid-Nineteenth-Century Massachusetts." *Law and History Review* 10 (1992): 323–56.

Ayers, Edward L. *Vengeance and Justice: Crime and Punishment in the Nineteenth-Century American South.* New York, 1984.

Baer, Judith. *The Chains of Protection: The Judicial Response to Women's Labor Legislation.* Westport, CT, 1978.

Baker, Paula. "The Domestication of Politics: Women and American Political Society, 1789–1920." *American Historical Review* 89 (1984): 620–47.

Banner, Stuart. *How the Indians Lost Their Land: Law and Power on the Frontier.* Cambridge, MA, 2005.

Bardaglio, Peter W. *Reconstructing the Household: Families, Sex, and the Law in the Nineteenth-Century South.* Chapel Hill, 1995.

Basch, Norma. "Marriage and Domestic Relations." In *The Cambridge History of Law in America, 3 vol.* Eds. Michael Grossberg and Christopher Tomlins. New York, 2008. 2:245–79.

Framing American Divorce: From the Revolutionary Generation to the Victorians. Berkeley, 1999.

In the Eyes of the Law: Women, Marriage, and Property in Nineteenth-Century New York. Ithaca, NY, 1982.

Baynton, Douglas C. "Disability and Immigration Policy." *Journal of American Ethnic History* 24 (2005): 31–69.

"Defectives in the Land: Disability and American Immigration Policy, 1882–1924." *Journal of American Ethnic History* 24 (2005): 31–44.

"Disability and the Justification of Inequality in American History." In *The New Disability History: American Perspectives*. Eds. Paul K. Longmore and Lauri Umansky. New York, 2001. 33–57.

Forbidden Signs: American Culture and the Campaign Against Sign Language. Chicago, 1996.

Beckert, Sven. "Emancipation and Empire: Reconstructing the Worldwide Web of Cotton Production in the Age of the American Civil War." *American Historical Review* 109 (2004): 1405–38.

Bederman, Gail. *Manliness and Civilization: A Cultural History of Gender and Race in the United States, 1880–1917*. Chicago, 1995.

Berlin, Ira. *Many Thousands Gone: The First Two Centuries of Slavery in North America*. Cambridge, MA, 1998.

Berlin, Ira, et al, eds. *Freedom: A Documentary History of Emancipation, 4 vols*. New York, 1982–1994.

Barbara J. Fields, Steven F. Miller, Joseph P. Reidy, Leslie S. Rowland, eds. *Free at Last: A Documentary History of Slavery, Freedom, and the Civil War*. New York, 1992.

Slaves Without Masters: The Free Negro in the Antebellum South. 1976; New York, 1992.

and Ronald Hoffman, eds. *Slavery and Freedom in the Age of the American Revolution*. Charlottesville, 1983.

Bilder, Mary Sarah. "The Struggle Over Immigration: Indentured Servants, Slaves, and Articles of Commerce." *Missouri Law Review* 61 (1996): 743–824.

Blackstone, William. *Commentaries on the Laws of England, 4 vols*. 1765–69. Reprint, Chicago, 1979.

Bloch, Ruth H. "The American Revolution, Wife Beating, and the Emergent Value of Privacy." *Early American Studies* 5 (2007): 223–51.

"The Gendered Meanings of Virtue in Revolutionary America." *Signs: Journal of Women in Culture and Society* 13 (1987): 37–58.

Blumenthal, Susanna L. "The Mind of a Moral Agent: Scottish Common Sense and the Problem of Responsibility in Nineteenth-Century American Law." *Law and History Review* 26 (2008): 99–159.

"The Default Legal Person." *UCLA Law Review* 54 (2007): 1135–1265.

"The Deviance of the Will: Policing the Bounds of Testamentary Freedom in Nineteenth-Century America." *Harvard Law Review* 119 (2006): 959–1035.

Boydston, Jeanne Boydston. *Home and Work: Housework, Wages, and the Ideology of Labor in the Early Republic*. New York, 1990.

Bredbenner, Candace Lewis. *A Nationality of Her Own: Women, Marriage, and the Law of Citizenship*. Berkeley, 1998.

Brewer, Holly. "The Transformation of Domestic Law." In *The Cambridge History of American Law, 3 vols*. Eds. Michael Grossberg and Christopher Tomlins. New York, 2008. 1: 288–323.

By Birth or Consent: Children, Law, and the Anglo-American Revolution in Authority. Chapel Hill, 2005.

Briggs, Laura. *Reproducing Empire: Race, Sex, Science, and U. S. Imperialism in Puerto Rico*. Berkeley, 2003.

Brophy, Alfred L. *Reconstructing the Dreamland: The Tulsa Riot of 1921: Race, Reparations, and Reconciliation*. New York, 2002.

Brown, Elizabeth Gaspar, in consultation with William Wirt Blume. *British Statutes in American Law, 1776–1836*. Ann Arbor, 1964.

Brown, Richard Maxwell. *No Duty to Retreat: Violence and Values in American History*. New York, 1991.

Brundage, W. Fitzhugh. *Lynching in the New South, Georgia, and Virginia, 1880–1930*. Urbana, 1993.

Bruyneel, Kevin. "Challenging American Boundaries: Indigenous People and the 'Gift' of U. S. Citizenship." *Studies in American Political Development* 18 (2004): 130–43.

Burgdorf, Marcia Pearce and Robert Burgdorf, Jr. "A History of Unequal Treatment: The Qualifications Of Handicapped Persons As A 'Suspect Class' Under the Equal Protection Clause." *Santa Clara Lawyer* 15 (1975): 855–910.

Burke, Joseph C. "The Cherokee Cases: A Study in Law, Politics, and Morality." *Stanford Law Review* 21 (1969): 500–31.

Burnett, Christina Duffy and Burke Marshall, eds. *Foreign in a Domestic Sense: Puerto Rico, American Expansion, and the Constitution*. Durham, 2001.

Burnett, Christina Duffy. " 'They say I am not an American …": The Noncitizen National and the Law of American Empire." *Virginia Journal of International Law* 48 (2007–2008): 659–718.

"Empire and the Transformation of Citizenship." In *Colonial Crucible: Empire in the Making of the Modern American*

State. Eds. Alfred W. McCoy and Francisco A. Scarano. New York, 2005. 332–41.

Cabranes, José A. *Citizenship and the American Empire*. New Haven, 1979.

Calavita, Kitty. "Law, Citizenship, and the Construction of (Some) Immigrant 'Others.'" *Law and Social Inquiry* 30 (2005): 401–20.

"The Paradoxes of Race, Class, Identity, and 'Passing': Enforcing the Chinese Exclusion Acts, 1882–1910." *Law and Social Inquiry* 25 (2000): 1–40.

Canaday, Margot. *The Straight State: Sexuality and Citizenship in Twentieth-Century America*. Princeton, 2009.

"Heterosexuality as a Legal Regime." In *The Cambridge History of Law in America, 3 vols*. Eds. Michael Grossberg and Christopher Tomlins. New York, 2008. 3: 442–71.

Carbado, Devon W. "Yellow by Law: The Story of *Ozawa v. United States*." In *Race Law Stories*. Eds. Rachel F. Moran and Devon W. Carbado. New York, 2008. 175–235.

"Racial Naturalization." In Legal Borderlands: Law and the Construction of American Borders. Eds. Mary L. Dudziak and Leti Volpp. *American Quarterly* 57 (2005): 633–58.

Carr, Raymond. *Puerto Rico: A Colonial Experiment*. New York, 1984.

Carrigan, William D. and Clive Webb. "The Lynching of Persons of Mexican Origin or Descent in the United States, 1848 to 1928." *Journal of Social History* 37 (2003): 411–38.

Carter, N. C. "Race and Power Politics as Aspects of Federal Guardianship over American Indians: Land-Related Cases, 1887–1924." *American Indian Law Journal* 4 (1976): 197–248.

Chan, Sucheng, ed. *Entry Denied: Exclusion and the Chinese Community in America, 1882–1943*. Philadelphia, 1994.

Chang, David A. *The Color of the Land: Race, Nation, and the Politics of Landownership in Oklahoma, 1866–1929*. Chapel Hill, 2010.

Chang, Robert S. *Disoriented: Asian Americans, Law, and the Nation State*. New York, 1999.

Chused, Richard H. "Late Nineteenth Century Married Women's Property Law: Reception of the Early Married Women's Property Acts by Courts and Legislatures." *American Journal of Legal History* 29 (1985): 3–35.

"Married Women's Property Law: 1800–1850." *Georgetown Law Journal* 71 (1983): 1359–1425.

Clark, Blue. *Lone Wolf v. Hitchcock: Treaty Rights and Indian Law at End of the Nineteenth Century*. Lincoln, NE, 1994.

Clark, Elizabeth B. "The Sacred Rights of the 'Weak': Pain, Sympathy, and the Culture of Individual Rights in Antebellum America." *Journal of American History* 82 (1995): 463–93.

"Matrimonial Bonds: Slavery and Divorce in Nineteenth-Century America." *Law and History Review* 8 (1990): 25–53.

"Self-Ownership and the Political Theory of Elizabeth Cady Stanton." *Connecticut Law Review* 21 (1989): 905–41.

Cohen, Felix S. *Handbook of Federal Indian Law*. Washington, DC, 1942.

Cole, Richard P. and Gabriel Chin. "Emerging from the Margins of Historical Consciousness: Chinese Immigrants and the History of American Law." *Law and History Review* 17 (1999): 325–64.

Cott, Nancy F. *Public Vows: A History of Marriage and the Nation*. Cambridge, MA, 2000.

"Marriage and Women's Citizenship in the United States, 1830–1934." *American Historical Review* 103 (1998): 1440–74.

"Giving Character to Our Whole Civil Polity: Marriage and the Public Order in the Late Nineteenth Century." In *U. S. History as Women's History*. Eds. Linda K. Kerber, Alice Kessler-Harris, Kathryn Kish Sklar. Chapel Hill, 1995. 107–121.

Crenshaw, Kimberlé, Neil Gotanda, Gary Peller, and Kendall Thomas, eds. *Critical Race Theory: The Key Writings that Formed the Movement*. New York, 1995.

Dailey, Jane. *Before Jim Crow: The Politics of Race in Postemancipation Virginia*. Chapel Hill, 2000.

Davis, David Brion. *Inhuman Bondage: The Rise and Fall of Slavery in the New World*. New York, 2006.

The Problem of Slavery in the Age of Revolution, 1770–1823, 2nd ed. New York, 1999.

Delaney, David. *Race, Place and the Law, 1836–1948*. Austin, 1998.

Delgado, Richard and Jean Stefancic, eds. *Critical Race Theory: The Cutting Edge*. Philadelphia, 2000.

Deloria, Jr., Vine and David E. Wilkins. *Tribes, Treaties, and Constitutional Tribulations*. Austin, 1999.

and Raymond J. DeMallie. *Documents of Indian Diplomacy: Treaties, Agreements, and Conventions, 1775–1979*, 2 vols. Norman, OK, 1999.

Dorr, Lisa Lindquist. *White Women, Rape, and the Power of Race in Virginia, 1900–1960*. Chapel Hill, 2004.

Douglass, Frederick. *Narrative of the Life of Frederick Douglass, An American Slave, Written by Himself*. 1845. Reprint, ed. David W. Blight. Boston, 1993.

Du Bois, W. E. B. *The Souls of Black Folk*. New York, 1903.

DuBois, Ellen Carol. *Woman Suffrage and Women's Rights*. New York, 1998.

The Elizabeth Cady Stanton ~ Susan B. Anthony Reader: Correspondence, Writings, Speeches. Boston, 1992.

Feminism and Suffrage: The Emergence of an Independent Women's Movement in America, 1848–1869. Ithaca, NY, 1978.

Dudziak, Mary L. and Leti Volpp, eds. Legal Borderlands: Law and the Construction of American Borders. *American Quarterly* 57 (2005).

Edwards, Laura F. *The People and Their Peace: Legal Culture and the Transformation of Inequality in the Post-Revolutionary South*. Chapel Hill, 2009.

Gendered Strife and Confusion: The Political Culture of Reconstruction. Urbana, 1997.

Einhorn, Robin L. *American Taxation, American Slavery*. Chicago, 2006.

Erman. Sam. "Meanings of Citizenship in the U. S. Empire: Puerto Rico, Isabel Gonzalez, and the Supreme Court, 1898 to 1905." *Journal of American Ethnic History* 27 (2008): 5–33.

Fairchild, Amy L. *Science at the Borders: Immigrant Medical Inspection and the Shaping of the Modern Industrial Labor Force*. Baltimore, 2003.

Fehrenbacher, Don E. *The Dred Scott Case, Its Significance in American Law and Politics*. New York, 1978.

Ferguson, Philip M. *Abandoned to Their Fate: Social Policy and Practice toward Severely Retarded People in America, 1820–1920*. Philadelphia, 1994.

Fields, Barbara Jeanne. *Slavery and Freedom in the Middle Ground: Maryland During the Nineteenth Century*. New Haven, 1985.

"Ideology and Race in American History." In *Region, Race, and Reconstruction: Essays in honor of C. Vann Woodward*. Eds. J. Morgan Kousser and James M. McPherson. New York, 1982. 143–77.

Finkelman, Paul. *Dred Scott v. Sandford: A Brief History with Documents*. Boston, 1997.

"Prelude to the Fourteenth Amendment: Black Legal Rights in the Antebellum North." *Rutgers Law Journal* 17 (1986): 415–82.

Flexnor, Eleanor. *Century of Struggle: The Woman's Rights Movement in the United States, rev. ed.* Cambridge, MA, 1975.

Foley, Neil. *The White Scourge: Mexicans, Blacks, and Poor Whites in Texas Cotton Culture*. Berkeley, 1998.

Foner, Eric. *Freedom's Lawmakers: A Directory of Black Office-holders During Reconstruction, rev. ed.* Baton Rouge, 1996.

"The Meaning of Freedom in the Age of Emancipation." *Journal of American History* 81 (1994): 435–60.

Reconstruction: America's Unfinished Revolution. New York, 1988.

"Rights and the Constitution in Black Life during the Civil War and Reconstruction." *Journal of American History* 74 (1987): 863–83.

Nothing But Freedom: Emancipation and Its Legacy. Baton Rouge, 1983. 39–73.

Forbath, William E. *Law and the Shaping of the American Labor Movement*. Cambridge, MA, 1989.

Forum. "Whiteness and Others: Mexican Americans and American Law." *Law and History Review* 21 (2003): 109–213.

"Citizenship as Refusal 'Outing' the Nation of Immigrants." *Law and History Review* 19 (2001): 583–660.

"Disability and Immigration Policy." *Journal of American Ethnic History* 24 (2005): 31–69.

Franke, Katherine. "Becoming a Citizen: Reconstruction Era Regulation of African American Marriages. *Yale Journal of Law and Humanities* 11 (1999): 251–309.

Fraser, Nancy and Linda Gordon. "Civil Citizenship against Social Citizenship?: On the Ideology of Contract-versus-Charity." In *The Condition of Citizenship*. Ed. Bart van Steenbergen. Thousand Oaks, CA, 1994. 90–107.

Unruly Practices: Power, Discourse and Gender in Contemporary Social Theory. Minneapolis, 1989.

Frederickson, George M. *The Black Image in the White Mind: The Debate on Afro-American Character and Destiny, 1817–1914*. New York, 1971.

Friedman, Lawrence M. *A History of American Law, 2nd ed.* New York, 1985.

Gardner, Martha. *The Qualities of a Citizen: Women, Immigration, and Citizenship, 1870–1965*. Princeton, 2005.

Garrison, Tim Allen. *The Legal Ideology of Removal: The Southern Judiciary and the Sovereignty of Native American Nations*. Athens, GA, 2003.

Gates, Henry Louis Jr., ed. and intro., coed. Donald Yacavone. *Lincoln on Race and Slavery*. Princeton, 2009.

Gellman, David N. *Emancipating New York: The Politics of Slavery and Freedom, 1777–1827*. New York, 2006.

Gellman, David N. and David Quigley. *Jim Crow New York: A Documentary History of Race and Citizenship, 1777–1877*. New York, 2003.

Gilmore, Glenda E. *Gender and Jim Crow: Women and the Politics of White Supremacy in North Carolina, 1896–1920*. Chapel Hill, 1996.

Glenn, Evelyn Nakano, *Unequal Freedom: How Race and Gender Shaped American Citizenship and Labor*. Cambridge, MA, 2002.

Glenn, Myra C. *Campaigns Against Corporal Punishment: Prisoners, Sailors, Women, and Children in Antebellum America*. Albany, 1984.

Gordon, Linda. *The Great Arizona Orphan Abduction*. Cambridge, MA, 1999.

Pitied But Not Entitled: Single Mothers and the History of Welfare. Cambridge, MA, 1994.

Woman's Body, Woman's Rights: Birth Control in America, rev. ed. New York, 1990.

ed. *Women, the State, and Welfare.* Madison, 1990.

Heroes of Their Own Lives: The Politics and History of Family Violence. New York, 1988.

Gotanda, Neil. "A Critique of 'Our Constitution is Color-Blind.'" *Stanford Law Review* 44 (1991): 1–68.

Graber, Mark A. *Dred Scott and the Problem of Constitutional Evil.* New York, 2006.

Greenwald, Emily. *Reconfiguring the Reservation: The Nez Perces, Jicarilla Apaches, and the Dawes Act.* Albuquerque, 2002.

Griswold, Robert L. Griswold. "The Evolution of the Doctrine of Mental Cruelty in Victorian American Divorce, 1790–1900." *Journal of Social History* 20 (1986): 127–48.

"Law, Sex, Cruelty and Divorce in Victorian America, 1840–1900." *American Quarterly* 38 (1986): 721–45.

Family and Divorce in California, 1850–1890. Albany, 1982.

Gross, Ariela J. *What Blood Won't Tell: A History of Race on Trial in America.* Cambridge, MA, 2009.

Double Character: Slavery and Mastery in the Antebellum Southern Courtroom. Princeton, 2000.

Grossberg, Michael. *A Judgment for Solomon: The D'Hauteville Case and Legal Experience in Antebellum America.* New York, 1996.

"Institutionalizing Masculinity: The Law as a Masculine Profession." In *Meanings for Manhood: Constructions of Masculinity in Victorian America.* Eds. Mark C. Carnes and Clyde Griffen. Chicago, 1990. 133–51.

Governing the Hearth: Law and the Family in Nineteenth-Century America. Chapel Hill, 1985.

Grossberg, Michael and Christopher Tomlins, eds. *The Cambridge History of Law in America, 3 vols.* New York, 2008.

Guglielmo, Thomas A. *White on Arrival: Italians, Race, Color, and Power in Chicago, 1890–1945.* New York, 2003.

Gunderson, Joan R. "Independence, Citizenship and the American Revolution." *Signs: Journal of Women in Culture* 13 (1987): 59–77.

Gutíerrez, David. *Walls and Mirrors: Mexican Americans, Mexican Immigrants, and the Politics of Ethnicity.* Berkeley, 1995.

Hadden, Sally E. *Slave Patrols: Law and Violence in Virginia and the Carolinas.* Cambridge, MA, 2001.

Hahn, Steven. *A Nation Under Our Feet: Black Political Struggles in the Rural South From Slavery to the Great Migration.* Cambridge, MA, 2003.

Hale, Grace Elizabeth. *Making Whiteness: The Culture of Segregation in the South, 1890–1940.* New York, 1998.

Hall, Jacquelyn Dowd. *Revolt Against Chivalry: Jessie Daniel Ames and the Women's Campaign Against Lynching, rev. ed.* New York, 1993.

" 'The Mind That Burns in Each Body': Women, Rape, and Racial Violence." *Southern Exposure* 12 (1984): 61–71.

Harring, Sidney L. *Crow Dog's Case: American Indian Sovereignty, Tribal Law, and United States Law in the Nineteenth Century.* New York, 1994.

Harris, Angela P. "Equality Trouble: Sameness and Difference in Twentieth-Century Race Law." *California Law Review* 88 (2000): 1923–2015.

Harris, Cheryl I. "Whiteness as Property." *Harvard Law Review* 106 (1993): 1709–91.

Hartog, Hendrik. *Man and Wife in America: A History.* Cambridge, MA, 2000.

"Lawyering, Husbands' Rights, and 'the Unwritten Law' in Nineteenth Century America," *Journal of American History* 84 (1997): 67–96.

"The Constitution of Aspiration and 'The Rights That Belong to Us All,' " *Journal of American History* 74 (1987): 1013–34.

"Mrs. Packard on Dependency." *Yale Journal of Law & Humanities* 79 (1988–89): 79–103.

Healy, David. *Drive to Hegemony: The United States in the Caribbean, 1898–1917.* Madison, 1988.

Hewitt, Nancy. *Women's Activism and Social Change: Rochester, New York, 1822–1872.* Ithaca, NY, 1984.

Higbie, Frank Tobias. *Indispensable Outcasts: Hobo Workers and Community in the American Midwest, 1880–1930.* Champaign, 2003.

Higham, John. *Strangers in the Land: Patterns of American Nativism, 1860–1925.* 1969 Reprint with new epilogue, New Brunswick, NJ, ACLS Humanities E-Book, 2002.

Hine, Darlene Clark. "Rape and the Inner Lives of Black Women in the Middle West: Preliminary Thoughts on the Culture of Dissemblance." *Signs: Journal of Women in Culture* 14 (1989): 912–20.

Hing, Bill Ong. *Making and Remaking Asian America Through Immigration Policy, 1850–1990.* Stanford, 1990.

Hodes, Martha. *White Women, Black Men: Illicit Sex in the 19th-Century South.* New Haven, 1997.

Horsman, Reginald. *Race and Manifest Destiny: The Origins of American Racial Anglo-Saxonism.* Cambridge, MA, 1981.

Horwitz, Morton, *The Transformation of American Law, 1780–1860.* Cambridge, MA, 1977.

Hoxie, Frederick E. *A Final Promise: The Campaign to Assimilate the Indians, 1880–1920.* Lincoln, NE, 1984.

Hurst, James Willard. *Law and the Conditions of Freedom in the Nineteenth-Century United States.* Madison, 1956.

Hutchinson, E. P. *Legislative History of American Immigration Policy, 1798–1965.* Philadelphia, 1981.

Hyman, Harold M. and William M. Wiecek. *Equal Justice Under the Law: Constitutional Development, 1835–1875.* New York, 1982.

Igra, Anna R. *Wives Without Husbands: Marriage, Desertion, and Welfare in New York, 1900–1935.* Chapel Hill, 2006.

Isenberg, Nancy. *Sex and Citizenship in Antebellum America.* Chapel Hill, 1998.

Jacobs, Harriet A. *Incidents in the Life of a Slave Girl, Written by Herself.* 1861. Reprint, Ed. Jean Fagan Yellin. Cambridge, MA, 1987.

Jacobson, Matthew Frye. *Barbarian Virtues: The United States Encounters Foreign Peoples at Home and Abroad, 1876–1917.* New York, 2000.

Whiteness of a Different Color: European Immigrants and the Alchemy of Race. Cambridge, MA, 1998.

Jensen, Laura. *Patriots, Settlers, and the Origins of American Social Policy.* New York, 2003.

Jew, Victor. " 'Chinese Demons': The Violent Articulation of Chinese Otherness and Interracial Sexuality in the U. S. Midwest, 1885–1889." *Journal of Social History* 37 (2003): 389–410.

Johnson, Walter. "Slavery, Reparations, and the Mythic March of Freedom." *Raritan* 27 (2007): 41–67.

Soul by Soul: Life Inside the Antebellum Slave Market. Cambridge, MA, 1999.

Jones, Jacqueline. *Labor of Love, Labor of Sorrow: Black Women, Work, and the Family from Slavery to the Present.* New York, 1985.

Jordan, Winthrop D. *White over Black: American Attitudes Toward the Negro, 1550–1812.* Chapel Hill, 1968.

Kaczorowski, Robert J. "To Begin the Nation Anew: Congress, Citizenship, and Civil Rights After the Civil War." *American Historical Review* 92 (1987): 45–68.

Kelly, Joan. *Women, History, and Theory: The Essays of Joan Kelly.* Chicago, 1984.

Kerber, Linda K. *No Constitutional Right to Be Ladies: Women and the Obligations of Citizenship.* New York, 1998.

"The Meanings of American Citizenship," *Journal of American Hist.* 94 (1997): 833–54.

"Can a Woman Be an Individual?: The Discourse of Self-Reliance," In *Toward an Intellectual History of Women.* Ed. Linda K. Kerber. Chapel Hill, 1997. 200–223.

Women of the Republic: Intellect and Ideology in Revolutionary America. New York, 1980.

Kessler-Harris, Alice. *In Pursuit of Equity: Women, Men, and the Quest for Economic Citizenship in 20th-Century America.* New York, 2001.

Kettner, James H. *The Development of American Citizenship, 1608–1870.* Chapel Hill, 1978.

Keyssar, Alexander. *The Right to Vote: The Contested History of Democracy in the United States.* New York, 2000.

Kline, Wendy. *Building a Better Race: Gender, Sexuality, and Eugenics from the Turn of the Century to the Baby Boom.* Berkeley, 2001.

Kolchin, Peter. "Whiteness Studies: The New History of Race in America." *Journal of American History* 89 (2002): 154–73.

Kousser, J. Morgan. *The Shaping of Southern Politics: Suffrage Restriction and the Establishment of the One-Party South, 1880–1910.* New Haven, 1974.

Kramer, Paul A. *The Blood of Government: Race, Empire, the United States, and the Philippines.* Chapel Hill, 2006.

Kraut, Alan M. *Silent Travelers: Germs, Genes, and the "Immigrant Menace."* Baltimore, 1994.

Kudlick, Catherine J. "Disability History: Why We Need Another 'Other'" *American Historical Review* 108 (2003): 763–93.

Labbé, Ronald M. and Jonathan Lurie. *The Slaughterhouse Cases: Regulation, Reconstruction and the Fourteenth Amendment.* Lawrence, 2003.

Ladd-Taylor, Molly. *Mother-Work: Women, Child Welfare, and the State, 1890–1930.* Urbana, 1994.

Lake, Marilyn. "Translating Needs into Rights: The Discursive Imperative of the Australian White Man, 1901–30." In *Masculinities in Politics and War: Gendering Modern History.* Eds. Stefan Dudink, Karen Hagemann, and John Tosh. Manchester, UK, 2004. 199–219.

"On Being a White Man, Australia, Circa 1900." In *Cultural History in Australia.* Eds. Hsu-Ming Teo and Richard White. Sydney, Australia, 2003. 98–112.

Langum, David. *Law and Community on the Mexican California Frontier: Anglo-American Expatriates and the Clash of Legal Traditions, 1821–1846.* Norman, OK, 1987.

Largent, Mark A. *Breeding Contempt: The History of Coerced Sterilization in the United States.* New Brunswick, NJ, 2008.

Larson, Edward J. *Sex, Race, and Science: Eugenics in the Deep South.* Baltimore, 1995.

Lebsock, Suzanne. *The Free Women of Petersburg: Status and Culture in a Southern Town, 1784–1864.* New York, 1984.

"Radical Reconstruction and the Property Rights of Southern Women." *Journal of Southern History* 43 (1977): 195–216.

Lee, Erika. "Birthright Citizenship, Immigration, and the U. S. Constitution: The Story of *United States v. Wong Kim Ark*." In *Race Law Stories*. Eds. Rachel F. Moran and Devon W. Carbado. New York, 2008. 89–109.

At America's Gates: Chinese Immigration During the Exclusion Era, 1882–1943. Chapel Hill, 2003.

Levinson, Sanford and Bartholomew H. Sparrow, eds. *The Louisiana Purchase and American Expansion, 1803–1898*. New York, 2005.

Lewis, Earl and Heidi Ardizzone. *Love on Trial: An American Scandal in Black and White*. New York, 2001.

Lichtenstein, Alex. *Twice the Work of Free Labor: The Political Economy of Convict Labor in the New South*. New York, 1996.

Limerick, Patricia Nelson. *The Legacy of Conquest: The Unbroken Past of the American West*. New York, 1987.

Lipsitz, George. *The Possessive Investment in Whiteness: How White People Profit from Identity Politics*. Philadelphia, 1998.

Litwack, Leon F. *Been in the Storm So Long: The Aftermath of Slavery*. New York, 1979.

North of Slavery: The Negro in the Free States, 1790–1860. Chicago, 1961.

Loewen, James W. *Sundown Towns: A Hidden Dimension of American Racism*. New York, 2005.

Lofgren, Charles A. *The Plessy Case: A Legal-Historical Interpretation*. New York, 1987.

Longmore, Paul K. and Lauri Umansky, eds. *The New Disability History: American Perspectives*. New York, 2001.

Why I Burned My Book and Other Essays on Disability. Philadelphia, 2003.

Lopez, Ian Haney. *White By Law: The Construction of Race*. New York, 1996.

Lowe, Lisa. *Immigrant Acts: On Asian American Cultural Politics*. Durham, 1996.

Lyman, Stanford M. "The Race Question and Liberalism: Casuistries in American Constitutional Law." *International Journal of Politics, Culture, and Society* 5 (1991): 183–247.

MacPherson, C. B. *The Political Theory of Possessive Individualism: Hobbes to Locke*. New York, 1962.

Mack, Kenneth. "Rethinking Civil Rights Lawyering and Politics in the Era Before *Brown*." *Yale Law Journal* 115 (2005): 256–354.

"A Social History of Everyday Practice: Sadie T. M. Alexander and the Incorporation of Black Women into the American Legal Profession, 1925–60." *Cornell Law Review* 87 (2002): 1405–74.

Maovet, Pedro A. " 'The Constitution Fellows the Flag...but Doesn't Quite Catch Up with It": The Story of *Downes v. Bidwell*." In *Race Law Stories*. Eds. Rachel F. Moran and Devon W. Carbado. New York, 2008. 175–235.

Mangum, Jr., Charles S. *The Legal Status of the Negro*. Chapel Hill, 1940.

Mann, Bruce. *Republic of Debtors: Bankruptcy in the Age of American Independence*. Cambridge, MA, 2002.

Martinez, George A. "The Legal Construction of Race: Mexican-Americans and Whiteness." *Harvard Latino Law Review* 2 (1997): 321–38.

McClintock, Megan J. "Civil War Pensions and the Reconstruction of Union Families." *Journal of American History* 83 (1996): 456–80.

McCoy, Alfred W. and Francisco A. Scarano, eds. *Colonial Crucible: Empire in the Making of the Modern American State*. Madison, 2009.

McCurry, Stephanie. *Masters of Small Worlds: Yeoman Households, Gender Relations, and the Political Culture of the Antebellum South Carolina Low Country*. New York, 1995.

McDowell, Janet A. *The Dispossession of the American Indian, 1887–1934*. Bloomington, 1991.

McLennan, Rebecca M. *The Crisis of Imprisonment: Protest, Politics, and the Making of the American Penal State, 1776–1941*. New York, 2008.

McMillen, Neil R. *Dark Journey: Black Mississippians in the Age of Jim Crow*. Urbana, 1989.

Melish, Joanne Pope. *Disowning Slavery: Gradual Emancipation and "Race" in New England, 1780–1860*. Ithaca, 1998.

Merry, Sally Engle. *Colonizing Hawaii: The Cultural Power of Law*. Princeton, 2000.

Mezey, Naomi. "Erasure and Recognition: The Census, Race, and the National Imagination." *Northwestern Law Review* 97 (2003): 1701–68.

Miles, Tiya. *Ties That Bind: The Story of an Afro-Cherokee Family in Slavery and Freedom*. Berkeley, 2005.

Mills, Charles W. *The Racial Contract*. Ithaca, NY, 1997.

Mitchell, David T. and Sharon L. Snyder, eds. *Narrative Prosthesis: Disability and the Dependencies of Discourse*. Ann Arbor, 2000.

"The Eugenic Atlantic: Race, Disability, and the Making of an International Eugenic Science, 1800–1945." *Disability & Society* 18 (2003): 843–64.

Mohr, James C. *Abortion in America: The Origins and Evolution of National Policy, 1800–1900*. New York, 1978.

Montoya, Maria. *Translating Property: The Maxwell Land Grant and the Conflict over Land in the American West, 1840–1900*. Berkeley, 2002.

Moran, Rachel F. and Devon W. Carbado, eds. *Race Law Stories.* New York, 2008.

Morantz, Alison D. "There's No Place Like Home: Homestead Exemption and Judicial Constructions of Family in Nineteenth-Century America." *Law and History Review* 24 (2006): 245–96.

Morris, Thomas D. *Southern Slavery and the Law, 1619–1860.* Chapel Hill, 1996.

Mossman, Mary Jane. *The First Women Lawyers: A Comparative Study of Gender, Law, and the Legal Professions.* Portland, OR, 2006.

Murray, Pauli, comp. and ed. *States' Laws on Race and Color.* 1951. Reprint, Athens, GA, 1997.

Myrdal, Gunnar. *An American Dilemma.* New York, 1944.

Nash, Gary B. *The Forgotten Fifth: African Americans in the Age of Revolution.* Cambridge, MA, 2006.

Nedelsky, Jennifer. *Private Property and the Limits of American Constitutionalism.* Chicago, 1990.

　 "Law, Boundaries, and the Bounded Self." *Representations* 30 (1990): 162–89.

　 "Reconceiving Autonomy: Sources, Thoughts and Possibilities. *Yale Journal of Law & Feminism* 1 (1989): 7–36.

Nelson, William E. *The Fourteenth Amendment: From Political Principle to Judicial Doctrine.* Cambridge, MA, 1988.

　 Americanization of the Common Law: The Impact of Legal Change on Massachusetts Society, 1760–1830. 1975. Reprint, Athens, GA, 1994.

Neuman, Gerald L. *Strangers to the Constitution: Immigrants, Borders, and Fundamental Law.* Princeton, 1996.

　 "The Lost Century of American Immigration Law (1776–1875)." *Columbia Law Review* 93 (1993): 1833–1901.

Ngai, Mae M. *Impossible Subjects: Illegal Aliens and the Making of Modern America.* Princeton, 2004.

　 "The Architecture of Race in American Immigration Law: A Re-Examination of the Immigration Act of 1924." *Journal of American History* 89 (1999): 67–92.

Nobles, Melissa. *Shades of Citizenship: Race and the Census in Modern Politics.* Stanford, 2000.

Norgren, Jill. *The Cherokee Cases: The Confrontation of Law and Politics.* New York, 1996.

Novak, William J. "The Legal Transformation of Citizenship in Nineteenth-Century America." In *The Democratic Experiment: New Directions in American Political History.* Eds. Meg Jacobs, William J. Novak, and Julian Zelizer. Princeton, 2003. 85–119.

Oberly, James W. *Sixty Million Acres: American Veterans and the Public Lands before the Civil War.* Kent, Ohio, 1990.

Orren, Karen. *Belated Feudalism: Labor, the Law, and Liberal Development in the United States.* New York, 1991.

Oshinsky, David M. *"Worse than Slavery": Parchman Farm and the Ordeal of Jim Crow Justice.* New York, 1996.

Ostler, Jeffrey. *The Plains Sioux and U. S. Colonialism from Lewis and Clark to Wounded Knee.* New York, 2004.

Parker, Kunal M. "Citizenship and Immigration Law, 1800–1924: Resolutions of Membership and Territory." In *The Cambridge History of Law in America, 3 vols.* Eds. Michael Grossberg and Christopher Tomlins. New York, 2008. 2: 168–203.

"Citizenship as Refusal 'Outing' the Nation of Immigrants." *Law and History Review* 19 (2001): 583–660.

"Making Blacks Foreigners: The Legal Construction of Former Slaves in Post-Revolutionary Massachusetts," *Utah Law Review* (2001): 75–124.

"From Poor Law to Immigration Law: Changing Visions of Territorial Community in Antebellum Massachusetts." *Historical Geography* 28 (2000): 61–85.

Pascoe, Peggy. *What Comes Naturally: Miscegenation Law and the Making of Race in America.* New York, 2009.

"Miscegenation Law, Court Cases and Ideologies of 'Race' in Twentieth Century America." *Journal of American History* 83 (1996): 44–69.

Pateman, Carole. *The Sexual Contract.* Stanford, 1988.

Peck, Gunther. *Reinventing Free Labor: Padrones and Immigrant Workers in the North American West, 1880–1930.* New York, 2000.

Penningroth, Dylan. *The Claims of Kinfolk: African American Property and Community in the Nineteenth-Century South.* Chapel Hill, 2003.

Perez, Lou. *The War of 1898: The United States and Cuba in History and Historiography.* Chapel Hill, 1998.

Perman, Michael. *Struggle for Mastery: Disfranchisement in the South, 1888–1908.* Chapel Hill, 2001.

Pleck, Elizabeth H. *Domestic Tyranny: The Making of Social Policy Against Family Violence From Colonial Times to the Present.* New York, 1987.

Rabinowitz, Howard N. *Race Relations in the Urban South, 1865–1890.* Urbana, 1980.

Rao, Gautham. "The Federal *Posse Comitatus* Doctrine: Slavery, Compulsion, and Statecraft in Mid-Nineteenth-Century America." *Law and History Review* 26 (2008): 1–56.

Reagan, Leslie J. *When Abortion Was a Crime: Women, Medicine, and Law in the United States, 1867–1973*. Berkeley, 1997.

Reeve, Tapping. *The Law of Baron and Femme, Parent and Child, Guardian and Ward, Master and Servant, and of the Powers of the Courts of Chancery*. New Haven, 1816.

Reilly, Philip R. *The Surgical Solution: A History of Involuntary Sterilization in the United States*. Baltimore, 1991.

Resch, John and Walter Sargent, eds. *War and Society in the American Revolution*. DeKalb, IL, 2007.

Ritter, Gretchen, *The Constitution as Social Design: Gender and Civic Membership in the American Constitutional Order*. Stanford, 2006.

"Jury Service and Women's Citizenship Before and After the Nineteenth Amendment." *Law and History Review* 20 (2002): 479–516.

Robertson, Lindsay G. *Conquest by Law: How the Discovery of America Dispossessed Indigenous Peoples of Their Lands*. New York, 2005.

Roediger, David R. *The Wages of Whiteness: Race and the Making of the American Working Class*. New York, 1991.

Rosen, Hannah. *Terror in the Heart of Freedom: Citizenship, Sexual Violence, and the Meaning of Race in the Postemancipation South*. Chapel Hill, 2009.

Rosenberg, Caroll Smith. "Dis-Covering the Subject of the 'Great Constitutional Discussion,' 1786–1789." *Journal of American History* 79 (1992): 841–73.

Disorderly Conduct: Visions of Gender in Victorian America. New York, 1985.

Ross, Michael A. *Justice of Shattered Dreams: Samuel Freeman Miller and the Supreme Court During the Civil War Era*. Baton Rouge, 2003.

Rothman, David J. *The Discovery of the Asylum*. Boston, 1980.

Rothman, Joshua D. *Notorious in the Neighborhood: Sex and Families Across the Color Line in Virginia, 1787–1861*. Chapel Hill, 2003.

Salmon, Marylynn. *Women and the Law of Property in Early America*. Chapel Hill, 1986.

Salyer, Lucy E. *Laws Harsh as Tigers: Chinese Immigrants and the Shaping of Modern Immigration Law*. Chapel Hill, 1995.

Sánchez-Eppler, Karen. *Touching Liberty: Abolition, Feminism, and the Politics of the Body*. Berkeley, 1993.

Saunt, Claudio *Black, White, and Indian: Race and the Unmaking of an American Family*. New York, 2005.

A New Order of Things: Property, Power, and the Transformation of the Creek Indians, 1733–1816. New York, 1999.

Saville, Julie. *The Work of Reconstruction: From Slave to Wage Laborer in South Carolina, 1860–1870.* New York, 1994.

Saxton, Alexander. *The Rise and Fall of the White Republic: Class Politics and Mass Culture in Nineteenth-Century America.* New York, 1990.

The Indispensable Enemy: Labor and the Anti-Chinese Movement. Berkeley, 1971.

Schweik, Susan M. *The Ugly Laws: Disability in Public.* New York, 2009.

"Begging the Question: Disability, Mendicancy, Speech and the Law." *Narrative* 15 (2007): 58–70.

Scott, Rebecca J. "Public Rights, Social Equality, and the Conceptual Roots of the *Plessy* Challenge." *Michigan Law Review* 106 (2008): 777–804.

Degrees of Freedom: Louisiana and Cuba after Slavery. Cambridge, MA, 2005.

Shafir, Gershon, ed. *The Citizenship Debates: A Reader.* Minneapolis, 1998.

Shah, Nayan. *Contagious Divides: Epidemics and Race in San Francisco's Chinatown.* Berkeley, 2001.

Shammas, Carole. "Re-assessing the Married Women's Property Acts." *Journal of Women's History* 6 (1994): 9–30.

Shaw, Angel Velasco and Luis H. Francia, eds. *Vestiges of War: The Philippine-American War and the Aftermath of an Imperial Dream, 1899–1999.* New York, 2002.

Siegel, Reva B. "She The People: The Nineteenth Amendment, Sex Equality, Federalism, and the Family." *Harvard Law Review* 115 (2001–2001): 947–1046.

"The Modernization of Marital Status Law: Adjudicating Wives' Rights to Earnings, 1860–1930." *Georgetown Law Journal* 82 (1994): 2127–2211.

"The First Woman's Rights Claims Concerning Wives' Household Labor, 1850–1880." *Yale Law Journal* 103 (1994): 1073–217.

Skocpol, Theda. *Protecting Soldiers and Mothers: The Political Origins of Social Policy in the United States.* Cambridge, MA, 1992.

Skogen, Larry C. *Indian Depredation Claims, 1796–1920.* Norman, OK, 1996.

Smith, Rogers M. *Civic Ideals: Conflicting Visions of Citizenship in U. S. History.* New Haven, 1997.

Smith-Rosenberg, Carroll. *Disorderly Conduct: Visions of Gender in Victorian America.* New York, 1985.

Snyder, Sharon L. and David T. Mitchell. "Out of the ashes of eugenics: diagnostic regimes in the United States and the making of a disability minority." *Patterns of Prejudice* 36 (2002): 79–103.

Sommerville, Diane Miller. *Rape and Race in the Nineteenth-Century South*. Chapel Hill, 2004.

Sparrow, Bartholomew H. *The Insular Cases and the Emergence of American Empire*. Lawrence, 2006.

"Empires External and Internal: Territories, Government Lands, and Federalism in the United States." In *The Louisiana Purchase and American Expansion, 1803–1898*. Eds. Sanford Levinson and Bartholomew H. Sparrow. New York, 2005. 231–49.

Stanley, Amy Dru. *From Bondage to Contract: Wage Labor, Marriage, and the Market in the Age of Slave Emancipation*. New York, 1998.

Steinfeld, Robert J. *Coercion, Contract, and Free Labor in the Nineteenth Century*. New York, 2001.

The Invention of Free Labor: The Employment Relation in English and American Law and Culture, 1350–1870. Chapel Hill, 1991.

"Property and Suffrage in the Early American Republic." *Stanford Law Review* 41 (1988–89): 335–376.

Stephenson, Gilbert Thomas. *Race Distinctions in American Law*. New York, 1910.

Stevens, Todd. "Tender Ties: Husbands' Rights and Racial Exclusion in Chinese Marriage Cases, 1882–1924." *Law and Social Inquiry* 27 (2002): 271–305.

Stern, Alexandra Minna. *Faults and Frontiers of Better Breeding in Modern America*. Berkeley, 2005.

Strickland, Rennard. "The Tribal Struggle for Indian Sovereignty: The Story of the *Cherokee Cases*." In *Race Law Stories*. Eds. Rachel F. Moran and Devon W. Carbado. New York, 2008. 37–57.

Fire and the Spirits: Cherokee Law from Clan to Court. Norman, OK, 1975.

Symposium. "Scholarly Controversy: Whiteness and the Historians' Imagination." *International Labor and Working Class History* 60 (2001): 1–92.

Sweet, John Wood. *Bodies Politic: Negotiating Race in the American North, 1730–1830*. Baltimore, 2003.

Takaki, Ronald. *Iron Cages: Race and Culture in 19th Century America*. New York, 1979.

Taves, Ann, ed. *Religion and Domestic Violence in Early New England: The Memoirs of Abigail Abbot Bailey*. Bloomington, 1989.

Taylor, Quintard. *In Search of the Racial Frontier: African Americans in the American West, 1528–1990*. New York, 1998.

Tehranian, John, "Performing Whiteness: Naturalization Litigation and the Construction of Racial Identity in America." *Yale Law Journal* 109 (2000): 817–48.

tenBroek, Jacobus. "The Right to Live in the World: The Disabled in the Law of Torts." *California Law Review* 54 (1966): 841–919.

Thomson, Rosemarie Garland. *Extraordinary Bodies: Figuring Physical Disability in American Culture and Literature.* New York, 1997.

Thorpe, Francis Newton, ed. and comp. *The Federal and State Constitutions, Colonial Charters, and Other Organic Laws of the States, Territories, and Colonies Now or Heretofore Forming the United States of America, 7 vols.* Washington, 1909.

Tomlins, Christopher L. *Law, Labor, and Ideology in the Early American Republic.* New York, 1993.

"A Mysterious Power: Industrial Accidents and the Legal Construction of Employment Relations in Massachusetts, 1800–1850." *Law and History Review* 6 (1988): 375–438.

Torpey, John C. *The Invention of the Passport: Surveillance, Citizenship, and the State.* New York, 2000.

Torruella, Juan R. *The Supreme Court and Puerto Rico: The Doctrine of Separate and Unequal.* Rio Piedras, P.R., 1988.

Trent, Jr., James W. *Inventing the Feeble Mind: A History of Mental Retardation in the United States.* Berkeley,1994.

Ulrich, Laurel Thatcher. *A Midwife's Tale: The Life of Martha Ballard, Based on her Diary, 1785–1812.* New York, 1990.

VanderVelde, Lea. *Mrs. Dred Scott: A Life on Slavery's Frontier.* New York, 2009.

and Sandhya Subramanian. "Mrs. Dred Scott." *Yale Law Journal* 106 (1997): 1033–1122.

Van Steenbergen, Bart, ed. *The Condition of Citizenship.* Thousand Oaks, CA, 1994.

Volpp, Leti. "Divesting Citizenship: On Asian American History and the Loss of Citizenship Through Marriage." *UCLA Law Review* 53 (2005): 405–83.

"'Obnoxious to Their very Nature': Asian Americans and Constitutional Citizenship." *Asian Law Journal* 8 (2001): 71–87.

Vorenberg, Michael. *Final Freedom: The Civil War, the Abolition of Slavery, and the Thirteenth Amendment.* New York, 2001.

Waldrep, Christopher. *The Many Faces of Judge Lynch: Extralegal Violence and Punishment in America.* New York, 2002.

Roots of Disorder: Race and Criminal Justice in the American South, 1817–1880. Urbana, 1998.

Wall, Wendy. "Gender and the Citizen Indian." In *Writing the Range: Race, Class, and Culture in the Women's West.* Eds. Elizabeth Jameson and Susan Armitage. Norman, OK, 1997. 202–29.

Walsh, Mary Roth. *"Doctors Wanted, No Women New Apply"*: *Sexual Barriers in the Medical Profession*. New Haven, 1977.

Weisberg, D. Kelly. "Barred from the Bar: Women and Legal Education in the United States, 1870–1890." In *Women and the Law: A Social Historical Perspective, vol. II, Property, Family and the Legal Profession*. Ed. D. Kelly Weisberg. Cambridge, MA, 1982. 231–58.

Welke, Barbara Y. "Rights of Passage: Gendered-Rights Consciousness and the Quest for Freedom, San Francisco, California, 1850–1870." In Quintard Taylor and Shirley Moore, eds. *African-American Women Confront the West, 1600–2000*. Norman, OK, 2003.

Recasting American Liberty: Gender, Race, Law and the Railroad Revolution, 1865–1920. New York, 2001.

"Beyond Plessy: Space, Status, and Race in the Era of Jim Crow," *Utah Law Review* (2000): 267–99.

"When All the Women Were White, and All the Blacks Were Men: Gender, Class, Race, and the Road to *Plessy*, 1855–1914," *Law and History Review* 13 (1995): 261–316.

"Unreasonable Women: Gender and the Law of Accidental Injury, 1870–1920," *Law and Social Inquiry* 19 (1994): 369–403.

Wells-Barnett, Ida B. *On Lynchings: Southern Horrors, A Red Record, Mob Rule in New Orleans*. 1892, 1895, 1900. Reprint, Salem, NH, 1993.

Wickberg, Daniel. "Heterosexual White Male: Some Recent Inversions in American Cultural History." *Journal of American History* 92 (2005): 136–57.

Wiecek, William. *The Sources of Anti-Slavery Constitutionalism in America, 1760–1848*. Ithaca, NY, 1977.

Wilkins, David. "Federal Policy, Western Movement, and Indigenous People, 1790–1920." In *The Cambridge History of Law in America, 3 vols*. Eds. Michael Grossberg and Christopher Tomlins. New York, 2008. 2: 204–44.

Wilkins, David. and K. Tsianina Lomawaima. *Uneven Ground: American Indian Sovereignty and Federal Law*. Norman, OK, 2001.

Williams, Patricia J. *The Alchemy of Race and Rights*. Cambridge, MA, 1991.

Williams, Jr., Robert A. *The American Indian in Western Legal Thought: The Discourses of Conquest*. New York, 1990.

Williams, Walter L. "United States Indian Policy and the Debate over Philippine Annexation: Implications for the Origins of American Imperialism." *Journal of American History* 66 (1980): 810–31.

Williamson, Joel. *The Crucible of Race: Black-White Relations in the American South Since Emancipation.* New York, 1984.

Willrich, Michael. *City of Courts: Socializing Justice in Progressive Era Chicago.* New York, 2003.

"Home Slackers: Men, the State, and Welfare in Modern America." *Journal of American History* 87 (2000): 460–89.

Wilson, Mark R. "Law and the American State, from the Revolution to the Civil War: Institutional Growth and Structural Change." In *Cambridge History of Law in America, 3 vols.* Eds. Michael Grossberg and Christopher L. Tomlins. New York, 2008. 2: 1–35.

Wing, Adrien Katherine, ed. *Critical Race Feminism: A Reader.* New York, 1997.

Witt, John Fabian. *The Accidental Republic: Crippled Workingmen, Destitute Widows, and the Remaking of American Law.* New York, 2004.

"From Loss of Services to Loss of Support: Wrongful Death, the Origins of Modern Tort Law, and the Making of the Nineteenth Century Family." *Law and Social Inquiry* 25 (2000): 717–55.

Woloch, Nancy. *Muller v. Oregon: A Brief History with Documents.* Boston, 1996.

Woodward, C. Vann. *The Strange Career of Jim Crow, 3rd rev. ed.* New York, 1974.

Wunder, John. "Anti-Chinese Violence in the American West, 1850–1910." In *Law for the Elephant, Law for the Beaver: Essays in the Legal History of the North American West.* Eds. John McLaren, Hamar Foster, and Chet Orloff. Regina, Saskatchewan, 1992. 212–36.

Yellin, Jean Fagan. *Women and Sisters: Anti-Slavery Feminists in American Culture.* New Haven, 1990.

ed. *Harriet A. Jacobs, Incidents in the Life of a Slave Girl, Written by Herself.* Cambridge, MA, 1987.

Zolberg, Aristide R. *A Nation by Design: Immigration Policy in the Fashioning of America.* Cambridge, MA, 2006.

INDEX

ability, personhood and, as
assumed in structure of
public space and public
accommodations, 55–56,
92
able white men, 21–60.
See also privilege, for able
white men
bans on testifying against,
80–81
borders of belonging for,
107–19
citizenship of, 34–37
claim to land by, 45–46
under coverture, 45–46
divorce for, 28
factors limiting significance
of class divisions among,
107–09, 122–23
father's rights to children
under common law for,
67–68
under Fourteenth
Amendment, 78
freedom of contract for, 3
as judges, 119–30
law of negligence by, 24
as lawyers, 119–30
military service by, 35–37

Native-American land
allotments and, 75
privilege of, 21, 94–96
property rights and, 23–24
right to dispose of property
by, 24–25
rights within marriage for,
25–26, 27–28, 64
self-defense for, 25–26
self-ownership for, 21–30
shared identity of, 8–9, 12
structure of law and, privilege
as result of, 130–40
suffrage rights for, 108, 114,
122–23
abortion, 87–89
criminalization of, 68, 148
Adams, Abigail, 26–27, 100
Adams, John, 8, 109
coverture and, 26–27
African-Americans.
See also Black Codes;
Jim Crow laws;
lynching
bans on testifying against
whites for, 124
citizenship for, 34–35
community among, as result
of exclusion, 101

229

public transit accommodations.
See also disabled persons;
Jim Crow
African-Americans and, 86,
102–03, 132–33
disabled persons
and, 55–56
resistance to discrimination
in, 103
Puerto Rico, 38

race
color definitions and, 117
immigration restriction and,
53–54
law and, 4
scientific racism and
definition of, 72
*Race Distinctions in American
Law* (Stephenson), 126,
131
racialized others, 63–93
birthright citizenship and,
69–70
borders of belonging and,
2–3, 9–10, 63–64
capitalism influenced
by, 146
citizenship of, 141–42,
143–44
education discrimination
against, 48, 51
empire and, 38–39, 110–11
employment discrimination
against, 48
illegality of, impact on
community from, 76,
87–88
immigration restriction and,
53
as jurors, discrimination
against, 120
legal remedies as resistance,
102–04, 105–07
miscegenation laws and, 50
property rights discrimination
against, 52

public transit
accommodations for,
50–51, 86
resistance by, 96–107
scientific racism, 137–38
sequestering of, 86–87
state law bans on testifying
against whites, 80–81,
124
U.S. Constitutional
Amendments and, 141–43
violence against, 82–86,
129–30
Rao, Gautham, 123
Reeve, Tapping, 131
reproduction, 116. *See also* disabled persons; eugenics;
sterilization laws
abortion laws restricting, 68,
87
birth control, 68
Reservation Policy (1867),
116
reservations, Native-Americans
on, 86–87, 116,
136–37
resistance, 96–107
by Chinese and Chinese-
Americans, 146
community as result of, 101
individual v. collective, 99
by Mexican-Americans, 98
by Native-Americans, 104
by newly freed African-
Americans, 96–98, 103
remedy of law as, 102–04,
105–07
to slavery, 97–98
by women, 98
restrictive covenants, 52
Buchanan v. Warley (1917),
52
Corrigan v. Buckley (1926),
52

scientific racism, 137–38.
See also eugenics